적중! 영어 독해

중등 2

교재 개발에 도움을 주신 선생님들께 감사드립니다.

강윤구 부산
김항중 서울
서동준 산본
이충기 화성
조재신 안동
권익재 대구
나규성 대전
오승준 부산
정도영 인천
지정림 김제
김광수 수원
노준환 화성
이신영 부산
정방현 익산
최수남 강릉
김동관 서울
류대국 광주
이장령 창원
정진원 안동
김연정 인천
박현도 전주
이제석 인천
조예은 양주

적중! 영어 독해

중등 2

구성과 특징 Structure

❶ 내가 아는 단어는 몇 개?

본문에 나오는 단어를 학습 전에 미리 확인해 볼 수 있습니다. 모르는 단어는 사진을 보고 뜻을 추측해 보고, 본문에서 뜻을 확인해 보세요.

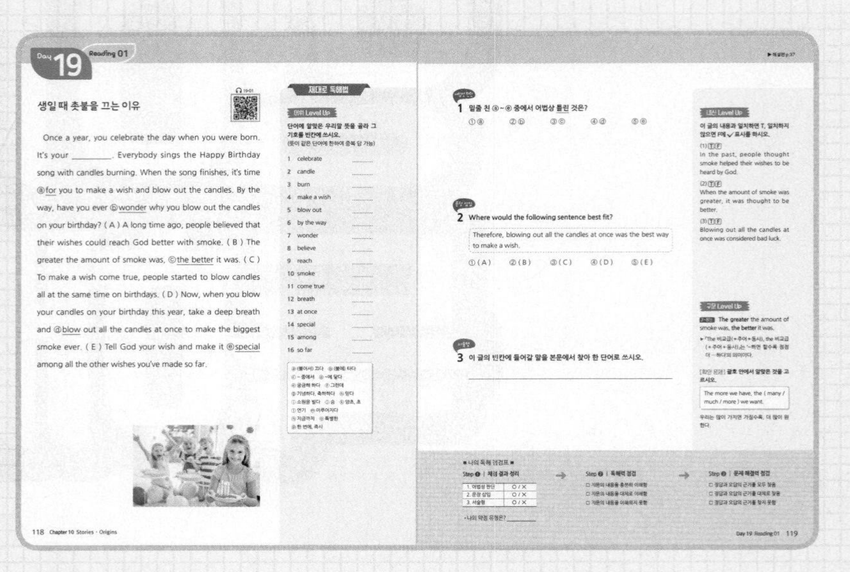

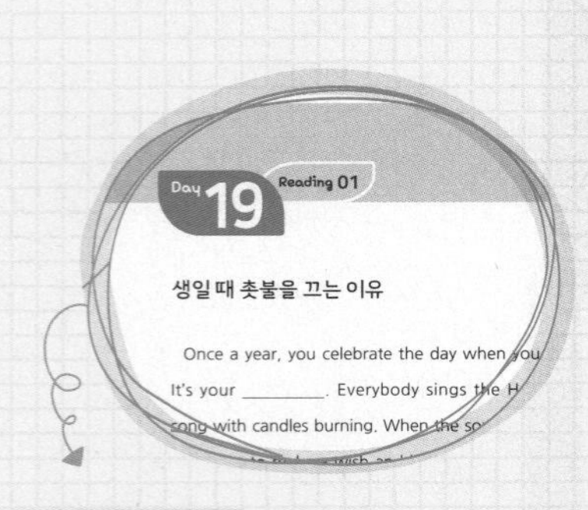

❷ Reading

흥미로운 소재의 지문들을 읽어 보세요. 모르는 단어들은 동그라미 표시를 해놓고, 지문을 다 읽고 난 후에 [어휘 Level Up] 문제를 풀면서 단어들의 뜻을 확인해 보세요.

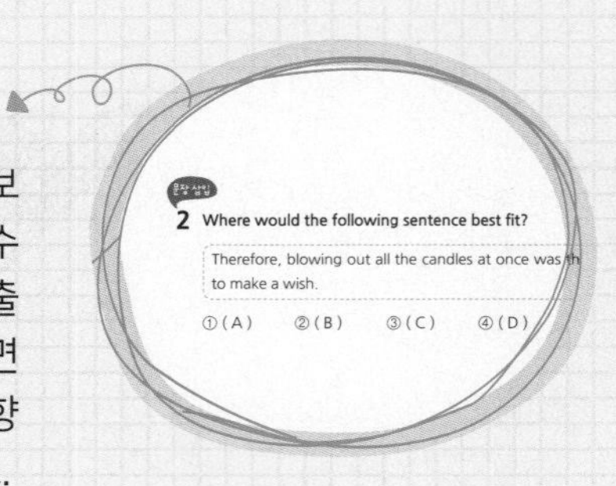

❹ English Only

영어로만 제시된 문제를 풀어 보세요. 처음에는 어렵게 느껴질 수 있지만, 매 지문마다 한 문제씩 출제된 영어 문제를 매일 풀다 보면 금방 익숙해지고 영어 실력이 향상되는 것을 느낄 수 있을 거예요.

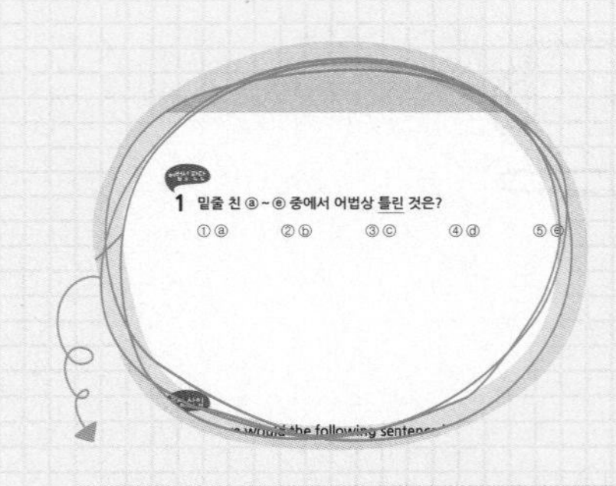

❸ 다양한 유형의 객관식 독해 문제

제목, 요지, 주장, 주제, 목적, 심경, 분위기, 지칭 추론, 내용 일치, 빈칸, 어휘, 어법, 무관한 문장, 문장 삽입, 글의 순서, 밑줄 추론, 요약문 완성 등의 다양한 독해 유형 문제를 풀어보세요.

❺ 서술형

매 지문마다 한 문제씩 출제된 서술형 문제를 매일 풀다 보면 학교 내신 서술형 문제가 더 이상 어렵게 느껴지지 않을 거예요.

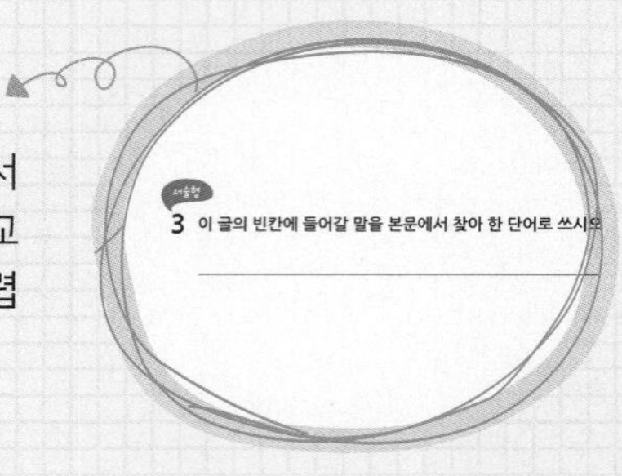

❻ 내신 Level Up · 구문 Level Up

학교 내신에 대비할 수 있는 추가 독해 문제도 풀어 보고, 지문에서 중요한 구문 풀이도 학습해 보세요. 독해력을 높일 수 있습니다.

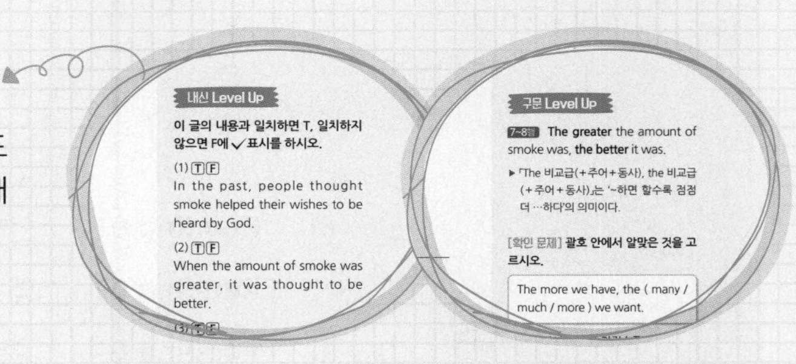

❼ QR코드

학습이 끝난 후에 원어민이 녹음한 파일을 들으면서 복습할 수 있습니다. 첫 번째는 눈을 감고 들으면서 내용을 확인하고, 두 번째는 지문을 보면서 따라 읽어보세요.

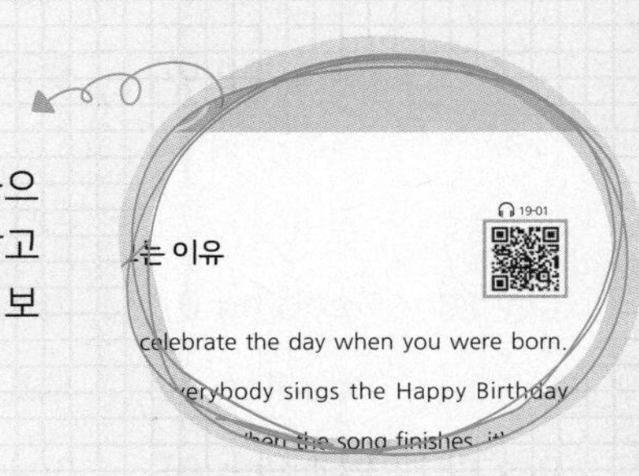

어휘 테스트

A 사진을 보고, 빈칸에 알맞은 단어를 골라 쓰시오.

aisles　entrances　fist　lined up　mirror　percentages

❽ 어휘 테스트

사진을 보고 문장 빈칸 채우기, 영영풀이 찾기 문제를 풀어 보세요. 본문에 나온 단어를 종합적으로 복습할 수 있습니다.

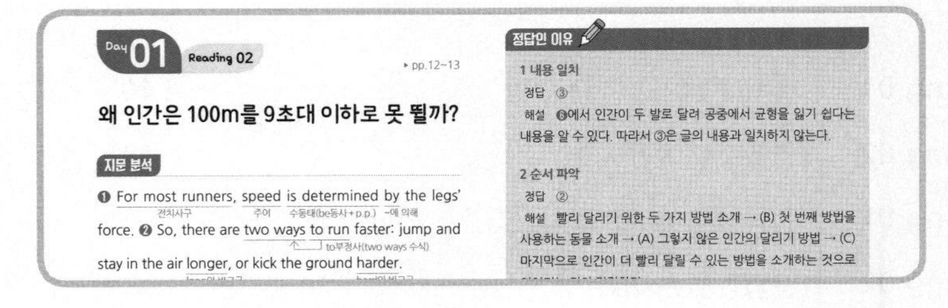

❾ 해설편

해석을 막힘없이 할 수 있도록 도와주는 지문 분석과 지문 해석, 정답의 이유를 알려주는 문제 해설로 구성된 해설편을 옆에 두고, 학습에 도움을 받아 보세요.

▶ 정답 p.46

DAY 08

Reading 01 기억을 잡아 두고 싶나요?

1 당신은 오른손잡이인가?
(you / a right-handed person / are / ?)

❿ 워크북

본문에 나온 단어들을 정리한 Word List와 간단한 확인 문제인 Word Test를 통해 단어를 암기하고 확인해 볼 수 있습니다.

Writing Test를 통해 주요 문장들을 복습하고 학교 내신 서술형 문제에도 대비할 수 있습니다.

차 례 Contents

PLAN_권장 학습 플랜

◎ 적중! 영어독해가 제시하는 표준 학습 계획입니다. 이를 참고하되, 반드시 자신만의 학습 플랜을 세워 보세요.

Chapter	Reading		문제편	해설편	워크북		학습 플랜		
					Word	Writing	중위	상위	스스로
Chapter 1	Day 01	Reading 01	pp.10-11	p.1	pp.3-4	p.25	1일	1일	
		Reading 02	pp.12-13	p.2					
	Day 02	Reading 01	pp.14-15	p.3		p.26	2일		
		Reading 02	pp.16-17	p.4					
	어휘 테스트		p.18	p.4					
Chapter 2	Day 03	Reading 01	pp.22-23	p.5	pp.5-6	p.27	3일	2일	
		Reading 02	pp.24-25	p.6					
	Day 04	Reading 01	pp.26-27	p.7		p.28	4일		
		Reading 02	pp.28-29	p.8					
	어휘 테스트		p.30	p.8					
Chapter 3	Day 05	Reading 01	pp.34-35	p.9	pp.7-8	p.29	5일	3일	
		Reading 02	pp.36-37	p.10					
	Day 06	Reading 01	pp.38-39	p.11		p.30	6일		
		Reading 02	pp.40-41	p.12					
	어휘 테스트		p.42	p.12					
Chapter 4	Day 07	Reading 01	pp.46-47	p.13	pp.9-10	p.31	7일	4일	
		Reading 02	pp.48-49	p.14					
	Day 08	Reading 01	pp.50-51	p.15		p.32	8일		
		Reading 02	pp.52-53	p.16					
	어휘 테스트		p.54	p.16					
Chapter 5	Day 09	Reading 01	pp.58-59	p.17	pp.11-12	p.33	9일	5일	
		Reading 02	pp.60-61	p.18					
	Day 10	Reading 01	pp.62-63	p.19		p.34	10일		
		Reading 02	pp.64-65	p.20					
	어휘 테스트		p.66	p.20					
Chapter 6	Day 11	Reading 01	pp.70-71	p.21	pp.13-14	p.35	11일	6일	
		Reading 02	pp.72-73	p.22					
	Day 12	Reading 01	pp.74-75	p.23		p.36	12일		
		Reading 02	pp.76-77	p.24					
	어휘 테스트		p.78	p.24					
Chapter 7	Day 13	Reading 01	pp.82-83	p.25	pp.15-16	p.37	13일	7일	
		Reading 02	pp.84-85	p.26					
	Day 14	Reading 01	pp.86-87	p.27		p.38	14일		
		Reading 02	pp.88-89	p.28					
	어휘 테스트		p.90	p.28					
Chapter 8	Day 15	Reading 01	pp.94-95	p.29	pp.17-18	p.39	15일	8일	
		Reading 02	pp.96-97	p.30					
	Day 16	Reading 01	pp.98-99	p.31		p.40	16일		
		Reading 02	pp.100-101	p.32					
	어휘 테스트		p.102	p.32					
Chapter 9	Day 17	Reading 01	pp.106-107	p.33	pp.19-20	p.41	17일	9일	
		Reading 02	pp.108-109	p.34					
	Day 18	Reading 01	pp.110-111	p.35		p.42	18일		
		Reading 02	pp.112-113	p.36					
	어휘 테스트		p.114	p.36					
Chapter 10	Day 19	Reading 01	pp.118-119	p.37	pp.21-22	p.43	19일	10일	
		Reading 02	pp.120-121	p.38					
	Day 20	Reading 01	pp.122-123	p.39		p.44	20일		
		Reading 02	pp.124-125	p.40					
	어휘 테스트		p.126	p.40					

◎ 자신의 학습 능력과 상황에 따라 스스로 학습 플랜을 완성하고, 학습에 반드시 활용해 보세요.

중위권을 위한 학습 플랜

공부한 날(월/일)	[학습 지문 수] 학습 내용
1일차 (월 일)	[2] Day 01 문제편+워크북
2일차 (월 일)	[2] Day 02 문제편+워크북
3일차 (월 일)	[2] Day 03 문제편+워크북
4일차 (월 일)	[2] Day 04 문제편+워크북
5일차 (월 일)	[2] Day 05 문제편+워크북
6일차 (월 일)	[2] Day 06 문제편+워크북
7일차 (월 일)	[2] Day 07 문제편+워크북
8일차 (월 일)	[2] Day 08 문제편+워크북
9일차 (월 일)	[2] Day 09 문제편+워크북
10일차 (월 일)	[2] Day 10 문제편+워크북
11일차 (월 일)	[2] Day 11 문제편+워크북
12일차 (월 일)	[2] Day 12 문제편+워크북
13일차 (월 일)	[2] Day 13 문제편+워크북
14일차 (월 일)	[2] Day 14 문제편+워크북
15일차 (월 일)	[2] Day 15 문제편+워크북
16일차 (월 일)	[2] Day 16 문제편+워크북
17일차 (월 일)	[2] Day 17 문제편+워크북
18일차 (월 일)	[2] Day 18 문제편+워크북
19일차 (월 일)	[2] Day 19 문제편+워크북
20일차 (월 일)	[2] Day 20 문제편+워크북

상위권을 위한 학습 플랜

공부한 날(월/일)	[학습 지문 수] 학습 내용
1일차 (월 일)	[4] Day 01~02 문제편+워크북
2일차 (월 일)	[4] Day 03~04 문제편+워크북
3일차 (월 일)	[4] Day 05~06 문제편+워크북
4일차 (월 일)	[4] Day 07~08 문제편+워크북
5일차 (월 일)	[4] Day 09~10 문제편+워크북
6일차 (월 일)	[4] Day 11~12 문제편+워크북
7일차 (월 일)	[4] Day 13~14 문제편+워크북
8일차 (월 일)	[4] Day 15~16 문제편+워크북
9일차 (월 일)	[4] Day 17~18 문제편+워크북
10일차 (월 일)	[4] Day 19~20 문제편+워크북

Chapter 1

Sports 스포츠
★
Leisure 레저

DAY 01
Reading 01 언제나 재밌게 즐기는 실내 스포츠, 탁구
Reading 02 왜 인간은 100m를 9초대 이하로 못 뛸까?

DAY 02
Reading 01 요즘 유행하는 방탈출 게임 해봤니?
Reading 02 볼링과 터키의 관계는?

내가 아는 단어는 몇 개?

▷▶ 다음 단어의 뜻을 추측해 보고, 알고 있는 단어에 ✔표시를 하시오.

☐ table tennis

☐ fast

☐ balance

☐ in the air

☐ exit

☐ password

☐ wall

☐ roll

☐ meat

Day 01 Reading 01

언제나 재밌게 즐기는 실내 스포츠, 탁구

01-01

In winter, it is not easy to enjoy outdoor sports. Then, why don't you try table tennis as an indoor sport? Table tennis, or ping-pong, only needs a table with a net in the center, rubber rackets, and a tiny ball. The rules are also simple. You just hit the ball over the net, and bounce it to the other player. If one misses or fails to return the ball, one score goes to the other player. If one player gets 15 points first, he or she wins. You have to move quickly because the ball speed is very fast. However, ㉠it doesn't give you much stress or physical demands, but it gives you ______________. If you want to spend winter time playing sports with your friends, table tennis is a good option.

제대로 독해법

어휘 Level Up

단어에 알맞은 우리말 뜻을 골라 그 기호를 빈칸에 쓰시오.
(뜻이 같은 단어에 한하여 중복 답 가능)

1 outdoor ....
2 table tennis ....
3 indoor ....
4 rubber ....
5 tiny ....
6 miss ....
7 fail ....
8 return ....
9 move ....
10 quickly ....
11 physical ....
12 demand ....
13 spend ....
14 option ....

ⓐ (시간을) 보내다 ⓑ 고무
ⓒ 놓치다
ⓓ (경기에서 공을) 받아치다[넘기다]
ⓔ 부담, 요구 ⓕ 빠르게 ⓖ 선택
ⓗ 신체적인 ⓘ 실내의 ⓙ 실패하다
ⓚ 아주 작은 ⓛ 야외의 ⓜ 움직이다
ⓝ 탁구

▶ 해설편 p.1

빈칸 추론

1 이 글의 빈칸에 들어갈 말로 가장 적절한 것은?

① good health
② painful injury
③ huge money
④ big noise
⑤ high intelligence

제목 추론

2 What is the best title for this passage?

① Do Not Play Sports in Winter
② How to Move Quickly in Table Tennis
③ Table Tennis Is Difficult but Fun
④ Nice Indoor Sports in Winter: Table Tennis
⑤ Outdoor Sports vs. Indoor Sports

서술형

3 탁구의 좋은 점을 본문에서 찾아 우리말로 쓰시오. (답 6개)

(1) ______________________
(2) ______________________
(3) ______________________
(4) ______________________
(5) ______________________
(6) ______________________

내신 Level Up

밑줄 친 ㉠it이 가리키는 것을 본문에서 찾아 두 단어로 쓰시오.

____

구문 Level Up

첫번째문장 In winter, **it** is not easy **to enjoy outdoor sports**.

▶ to부정사구가 주어로 쓰이는 경우, 주어 자리에 가주어 it을 쓰고 to부정사를 뒤로 보내는 것이 자연스럽다. 이때, 뒤로 보낸 to부정사구를 진주어라고 한다.

[확인 문제] 다음 문장을 가주어 It을 사용하여 바꿔 쓰시오.

1. To become an actor is his dream.
→ ______________________
배우가 되는 것은 그의 꿈이다.

2. To walk against the traffic light is dangerous.
→ ______________________
____
교통 신호를 지키지 않고 걷는 것은 위험하다.

■ 나의 독해 점검표 ■

Step ❶ | 채점 결과 정리

1. 빈칸 추론	O / X
2. 제목 추론	O / X
3. 서술형	O / X

• 나의 약점 유형은? __________

Step ❷ | 독해력 점검

□ 지문의 내용을 충분히 이해함
□ 지문의 내용을 대체로 이해함
□ 지문의 내용을 이해하지 못함

Step ❸ | 문제 해결력 점검

□ 정답과 오답의 근거를 모두 찾음
□ 정답과 오답의 근거를 대체로 찾음
□ 정답과 오답의 근거를 찾지 못함

Day 01 Reading 02

왜 인간은 100m를 9초대 이하로 못 뛸까?

01-02

For most runners, speed is determined by the legs' force. So, there are two ways to run faster: jump and stay in the air longer, or kick the ground harder.

(A) However, people cannot do this because they run with two legs and it's easy to lose their balance in the air. So the second way is the only option for humans to run faster.

(B) Fast animals such as cheetahs use the first method. They run with four legs to jump and to stay in the air longer. They can move forward much faster when they are in the air.

(C) In that way, it is important to hit the ground ㉠<u>harder</u>. The fastest runner in the world hits the ground 2.5 times stronger than his body weight. If we made the power stronger, it would break the world's record.

제대로 독해법

어휘 Level Up

단어에 알맞은 우리말 뜻을 골라 그 기호를 빈칸에 쓰시오.
(뜻이 같은 단어에 한하여 중복 답 가능)

1 determine ....
2 force ....
3 fast ....
4 stay ....
5 ground ....
6 lose ....
7 balance ....
8 in the air ....
9 such as ....
10 forward ....
11 important ....
12 weight ....
13 break ....

ⓐ ~와 같은 ⓑ 결정하다
ⓒ 공중에서 ⓓ 균형 ⓔ 깨다 ⓕ 땅
ⓖ 머무르다 ⓗ 무게 ⓘ 빠른; 빠르게
ⓙ 앞으로 ⓚ 잃다 ⓛ 중요한 ⓜ 힘

▶ 해설편 p.2

1 이 글의 내용과 일치하지 않는 것은?

① 달리는 속도는 다리 힘에 의해 결정된다.
② 치타는 달리는 속도가 빠른 동물이다.
③ 인간은 두 발로 달리기 때문에 공중에서 균형을 잘 잡는다.
④ 인간은 땅을 더 세게 차면 더 빨리 달릴 수 있다.
⑤ 세계에서 가장 빠른 달리기 선수는 자기 몸무게보다 2.5배 강하게 땅을 박차다.

2 What is the right order to read?

① (A) — (C) — (B)
② (B) — (A) — (C)
③ (B) — (C) — (A)
④ (C) — (A) — (B)
⑤ (C) — (B) — (A)

3 치타와 인간이 빨리 달리는 방법을 본문에서 찾아 우리말로 쓰시오.

(1) 치타가 빨리 달리는 방법 :

____

(2) 인간이 빨리 달리는 방법 :

____

내신 Level Up

밑줄 친 ⓐ harder와 의미가 가장 가까운 한 단어를 본문에서 찾아 쓰시오.

____

마지막 문장 If we **made** the power stronger, it **would break** the world's record.

▶ 「If+주어+동사의 과거형(made) ~, 주어+조동사의 과거형(would)+동사원형(break)」 형태의 가정법 과거 문장으로, 현재 사실과 반대되는 상황을 가정한다.

[확인 문제] 괄호 안에서 알맞은 것을 고르시오.

1. If I had good friends, I (will / would) be happy.

   만약 내게 좋은 친구들이 있으면, 나는 행복할 텐데.

2. If she (comes / came) earlier, she could take the bus.

   만약 그녀가 더 일찍 오면, 그녀는 그 버스를 탈 수 있을 텐데.

■ 나의 독해 점검표 ■

Step ❶ | 채점 결과 정리

1. 내용 일치	O / X
2. 순서 파악	O / X
3. 서술형	O / X

• 나의 약점 유형은? __________

Step ❷ | 독해력 점검

□ 지문의 내용을 충분히 이해함
□ 지문의 내용을 대체로 이해함
□ 지문의 내용을 이해하지 못함

Step ❸ | 문제 해결력 점검

□ 정답과 오답의 근거를 모두 찾음
□ 정답과 오답의 근거를 대체로 찾음
□ 정답과 오답의 근거를 찾지 못함

02-01

요즘 유행하는 방탈출 게임 해봤니?

Do you like playing room escape games? In these games, you will be locked up in a certain room. There is no explanation and no exit at all. You need to look around the room, check everything, and (A) [gather / gathering] hints and items in the room. It usually provides some puzzles to find an exit. (ⓐ) ㉠They are really fun and (B) [interested / interesting] to solve. (ⓑ) For example, you may need to find an invisible password on a wall with special goggles, then (C) [put it in / put in it] the keypad to go to the next stage. (ⓒ) Escaping room games usually take you about one hour. (ⓓ) Generally, you need to escape in a given time. (ⓔ)

*goggles 고글(물·바람·먼지 등이 들어가지 않게 얼굴에 밀착되게 쓰는 안경)

제대로 독해법

어휘 Level Up

단어에 알맞은 우리말 뜻을 골라 그 기호를 빈칸에 쓰시오.
(뜻이 같은 단어에 한하여 중복 답 가능)

1 escape ....
2 be locked up ....
3 certain ....
4 explanation ....
5 exit ....
6 at all ....
7 look around ....
8 gather ....
9 solve ....
10 for example ....
11 invisible ....
12 password ....
13 wall ....
14 stage ....
15 generally ....

ⓐ 풀다, 해결하다 ⓑ 갇히다
ⓒ 눈에 보이지 않는 ⓓ 단계, 무대
ⓔ 둘러보다 ⓕ 모으다 ⓖ 벽, 담
ⓗ 설명 ⓘ 암호 ⓙ 어떤
ⓚ 예를 들어 ⓛ 일반적으로 ⓜ 전혀
ⓝ 출구 ⓞ 탈출; 탈출하다

▶ 해설편 p.3

어법성 판단

1 (A), (B), (C)의 각 네모 안에서 어법에 맞는 표현으로 가장 적절한 것은?

	(A)		(B)		(C)
①	gather	----	interesting	----	put in it
②	gather	----	interested	----	put it in
③	gathering	----	interested	----	put in it
④	gathering	----	interesting	----	put in it
⑤	gather	----	interesting	----	put it in

문장 삽입

2 Where would the following sentence best fit?

> If you can't, you have to pay extra money for more hints or give up the game.

① ⓐ ② ⓑ ③ ⓒ ④ ⓓ ⑤ ⓔ

서술형

3 방탈출 게임에서 퍼즐을 푸는 방법의 예를 본문에서 찾아 우리말로 쓰시오.

____

내신 Level Up

밑줄 친 ㉠ They가 가리키는 것을 본문에서 찾아 두 단어로 쓰시오.

____

구문 Level Up

3~5행 You need to **look** around the room, **check** everything, **and gather** hints and items in the room.

▶ look ~, check ~, and gather ~는 접속사(and)로 연결되어 병렬구조를 이루고 있으므로 형태가 같아야 한다.

[확인 문제] 괄호 안에서 알맞은 것을 고르시오.

1. She likes to read, listen to music, and (jog / to jog).

   그녀는 독서하고, 음악을 듣고, 조깅하는 것을 좋아한다.

2. I like monkeys, elephants, and (going to the zoo / camels).

   나는 원숭이, 코끼리, 그리고 낙타를 좋아한다.

■ 나의 독해 점검표 ■

Step ❶ | 채점 결과 정리

1. 어법성 판단	O / X
2. 문장 삽입	O / X
3. 서술형	O / X

• 나의 약점 유형은? __________

Step ❷ | 독해력 점검

□ 지문의 내용을 충분히 이해함
□ 지문의 내용을 대체로 이해함
□ 지문의 내용을 이해하지 못함

Step ❸ | 문제 해결력 점검

□ 정답과 오답의 근거를 모두 찾음
□ 정답과 오답의 근거를 대체로 찾음
□ 정답과 오답의 근거를 찾지 못함

볼링과 터키의 관계는?

02-02

"Turkey" has several meanings. It may be a kind of bird or a country in Europe. But few people come up with ㉠another meaning. This word may mean triple strikes in a bowling game. Bowling is a sport with a heavy ball and 10 pins. You have to roll the ball to knock down as many pins as possible. If you knock over all of them at once, you call it a strike. And if you do this three times in a row, you call it a turkey. Then, why is it called a turkey? In America, turkey meat was a common prize in the past. One owner of the bowling game center decided to give a turkey to people if they made three strikes in a row. From that time on, bowling players named it a turkey and still use the word.

제대로 독해법

어휘 Level Up

단어에 알맞은 우리말 뜻을 골라 그 기호를 빈칸에 쓰시오.
(뜻이 같은 단어에 한하여 중복 답 가능)

1 several ....
2 meaning ....
3 kind ....
4 come up with ....
5 mean ....
6 triple ....
7 roll ....
8 knock down ....
9 at once ....
10 in a row ....
11 meat ....
12 common ....
13 owner ....
14 decide ....

ⓐ 3중의; [볼링] 3연속 스트라이크
ⓑ 결정하다 ⓒ 고기 ⓓ 굴리다
ⓔ (해답·아이디어 등을) 내놓다
ⓕ 넘어뜨리다 ⓖ 여러 가지의
ⓗ 연속으로 ⓘ 의미 ⓙ 의미하다
ⓚ 종류; 친절한 ⓛ 소유자, 주인
ⓜ 한 번에, 동시에 ⓝ 흔한

▶ 해설편 p.4

요약문 완성

1 이 글의 내용을 요약할 때 빈칸 (A), (B)에 들어갈 말로 가장 적절한 것은?

> Making triple strikes in a bowling game is called ____(A)____, and this word was from a(n) ____(B)____ in the past.

(A) ---- (B)

① chicken ---- bowling player
② turkey ---- country name
③ turkey ---- winning prize
④ chicken ---- turkey meat
⑤ turkey ---- American dream

주제 추론

2 What is the main idea of this passage?

① The origin of turkey in a bowling game
② How to hunt a turkey in the wild
③ Playing bowling games in the funniest way
④ The way to get high score in a bowling game
⑤ The history of European country, Turkey

서술형

3 'turkey'가 의미하는 것을 본문에서 모두 찾아 우리말로 쓰시오. (답 3개)

(1) ______________________________
(2) ______________________________
(3) ______________________________

내신 Level Up

밑줄 친 ㉠another meaning이 가리키는 것을 본문에서 찾아 6단어로 쓰시오.

____

구문 Level Up

6~7행 And if you do this three times in a row, **you call it a turkey**.

▶ you call it a turkey는 「주어 + 동사 + 목적어 + 목적격보어」 형태의 5형식 문장이다.

7~8행 Then, why **is it called a turkey**?

▶ 「주어 + 동사 + 목적어 + 목적격보어」의 형태를 가지는 5형식 문장은 목적어를 주어로 하여 수동태(be동사 + p.p.)를 만들 수 있다. 이때, 목적격보어는 「be동사 + p.p.」 뒤에 써 준다.
You call **it** a turkey. (능동태)
→ **It is called** a turkey (by you). (수동태)

[확인 문제] **다음 문장을 수동태로 바꿀 때, 빈칸에 알맞은 말을 쓰시오.**

> I made him angry.
> → He ______ ______ ______ by me.

나는 그를 화나게 만들었다.
→ 그는 나에 의해 화가 났다.

■ 나의 독해 점검표 ■

Step ❶ | 채점 결과 정리

1. 요약문 완성	O / X
2. 주제 추론	O / X
3. 서술형	O / X

• 나의 약점 유형은? __________

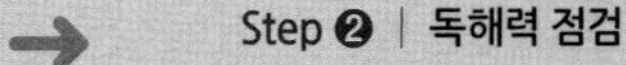

Step ❷ | 독해력 점검

□ 지문의 내용을 충분히 이해함
□ 지문의 내용을 대체로 이해함
□ 지문의 내용을 이해하지 못함

Step ❸ | 문제 해결력 점검

□ 정답과 오답의 근거를 모두 찾음
□ 정답과 오답의 근거를 대체로 찾음
□ 정답과 오답의 근거를 찾지 못함

▶ 해설편 p.4

어휘 테스트

A 사진을 보고, 빈칸에 알맞은 단어를 골라 쓰시오.

balance	exit	faster	meat	roll	table tennis

1 Why don't you try __________ as an indoor sport?

2 There are two ways to run __________.

3 It's easy to lose their __________ in the air.

4 It provides some puzzles to find a(n) __________.

5 You have to __________ the ball to knock down pins.

6 Turkey __________ was a common prize in the past.

B 다음 각 단어에 해당하는 의미를 짝지으시오.

1 physical •   • ⓐ towards the direction that is in front of you

2 forward •   • ⓑ impossible to see

3 invisible •   • ⓒ relating to the body

레저 스포츠 즐기기

스케이트보드

파도타기 애호가들이 파도가 없는 잔잔한 바다에서는 파도타기를 할 수 없게 되자 서핑보드가 육지로 올라오면서 점차 스케이트보드의 형태를 갖추게 되었다. 스케이트보드를 즐기기 위해서는 평탄한 장소만 있으면 어디든지 가능하다. 그러나 보다 난이도 높은 퍼포먼스를 위해서는 특별한 시설물을 만들어 그 위를 활주하면서 묘기를 부린다.

스포츠 클라이밍

스포츠 클라이밍은 산악 등지에서 경험할 수 있는 암벽 등반을 인공 시설물을 이용하여 즐기는 스포츠다. 스포츠 클라이밍은 건물 벽면이나 암벽을 연상케 하는 거대한 합판 등의 구조물에 인공 홀드를 설치해 놓고 손과 발만을 이용해 벽면을 따라 이동하는 스포츠다.

하강 시설(짚라인)

양편의 나무 또는 지주대 사이로 튼튼한 와이어를 설치하고 탑승자와 연결된 도르래를 와이어에 걸어 빠른 속도로 반대편으로 이동하여 스릴과 함께 자연을 느낄 수 있는 야외 레포츠이다. 와이어를 타고 이동할 때 트롤리와 와이어의 마찰음이 '짚~(zip)'과 비슷하게 들리는 점을 의성어로 착안하여 '짚라인'으로 브랜드명을 정하였다.

Chapter 2

Environment 환경

내가 아는 단어는 몇 개?

▷▶ 다음 단어의 뜻을 추측해 보고, 알고 있는 단어에 ✓표시를 하시오.

☐ satellite

☐ temperature

☐ recycle

☐ fisherman

☐ land

☐ crop

☐ freezing

☐ feather

☐ goose

Day 03 Reading 01

기후 변화의 원인에 대한 논쟁

03-01

Scientists are arguing why climate change is happening. Most of them believe that the recent climate change is due to human activity. Many data from satellite support the fact that the development of cities and factories actually is causing climate change. Researchers also agree that fossil fuel gas from cars is raising the temperature of the Earth. However, some people question the truth of ㉠ this argument. ⓐ They are saying that climate change is a part of the natural change in Earth's climate and temperature. ⓑ The Earth gets most energy from the Sun. ⓒ They think it is difficult to connect climate change and certain weather events. ⓓ For example, the summer is getting hotter and hotter around the world, but nobody knows the reason exactly. ⓔ Some people say it might be a natural change as the Earth ages.

*fossil fuel 화석 연료(석유)

제대로 독해법

어휘 Level Up

단어에 알맞은 우리말 뜻을 골라 그 기호를 빈칸에 쓰시오.
(뜻이 같은 단어에 한하여 중복 답 가능)

1 argue ....
2 climate ....
3 recent ....
4 due to ....
5 activity ....
6 satellite ....
7 support ....
8 development ....
9 actually ....
10 cause ....
11 researcher ....
12 agree ....
13 raise ....
14 temperature ....
15 question ....
16 connect ....
17 certain ....
18 exactly ....

ⓐ ~ 때문에 ⓑ ~을 일으키다; 원인
ⓒ 기후 ⓓ 논쟁하다 ⓔ 동의하다
ⓕ 뒷받침하다, 지원하다 ⓖ 발전
ⓗ 사실상 ⓘ 연관 짓다, 연결하다
ⓙ 연구자 ⓚ 온도, 기온
ⓛ (양·수준 등을) 올리다 ⓜ 위성
ⓝ ~을 의심하다; 문제 ⓞ 활동
ⓟ 정확히 ⓠ 최근의 ⓡ 특정한, 어떤

▶ 해설편 p.5

1 ⓐ ~ ⓔ 중에서 이 글의 전체 흐름과 관계없는 문장은?

① ⓐ ② ⓑ ③ ⓒ ④ ⓓ ⑤ ⓔ

2 What is the best title for this passage?

① Why Is Climate Change Happening?
② The Essentials of Human Activity: Cities and Factories
③ The Weather Changed by Human Activities
④ The Older the Earth Is, the Worse the Climate Is
⑤ The Climate Change: A Natural Thing to the Earth

서술형

3 밑줄 친 ㉠ this argument가 의미하는 것을 본문에서 찾아 우리말로 쓰시오.

____

내신 Level Up

기후 변화의 원인을 본문에서 찾아 우리말로 쓰시오. (답 2개)

(1) ____________________

(2) ____________________

구문 Level Up

2~3행 Most of them believe **that** *the recent climate change is due to human activity.*

▶ 접속사 that은 주어, 목적어, 보어의 역할을 하는 명사절을 이끈다. 여기서는 접속사 that이 이끄는 명사절(that the recent climate change is due to human activity)이 동사 believe의 목적어 역할을 하는 목적절이다. 이 경우, 목적절을 이끄는 접속사 that은 생략이 가능하다.

[확인 문제] 우리말과 뜻이 같도록 괄호 안에 주어진 단어들을 배열하여 문장을 완성하시오.

1. 나는 우리가 그것을 할 수 있다고 믿는다. (do / it / can / that / we)
→ I believe ____________________.

2. 나는 네가 고등학교 교사였다는 것을 들었다. (a / teacher / high school / that / were / you)
→ I've heard ____________________
____________________.

■ 나의 독해 점검표 ■

Step ❶ | 채점 결과 정리

1. 무관한 문장	O / X
2. 제목 추론	O / X
3. 서술형	O / X

• 나의 약점 유형은? __________

Step ❷ | 독해력 점검

□ 지문의 내용을 충분히 이해함
□ 지문의 내용을 대체로 이해함
□ 지문의 내용을 이해하지 못함

Step ❸ | 문제 해결력 점검

□ 정답과 오답의 근거를 모두 찾음
□ 정답과 오답의 근거를 대체로 찾음
□ 정답과 오답의 근거를 찾지 못함

Day 03 Reading 02

우리는 매일 플라스틱을 먹고 있다

03-02

We are eating plastic every day, but few of us realize it. The biggest reason is that we don't care whether it returns to us.

(A) Many fish and sea creatures are dying because of plastic concentration inside their body. It could be the same to human. Therefore, scientists suggest that we stop using plastic products and recycle them as much as possible.

(B) Finally, fishermen catch ⓐthem and then the tiny plastic pieces go into our food. We don't know much about its effect to the human body. However, ⓑthey do not seem good for our health.

(C) Let me give you an example. If we throw plastic pieces into the ocean, ⓒthey are broken down into smaller and smaller pieces. ⓓThey sink deep into the ocean and plankton absorbs ⓔthem. Then, some fish eat the plankton and the plastic pieces stay in the fish.

*sea creatures 해양 생물

제대로 독해법

어휘 Level Up

단어에 알맞은 우리말 뜻을 골라 그 기호를 빈칸에 쓰시오.
(뜻이 같은 단어에 한하여 중복 답 가능)

1 plastic ....
2 care ....
3 return ....
4 concentration ....
5 suggest ....
6 recycle ....
7 fisherman ....
8 tiny ....
9 piece ....
10 effect ....
11 ocean ....
12 break ~ down ....
13 sink ....
14 plankton ....
15 absorb ....
16 stay ....

ⓐ ~을 분해하다 ⓑ 가라앉다
ⓒ 남다 ⓓ 농축물, 집중
ⓔ 돌아오다 ⓕ 바다 ⓖ 신경 쓰다
ⓗ 아주 작은 ⓘ 어부 ⓙ 영향
ⓚ 재활용하다 ⓛ 제안하다 ⓜ 조각
ⓝ 플라스틱 ⓞ 플랑크톤
ⓟ 흡수하다

▶ 해설편 p.6

1 밑줄 친 ⓐ ~ ⓔ 중에서 가리키는 대상이 나머지 넷과 다른 것은?

① ⓐ ② ⓑ ③ ⓒ ④ ⓓ ⑤ ⓔ

순서 파악

2 What is the right order to read?

① (A) — (C) — (B)
② (B) — (A) — (C)
③ (B) — (C) — (A)
④ (C) — (A) — (B)
⑤ (C) — (B) — (A)

서술형

3 플라스틱이 우리 몸에 들어오는 과정에 따라 다음 빈칸을 완성하시오.

플라스틱 쓰레기 → ______ → ______ → ______ → ______ → (사람이 먹는) 음식

내신 Level Up

다음 영영풀이가 뜻하는 단어를 본문에서 찾아 쓰시오.

______ : to use something again for a different purpose

구문 Level Up

(A) 3행 Therefore, scientists suggest that we **stop using** plastic products and recycle them as much as possible.

▶ 「stop + -ing」는 '~하는 것을 멈추다[그만두다]'라는 의미이다. stop 뒤에 to부정사가 오는 경우에는 '~하기 위해 멈추다[그만두다]'라는 목적의 의미를 나타내는 부사적 용법으로 쓰인다.

[확인 문제] 우리말과 뜻이 같도록 괄호 안에서 알맞은 것을 고르시오.

1. 그녀는 그녀의 친구와 이야기하는 것을 멈추었다.
   She stopped (to chat / chatting) with her friend.

2. 그는 건강을 위해 당분간 커피 마시는 것을 그만두었다.
   He stopped (to drink / drinking) coffee for his health for a while.

■ 나의 독해 점검표 ■

Step ❶ | **채점 결과 정리**

1. 지칭 추론	O / X
2. 순서 파악	O / X
3. 서술형	O / X

• 나의 약점 유형은? ______

Step ❷ | **독해력 점검**

□ 지문의 내용을 충분히 이해함
□ 지문의 내용을 대체로 이해함
□ 지문의 내용을 이해하지 못함

Step ❸ | **문제 해결력 점검**

□ 정답과 오답의 근거를 모두 찾음
□ 정답과 오답의 근거를 대체로 찾음
□ 정답과 오답의 근거를 찾지 못함

Day 04 Reading 01

아보카도는 과연 좋기만 할까?

04-01

Do you like eating avocados? Avocados are favored around the world because they taste like butter, but are much ⓐhealthier than real butter. So many restaurants are inventing menu with avocados. However, there are problems about this green fruit. They usually grow in Mexico and need a lot of water. Many researchers say that it makes the land of Mexico drier and drier like ⓑthe desert. In other words, they are killing the land. They also ⓒharm the economy in Mexico. Because many local farmers prefer planting avocados to any other crop, they spend a lot of money on the seeds. However, the supply is ⓓlimitless, and the price keeps going up. So the farmers need to pay more and more for avocado farms. Some even call it a blood avocado because a number of people ⓔlose money and leave their farms.

제대로 독해법

어휘 Level Up

단어에 알맞은 우리말 뜻을 골라 그 기호를 빈칸에 쓰시오.
(뜻이 같은 단어에 한하여 중복 답 가능)

1 favor ....
2 taste ....
3 invent ....
4 a lot of ....
5 land ....
6 economy ....
7 local ....
8 prefer ....
9 crop ....
10 spend ....
11 seed ....
12 supply ....
13 price ....
14 go up ....
15 farm ....
16 even ....
17 leave ....

ⓐ (가격이) 오르다
ⓑ (돈·시간을) 쓰다 ⓒ ~도[조차]
ⓓ ~한 맛이 나다 ⓔ 가격 ⓕ 경제
ⓖ 공급 ⓗ 농장 ⓘ 땅 ⓙ 떠나다
ⓚ 많은 ⓛ 개발하다, 발명하다
ⓜ 선호하다 ⓝ (농)작물
ⓞ 종자, 씨앗 ⓟ 지역의

▶ 해설편 p.7

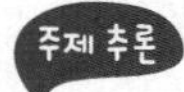

1 이 글의 주제로 가장 적절한 것은?

① 아보카도의 좋은 점
② 아보카도 재배 방법
③ 아보카도 맛의 특징
④ 아보카도 경작의 문제점
⑤ 아보카도가 들어간 음식 메뉴 개발

2 Which is NOT a suitable word in ⓐ ~ ⓔ?

① ⓐ ② ⓑ ③ ⓒ ④ ⓓ ⑤ ⓔ

서술형

3 아보카도가 전 세계에서 인기 있는 이유를 본문에서 찾아 우리말로 쓰시오.

____

내신 Level Up

이 글의 내용과 일치하도록 빈칸에 알맞은 말을 본문에서 찾아 쓰시오.

Many local farmers prefer planting avocados to any other (1)__________.

The farmers (2)__________ a lot of money on the seeds.

↓

A number of people lose money and (3)__________ their farms.

구문 Level Up

1~3행 ~, but are **much healthier than** real butter.

▶ 「비교급+than」은 '~보다 더 …한[하게]'의 의미를 가진다. much, even, still, far, a lot은 비교급 앞에서 비교급을 강조하여 '훨씬'의 의미를 나타낸다.

[확인 문제] 괄호 안에서 알맞은 것을 고르시오.

The church is (very / much) older than the library.

그 교회는 그 도서관보다 훨씬 더 오래되었다.

■ 나의 독해 점검표 ■

Step ❶ | 채점 결과 정리

1. 주제 추론	O / X
2. 어휘 파악	O / X
3. 서술형	O / X

• 나의 약점 유형은? __________

Step ❷ | 독해력 점검

□ 지문의 내용을 충분히 이해함
□ 지문의 내용을 대체로 이해함
□ 지문의 내용을 이해하지 못함

Step ❸ | 문제 해결력 점검

□ 정답과 오답의 근거를 모두 찾음
□ 정답과 오답의 근거를 대체로 찾음
□ 정답과 오답의 근거를 찾지 못함

04-02

따뜻한 롱패딩을 위해 죽어 가는 동물들

Long padding coats, or bench coats, are in trend these days, because they can make us warm even if the weather is freezing. However, you should know that quite a few animals are killed for this trend. Most of these coats contain thick volume of birds' feathers. (ⓐ) In clothing factories, the workers pull feathers from ducks and geese. (ⓑ) Mammals such as rabbits, racoons, or foxes are also losing their lives for this fashion. (ⓒ) Because their fur is colorful and smooth, fashion designers want to use it for styling the hoods and collars of these coats. (ⓓ) Consumers should be aware of ㉠these facts and be more careful when they buy long padding coats. (ⓔ)

*mammals 포유류 **racoon 라쿤(미국너구리)

제대로 독해법

어휘 Level Up

단어에 알맞은 우리말 뜻을 골라 그 기호를 빈칸에 쓰시오.
(뜻이 같은 단어에 한하여 중복 답 가능)

1 freezing ....
2 contain ....
3 thick ....
4 feather ....
5 pull ....
6 duck ....
7 goose ....
8 fur ....
9 colorful ....
10 smooth ....
11 hood ....
12 collar ....
13 consumer ....
14 be aware of ....
15 careful ....

ⓐ (털이) 윤이 나는, 매끄러운
ⓑ ~을 알다 ⓒ 거위 ⓓ 깃털
ⓔ 엄청[몹시] 추운 ⓕ 다채로운
ⓖ 두꺼운 ⓗ 모자 ⓘ 모피, 털
ⓙ 소비자 ⓚ 신중한 ⓛ 오리
ⓜ 옷깃 ⓝ (새 등의) 털을 뽑다
ⓞ 포함하다

▶ 해설편 p.8

1 이 글의 흐름으로 보아, 주어진 문장이 들어가기에 가장 적절한 곳은?

The birds stay still but feel strong pain because they are alive during this process.

① ⓐ ② ⓑ  ③ ⓒ  ④ ⓓ ⑤ ⓔ

주제 추론

2 What is the main idea of this passage?

① Bench coats are not warm enough.
② We should not kill animals in any way for the fashion.
③ Many animals are killed in pain for the bench coat trend.
④ Fashion trend is always changing.
⑤ Animals have their own soul and feel pain.

3 패션 디자이너들이 토끼나 여우의 모피를 사용하는 이유를 본문에서 찾아 우리말로 쓰시오.

____

내신 Level Up

밑줄 친 ㉠these facts가 가리키는 것을 본문에서 찾아 영어로 쓰시오. (9단어)

____

____

구문 Level Up

1~3행 ~, because they can **make us warm even if** the weather is freezing.

▶ 「make + 목적어(us) + 목적격보어(warm)」 형태의 5형식 문장으로, 5형식 동사 make의 목적격보어로는 형용사, 명사, 동사원형, 분사가 올 수 있다.

▶ even if는 양보를 나타내는 접속사로 '(비록) ~이지만, ~일지라도, ~하더라도'의 의미를 가진다. (= although, though, even though)

[확인 문제] 우리말과 뜻이 같도록 괄호 안에 주어진 단어들을 배열하여 문장을 완성하시오.

1. 그는 의자가 낡았다고 생각했다.
(old / thought / the chair)
→ He _______________.

2. 할머니는 문을 열어 두셨다.
(open / left / the door)
→ Grandma _______________.

■ 나의 독해 점검표 ■

Step ❶ | 채점 결과 정리

1. 문장 삽입	O / X
2. 주제 추론	O / X
3. 서술형	O / X

• 나의 약점 유형은? _______________

Step ❷ | 독해력 점검

□ 지문의 내용을 충분히 이해함
□ 지문의 내용을 대체로 이해함
□ 지문의 내용을 이해하지 못함

Step ❸ | 문제 해결력 점검

□ 정답과 오답의 근거를 모두 찾음
□ 정답과 오답의 근거를 대체로 찾음
□ 정답과 오답의 근거를 찾지 못함

▶ 해설편 p.8

어휘 테스트

A 사진을 보고, 빈칸에 알맞은 단어를 골라 쓰시오.

crop	feathers	freezing	geese	land	recycle

1 We should ___________ plastic products.

2 Avocados are killing the ___________.

3 They prefer planting avocados to any other ___________.

4 They can make us warm even if the weather is ___________.

5 They contain thick volume of birds' ___________.

6 They pull feathers from ducks and ___________.

B 다음 각 단어에 해당하는 의미를 짝지으시오.

1 agree •   • ⓐ to like, choose, or want one thing rather than another

2 prefer •   • ⓑ to have the same opinion

3 consumer •   • ⓒ a person who buys goods or services for their own use

세계 속 독특한 분리수거 방법

재활용 쓰레기가 학용품으로?

1980년 세계 최초 도시 차원의 분리수거 프로그램을 도입해 유엔 환경 프로그램을 수상한 브라질의 쿠리치바(Curytiba)! 공공장소 쓰레기통에 플라스틱/유리/캔/비닐/종이 모양으로 디자인된 스티커를 부착해 시민들이 쉽게 쓰레기를 분리해 버릴 수 있도록 했습니다. 특히 분리수거 프로그램 중 하나인 '녹색 교환'은 재활용이 가능한 쓰레기를 가져오면 학용품이나 식품으로 교환해 주어 어린 학생들까지 쓰레기 분리수거에 적극 동참했다고 합니다.

분리수거로 투표하기

위컵(Wecup)은 2014년 네덜란드 로테르담(Rotterdam)에서 열린 한 축제에 등장해 쓰레기 분리와 쓰레기 수거, 재미까지 세 마리의 토끼를 한 번에 잡는 데 성공한 분리수거 방법입니다. 두 개의 투명한 원통형 쓰레기통을 놓고 그 위에 '엘비스 프레슬리(Elvis Presley)가 돌아오면 좋겠다 vs. 마이클 잭슨(Michael Jackson)이 돌아오면 좋겠다'와 같은 주제를 제시해 원하는 쪽으로 플라스틱 컵을 버려 투표 결과를 확인할 수 있는 위컵은 사람들의 승부욕을 자극해 쓰레기를 스스로 분리해 버리도록 유도합니다.

페트병으로 동물 사랑

터키에는 플라스틱 병을 넣으면 즉석으로 동물들의 사료가 공급되는 '동물먹이 자판기'가 있습니다. 자판기 투입구에 다 먹고 난 음료수 병을 넣으면 하단에 있는 배출구를 통해 동물들이 먹을 수 있는 사료와 물이 공급됩니다. 이는 터키에 있는 15만 마리의 유기견과 유기묘를 위해 한 회사에서 발명해 낸 것으로 시민들의 분리수거를 장려하는 한편 주인 없는 동물들도 함께 도울 수 있습니다.

Chapter 3

Travel 여행
★
Places 장소

내가 아는 단어는 몇 개?

▷▶ 다음 단어의 뜻을 추측해 보고, 알고 있는 단어에 ✓표시를 하시오.

☐ tropical fish

☐ squid

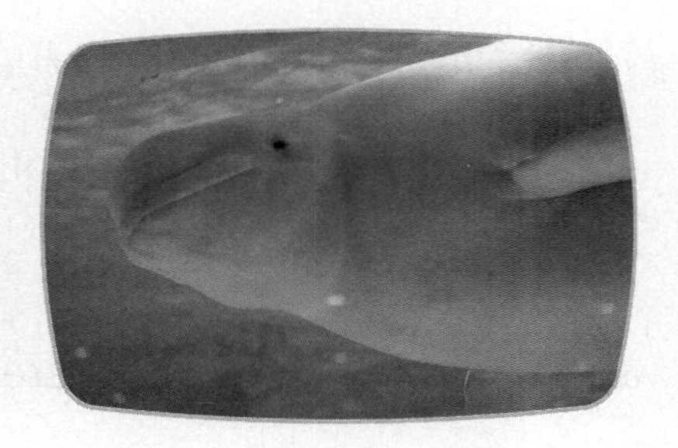

☐ whale

☐ traveler

☐ concerned

☐ scuba-diving

☐ kayaking

☐ measure

☐ weight

몰디브에서 볼 수 있는 동물은?

Maldives have beautiful blue seas and white beaches. There are more than 2,000 kinds of tropical fish around the islands. Sea creatures like jellyfish, octopus, squid, and clams are also common. Coral reefs are very popular with the seasonal movement of fish and whales. Maldives' oceans and beaches are becoming one of the most popular tourist attractions in the world to see these colorful sea creatures, including aquariums. However, if you are looking for zoos, you may be disappointed. There are very few land animals, and even no house dogs live in Maldives. In fact, Maldives are a group of very small islands and most animals live in the water. They simply don't have ________________________________.

*jellyfish 해파리 **clam 조개 ***coral reef 산호초

몰디브 공화국
인도양 중북부에 있는 섬나라로 인도와 스리랑카 남서쪽에 위치하는 남아시아 국가이다. 섬의 총수는 1,192개이다.

제대로 독해법

어휘 Level Up

단어에 알맞은 우리말 뜻을 골라 그 기호를 빈칸에 쓰시오.
(뜻이 같은 단어에 한하여 중복 답 가능)

1 beach ....
2 tropical fish ....
3 sea creature ....
4 octopus ....
5 squid ....
6 common ....
7 seasonal ....
8 movement ....
9 whale ....
10 tourist attraction ....
11 aquarium ....
12 disappointed ....
13 land ....
14 simply ....

ⓐ 계절의 ⓑ 고래 ⓒ 관광지
ⓓ 단지, 단순히 ⓔ 문어
ⓕ 아쿠아리움, 수족관 ⓖ 실망한
ⓗ 열대어 ⓘ 오징어
ⓙ 육지, 땅 ⓚ 이동 ⓛ 해변
ⓜ 해양 생물 ⓝ 흔한

▶ 해설편 p.9

요약문 완성

1 **이 글의 내용을 요약할 때, 빈칸 (A), (B)에 들어갈 말로 가장 적절한 것은?**

In Maldives, one of the most famous ____(A)____, most animals don't live on land, but in ____(B)____.

	(A)		(B)
①	urban areas	----	water
②	trading nations	----	aquariums
③	tourist attractions	----	water
④	volcano islands	----	caves
⑤	historic sites	----	caves

빈칸 추론

2 **What is the best choice for the blank?**

① enough budget to run zoos
② enough space to raise land animals
③ the good weather for land animals
④ animal trainers to feed land animals
⑤ markets for importing land animals

서술형

3 **몰디브가 세계적인 관광지로 인기 있는 이유를 본문에서 찾아 우리말로 쓰시오.**

____

내신 Level Up

몰디브에서 볼 수 있는 동물들을 본문에서 찾아 우리말로 쓰시오. (5개 이상)

____
____
____

구문 Level Up

1~2행 **There are** more than 2,000 kinds of tropical fish around the islands.

▶「There + be동사 + 주어 ~」 형태의 1형식 문장이다. 주어의 수에 be동사의 수를 일치시킨다. There is/are ~는 '~(들)이 있다'의 의미를 가진다.

[확인 문제] 괄호 안에서 알맞은 것을 고르시오.

1. There (is / are) a cow in the field.
들판에 소 한 마리가 있다.

2. There (isn't / aren't) many trees in the park.
그 공원에 나무가 많지 않다.

■ 나의 독해 점검표 ■

Step ❶ | 채점 결과 정리

1. 요약문 완성	O / X
2. 빈칸 추론	O / X
3. 서술형	O / X

• 나의 약점 유형은? __________

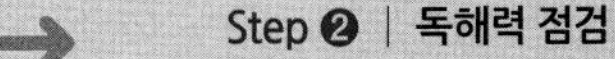

Step ❷ | 독해력 점검

□ 지문의 내용을 충분히 이해함
□ 지문의 내용을 대체로 이해함
□ 지문의 내용을 이해하지 못함

Step ❸ | 문제 해결력 점검

□ 정답과 오답의 근거를 모두 찾음
□ 정답과 오답의 근거를 대체로 찾음
□ 정답과 오답의 근거를 찾지 못함

당신은 어떤 유형의 여행자인가요?

05-02

Here are three types of travelers. Read and check what type of traveler you are.

1. The Lifetime Traveler

   They live to travel. When they aren't traveling, they are thinking about the next place to go. They just enjoy traveling and are not concerned about whether their situation during the journey is good or bad.

2. The Athlete Traveler

   They like to plan vacations around sports. They go on golfing, mountain-climbing, or scuba-diving vacations. They may love to sit on a beach but only after sailing or kayaking.

3. The Comfort Traveler

   They are almost the opposite of the athlete travelers. They love traveling only when it is easy and comfortable. One thing that's important to them is the view from their room or from warm and sunny beaches.

제대로 독해법

어휘 Level Up

단어에 알맞은 우리말 뜻을 골라 그 기호를 빈칸에 쓰시오.
(뜻이 같은 단어에 한하여 중복 답 가능)

1 type ....
2 traveler ....
3 travel ....
4 concerned ....
5 situation ....
6 journey ....
7 plan ....
8 vacation ....
9 golfing ....
10 mountain-climbing ....
11 scuba-diving ....
12 sailing ....
13 kayaking ....
14 opposite ....
15 athlete ....
16 comfortable ....
17 view ....

ⓐ 걱정하는 ⓑ 계획하다 ⓒ 골프
ⓓ 등산 ⓔ 반대의 ⓕ 보트 타기
ⓖ 상황 ⓗ 스쿠버 다이빙 ⓘ 여행
ⓙ 여행자 ⓚ 여행하다 ⓛ 운동선수
ⓜ 유형 ⓝ 풍경, 경치 ⓞ 카약 타기
ⓟ 편안한 ⓠ 휴가, 방학

▶ 해설편 p.10

목적 추론

1 **이 글의 목적으로 가장 적절한 것은?**

① to confirm the reservation
② to complain about the trip
③ to advertise tourist attraction
④ to warn about dangerous places
⑤ to introduce different types of travelers

2 **What is NOT true according to this passage?**

① There are three types of travelers.
② The lifetime travelers like planning a new trip.
③ The athlete travelers tend to work out while travelling.
④ The comfort travelers are totally different from the athlete travelers.
⑤ All of the types are concerned about time and money for travel.

3 **다음 글에 가장 잘 어울리는 여행자 유형을 본문에서 찾아 쓰고, 그 유형의 특징 두 가지를 우리말로 쓰시오.**

You can stay in a hotel with great services. On a private beach, you are able to sunbathe and relax with a nice view. Even more, you can get a massage anytime.

(1) 유형: ______________________
(2) 특징: ① ______________________
② ______________________

내신 Level Up

빈칸에 알맞은 말을 본문에서 찾아 쓰시오.

(1) The ________ Traveler
"I plan to go bungee jumping during this summer vacation."

(2) The ________ Traveler
"I just want to read novels while lying on a beach chair."

(3) The ________ Traveler
"Seriously, traveling is everything in my life."

구문 Level Up

마지막문장 *One thing* **that's important to them** is the view from their room or from warm and sunny beaches.

▶ 주격 관계대명사 that이 이끄는 관계절(that's ~ them)이 선행사 One thing을 수식한다.
▶ 두 개의 전치사구(from their room, from warm and sunny beaches)가 접속사 or로 연결되어 병렬구조를 이룬다.

[확인 문제] 괄호 안에서 알맞은 것을 고르시오.

An inventor is someone that (make / makes) new things.

발명가는 새로운 물건을 만드는 사람이다.

■ 나의 독해 점검표 ■

Step ❶ | **채점 결과 정리**

1. 목적 추론	O / X
2. 내용 일치	O / X
3. 서술형	O / X

• 나의 약점 유형은? __________

Step ❷ | **독해력 점검**

□ 지문의 내용을 충분히 이해함
□ 지문의 내용을 대체로 이해함
□ 지문의 내용을 이해하지 못함

Step ❸ | **문제 해결력 점검**

□ 정답과 오답의 근거를 모두 찾음
□ 정답과 오답의 근거를 대체로 찾음
□ 정답과 오답의 근거를 찾지 못함

Day 06 Reading 01

미국의 가장 특이한 주, 알래스카

06-01

Alaska, a state of the United States, is a really interesting place in the world. People usually think ⓐit is cold all year long, but it actually has four seasons, too. The temperature even rose up to about 38 degree Celsius in the summer of 1915. However, ⓑit is true that Alaska freezes all over during wintertime. The sea between Alaska and Russia also freezes in winter, so some travelers successfully crossed the sea border on foot. ㉠The land has another interesting point. ⓒIt has the highest mountain in North America, Denali, and the longest coastline among the States. Although ⓓits size is quite big and wide, Alaska has the smallest population in the country. For your information, one of ⓔits towns, Barrow, has the longest and the shortest daytime records in the U.S. at the same time.

*Celsius 섭씨의

제대로 독해법

어휘 Level Up

단어에 알맞은 우리말 뜻을 골라 그 기호를 빈칸에 쓰시오.
(뜻이 같은 단어에 한하여 중복 답 가능)

1 state ....
2 place ....
3 temperature ....
4 rise ....
(rise - rose - risen)
5 up to ....
6 degree ....
7 freeze ....
8 successfully ....
9 border ....
10 on foot ....
11 coastline ....
12 although ....
13 wide ....
14 population ....
15 record ....
16 at the same time ....

ⓐ (온도 단위인) 도 ⓑ ~까지
ⓒ 비록 ~이지만 ⓓ 해안선
ⓔ 걸어서 ⓕ 국경
ⓖ 기록; 기록하다 ⓗ 넓은
ⓘ 동시에 ⓙ 주(州) ⓚ 성공적으로
ⓛ 얼다, 얼리다 ⓜ 장소
ⓝ (높은 위치·수준 등으로) 오르다
ⓞ 기온, 온도 ⓟ 인구

지칭 추론

1 밑줄 친 ⓐ ~ ⓔ 중에서 가리키는 대상이 나머지 넷과 다른 것은?

① ⓐ ② ⓑ ③ ⓒ ④ ⓓ  ⑤ ⓔ 

내용 일치

2 Which is TRUE according to this passage?

① Alaska is cold all year long.
② Nobody crossed the sea between Alaska and Russia on foot.
③ Alaska has the highest mountain in North America.
④ There is no coastline in Alaska.
⑤ Alaska has more population than any other state in the U.S.

서술형

3 알래스카가 가진 최고 기록을 본문에서 찾아 우리말로 쓰시오. (답 4개)

(1) ______________________________
(2) ______________________________
(3) ______________________________
(4) ______________________________

내신 Level Up

밑줄 친 ㉠The land가 가리키는 것을 본문에서 찾아 한 단어로 쓰시오.

____

구문 Level Up

5~6행 However, **it** is true **that** *Alaska freezes all over during wintertime.*

▸ that절(that Alaska ~ wintertime)이 주어 역할을 할 때 대개 주어 자리에 가주어 it을 쓰고, that절은 뒤로 보낸다. 이 경우, 가주어 it은 해석하지 않는다.

[확인 문제] **우리말과 뜻이 같도록 주어진 단어들을 배열하시오.**

그가 공부를 잘하는 것은 사실이다.
(studies / he / that / well)

→ It is true ______________________.

■ 나의 독해 점검표 ■

Step ❶ | 채점 결과 정리

1. 지칭 추론	O / X
2. 내용 일치	O / X
3. 서술형	O / X

• 나의 약점 유형은? ____________

Step ❷ | 독해력 점검

☐ 지문의 내용을 충분히 이해함
☐ 지문의 내용을 대체로 이해함
☐ 지문의 내용을 이해하지 못함

Step ❸ | 문제 해결력 점검

☐ 정답과 오답의 근거를 모두 찾음
☐ 정답과 오답의 근거를 대체로 찾음
☐ 정답과 오답의 근거를 찾지 못함

Day 06 Reading 02

세계에서 가장 깊은 곳, 마리아나 해구

06-02

Mariana Trench, located near the Philippines, is the deepest place in the Earth's oceans. In 2010, American researchers measured ㉠이곳이 얼마나 깊은지.

(A) For example, if you put a can into Mariana Trench, it will be flat right away by the amazing pressure of water. Adventurers around the world tried to dive into the ground of this point, but many of them were killed or hurt by the water's pressure.

(B) Thanks to recent technology, however, a famous movie director, James Cameron, successfully reached the bottom of this place and recorded the unbelievable view of Mariana Trench.

(C) They found that it is 1.6 km deeper than Mount Everest, the highest mountain on Earth. This place is also famous for its pressure by the weight of water above.

*Mariana Trench 마리아나 해구

해구(海溝)
대양(大洋) 밑바닥에 좁고 길게 도랑 모양으로 움푹 들어간 곳을 가리킨다. 제일 깊은 곳의 수심이 6,000미터 이상인 것을 이르며, 횡단면은 'V'자 모양을 이루어 경사가 급하다.

제대로 독해법

어휘 Level Up

단어에 알맞은 우리말 뜻을 골라 그 기호를 빈칸에 쓰시오.
(뜻이 같은 단어에 한하여 중복 답 가능)

1 ocean ....
2 researcher ....
3 measure ....
4 flat ....
5 amazing ....
6 pressure ....
7 adventurer ....
8 dive ....
9 hurt ....
10 recent ....
11 technology ....
12 movie director ....
13 bottom ....
14 unbelievable ....
15 weight ....

ⓐ 기술 ⓑ 압력 ⓒ 납작한
ⓓ 측정하다 ⓔ 다치게 하다; 다친
ⓕ 뛰어들다 ⓖ 모험가 ⓗ 무게
ⓘ 믿기 어려울 정도인 ⓙ 바다
ⓚ 바닥 ⓛ 엄청난, 놀라운
ⓜ 연구자 ⓝ 영화감독 ⓞ 최근의

▶ 해설편 p.12

1 Mariana Trench에 관한 글의 내용과 일치하지 않는 것은?

① 필리핀 근처에 위치해 있다.

② 에베레스트 산의 높이보다 더 깊은 바다에 있다.

③ 수압이 매우 높다.

④ 많은 모험가들이 이곳을 찾았다.

⑤ 아무도 이곳의 해저면에 도달하지 못했다.

2 What is the right order to read?

① (A) — (C) — (B)

② (B) — (A) — (C)

③ (B) — (C) — (A)

④ (C) — (A) — (B)

⑤ (C) — (B) — (A)

3 Mariana Trench에 캔을 놓으면 일어나는 일과 그 이유를 우리말로 쓰시오.

____

내신 Level Up

밑줄 친 ㉠의 우리말에 맞게 괄호 안에 주어진 단어들을 배열하시오.

㉠ 이곳이 얼마나 깊은지
(it / is / how deep)

→ ______________________

구문 Level Up

(A) 1~2행 For example, **if** you **put** a can into Mariana Trench, it **will be** flat right away by the amazing pressure of water.

▶ 시간·조건을 나타내는 부사절에서는 현재시제가 미래를 나타내므로, 이 문장에서는 if절에 put(현재시제), 주절에 will be(미래시제)가 쓰인다.

[확인 문제] **다음 밑줄 친 부분을 어법에 맞게 고쳐 쓰시오.**

1. I will carry my umbrella if it will rain tomorrow.

→ ______________________

내일 비가 오면 나는 우산을 가져갈 것이다.

2. Sam will do well in his piano concert if he will practice regularly.

→ ______________________

Sam이 규칙적으로 연습한다면 그는 피아노 연주회를 잘할 것이다.

■ 나의 독해 점검표 ■

Step ❶ | 채점 결과 정리

1. 내용 일치	O / X
2. 순서 파악	O / X
3. 서술형	O / X

• 나의 약점 유형은? ________

Step ❷ | 독해력 점검

□ 지문의 내용을 충분히 이해함
□ 지문의 내용을 대체로 이해함
□ 지문의 내용을 이해하지 못함

Step ❸ | 문제 해결력 점검

□ 정답과 오답의 근거를 모두 찾음
□ 정답과 오답의 근거를 대체로 찾음
□ 정답과 오답의 근거를 찾지 못함

▶ 해설편 p.12

어휘 테스트

A 사진을 보고, 빈칸에 알맞은 단어를 골라 쓰시오.

kayaking	measured	scuba-diving	squid	travelers	tropical fish

1 Here are three types of ____________.

2 They go on ____________ vacations.

3 They may love to sit on a beach but only after sailing or ____________.

4 There are more than 2,000 kinds of ____________ around the islands.

5 Sea creatures like jellyfish, octopus, ____________, and clams are also common.

6 American researchers ____________ how deep it is.

B 다음 각 단어에 해당하는 의미를 짝지으시오.

1 border •　　• ⓐ an area of sand or small stones near the sea

2 beach •　　• ⓑ the line that divides one country from another

3 recent •　　• ⓒ happening or starting from a short time ago

겨울방학에 가기 좋은 국내 여행지

거제도

거제도가 특히 겨울에 더 인기가 좋은 이유는 따뜻한 날씨 때문입니다. 겨울이 되어도 기온이 영하로 떨어지는 일이 거의 없는 따뜻한 남단에 위치한 거제도는 파라다이스라고 불리는 만큼 볼거리도 많고, 살기에 좋은 적합한 기후를 가지고 있습니다.
다도해의 아름다운 풍광을 감상할 수 있는 바람의 언덕은 여러 드라마 속 배경지로 유명해졌습니다. 특히 언덕의 풍차가 돌아가는 이국적인 풍경은 바람이 많이 부는 계절에만 주어진 선물입니다.

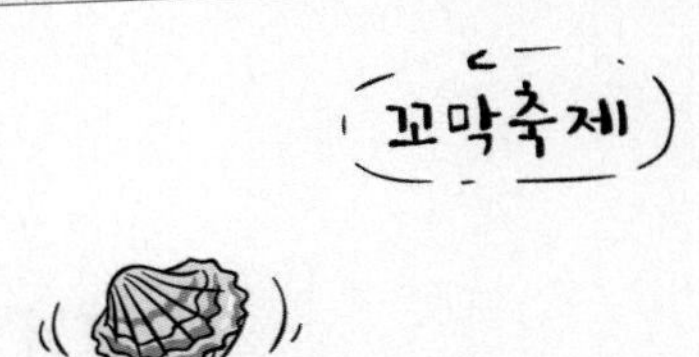

보성 벌교

한 여름 녹차 밭만이 보성의 자랑은 아닙니다. 겨울이 되면 전남 특산물인 꼬막을 마음껏 채취할 수 있는 벌교 갯벌로 전국의 관광객들이 몰리기 때문입니다. 국내 꼬막 생산량의 64%를 차지하는 벌교에서는 꼬막 따기 체험을 통해 가족 단위의 관광객에게 즐거움을 선사하고 있습니다.

여수

비교적 날씨가 온화한 남쪽의 이점과 아름다운 풍경이 더해진 여수는 우리나라에서 손꼽는 대표적인 물의 도시입니다.
여수에는 엑스포를 위해 지었던 전시관과 아쿠아플라넷 등이 있어 볼거리가 많습니다. 엑스포 근처에는 한려해상 국립공원인 오동도가 있는데 여수 바다 위로 다니는 케이블카로도 갈 수 있습니다.

Information 정보

내가 아는 단어는 몇 개?

▷▶ 다음 단어의 뜻을 추측해 보고, 알고 있는 단어에 ✓표시를 하시오.

☐ entrance

☐ aisle

☐ counter

☐ percentage

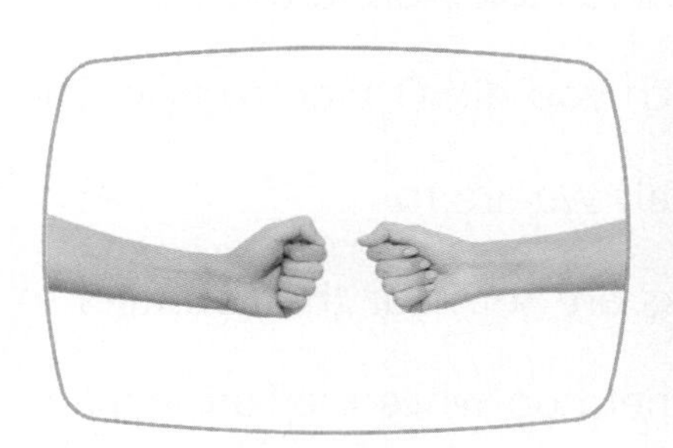

☐ fist

☐ mirror

☐ line up

☐ emotion

☐ arch-shaped

Day 07 Reading 01

07-01

슈퍼마켓에 이런 전략이!

Can you easily find milk in supermarkets? Probably not. Here lies a marketing strategy. It is usually placed on the opposite ends from the entrances. It means that if you want to buy it, you have to walk passed all of the aisles. Then, you may buy items which you didn't plan to. Some big-box retailers change the display of goods so that customers must wander around the store. Why do you think they do that? It is the same reason. They want you to look around the store and pick up some more items which you didn't plan to buy. The more we wander, the more likely we are to __________. Also, chewing gum and other snacks are set near the counters to encourage customers to pick them up while they are waiting in line to pay.

*big-box retailer 대형 할인점

제대로 독해법

어휘 Level Up

단어에 알맞은 우리말 뜻을 골라 그 기호를 빈칸에 쓰시오.
(뜻이 같은 단어에 한하여 중복 답 가능)

1 probably ....
2 lie ....
3 strategy ....
4 opposite ....
5 entrance ....
6 aisle ....
7 display ....
8 goods ....
9 customer ....
10 wander ....
11 pick up ....
12 counter ....
13 encourage ....
14 pay ....

ⓐ (돈을) 지불하다 ⓑ 통로
ⓒ ~을 집다 ⓓ 고객
ⓔ 권하다, 권장하다 ⓕ 돌아다니다
ⓖ 상품 ⓗ 아마
ⓘ 있다, 눕다; 거짓말하다 ⓙ 전략
ⓚ 정반대의 ⓛ 진열; 진열하다
ⓜ 출입구 ⓝ 카운터, 계산대

▶ 해설편 p.13

1 이 글의 빈칸에 들어갈 말로 가장 적절한 것은?

① find milk
② become hungry
③ buy items
④ meet people
⑤ pay less

2 What is the purpose of this passage?

① To explain why walking is good for us
② To promote milk products good for health
③ To persuade us to buy more milk for farmers
④ To encourage us to shop less to reduce waste
⑤ To let us know a marketing strategy

서술형

3 대형 할인점이 상품 진열을 바꾸는 이유를 우리말로 쓰시오.

____

내신 Level Up

이 글의 내용과 일치하면 T, 일치하지 않으면 F에 ✓ 표시를 하시오.

(1) T F
우유는 계산대와 가장 가까운 곳에 놓인다.

(2) T F
가게 안을 돌아다니다 보면 사려고 하지 않았던 것들을 사기 쉽다.

(3) T F
껌이나 다른 간식거리들은 출입구의 정 반대 끝에 놓인다.

구문 Level Up

7행 **Why do you think** they do that?

▶ 간접의문문이 동사 think, guess, imagine, believe, suppose 등의 목적어일 경우, 의문사가 문장의 맨 앞에 온다. 「의문사 + think / guess / imagine / believe / suppose 등 + 주어 + 동사?」의 어순으로 쓴다.

[확인 문제] **다음 주어진 두 문장을 연결하여 한 문장으로 바꿔 쓰시오.**

Do you think? + What did he do there?
→ ______________________

당신은 그가 거기에서 무엇을 했다고 생각하나요?

■ 나의 독해 점검표 ■

Step ❶ | 채점 결과 정리

1. 빈칸 추론	O / X
2. 목적 추론	O / X
3. 서술형	O / X

• 나의 약점 유형은? __________

Step ❷ | 독해력 점검

□ 지문의 내용을 충분히 이해함
□ 지문의 내용을 대체로 이해함
□ 지문의 내용을 이해하지 못함

Step ❸ | 문제 해결력 점검

□ 정답과 오답의 근거를 모두 찾음
□ 정답과 오답의 근거를 대체로 찾음
□ 정답과 오답의 근거를 찾지 못함

혈액형 이야기

What's your blood type? Here is the ratio of blood types.

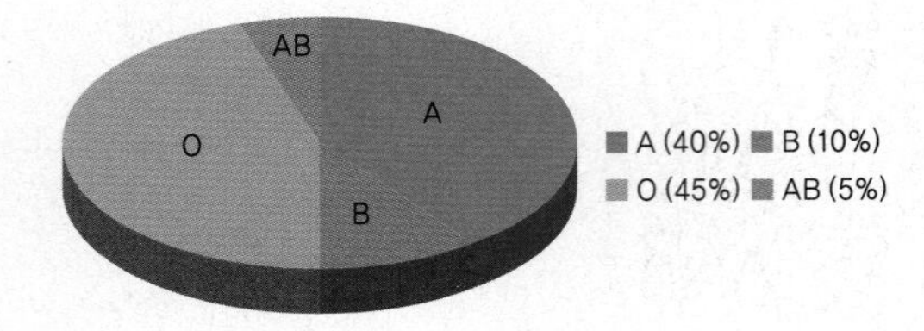

There are four basic blood types: A, B, O, and AB. The most common is type O. About 40 to 60% of the world's population has this blood type. The rarest is type AB. (ⓐ) However, blood type percentages vary among different countries. (ⓑ) For example, although type O is the most common in most countries, type A is the most common among Scandinavians and Australians. (ⓒ) Do you know why? (ⓓ) In an emergency, type O blood can be given to people of any blood type. (ⓔ) On the other hand, type AB can receive blood from any blood type.

*blood type 혈액형

제대로 독해법

어휘 Level Up

단어에 알맞은 우리말 뜻을 골라 그 기호를 빈칸에 쓰시오.
(뜻이 같은 단어에 한하여 중복 답 가능)

1 ratio ....
2 basic ....
3 common ....
4 population ....
5 rare ....
6 percentage ....
7 vary ....
8 among ....
9 emergency ....
10 on the other hand ....
11 receive ....

ⓐ ~ 사이에 ⓑ 흔한 ⓒ 기본적인
ⓓ 다르다 ⓔ 드문 ⓕ 반면에
ⓖ 받다 ⓗ 비율 ⓘ 응급, 비상
ⓙ 인구 ⓚ 퍼센트, 비율

▶ 해설편 p.14

1 이 글의 흐름으로 보아, 주어진 문장이 들어가기에 가장 적절한 곳은?

Type O is not only the most common, but it is the most generous blood type.

① ⓐ ② ⓑ ③ ⓒ ④ ⓓ ⑤ ⓔ

2 What is NOT true according to this passage?

① Blood types can be divided into 4 categories.
② The least common blood is type AB.
③ Each country has different blood type rates.
④ Type O blood can be given to any kind of blood types.
⑤ Type AB blood is the most useful blood in hospital.

서술형

3 혈액형 O형의 특징을 본문에서 찾아 우리말로 쓰시오. (답 2개)

(1) ______________________

(2) ______________________

내신 Level Up

혈액형 AB형의 특징을 본문에서 찾아 우리말로 쓰시오. (답 2개)

(1) ______________________

(2) ______________________

1행 **Here is** the ratio of blood types.

▶ 장소나 방향을 나타내는 부사가 강조되어 문장 앞에 오면 어순이 도치되어 「장소부사(Here) + 동사(is) + 주어(the ratio of blood types)」의 형태로 쓴다. 주어가 대명사인 경우에는 도치가 일어나지 않는다. (*ex.* Here **she comes**. 여기 그녀가 온다.)

[확인 문제] 다음 밑줄 친 부분을 강조하는 문장으로 바꿔 쓰시오.

A new computer was in the room.
→ In the room ______________ ______________.

방 안에 새 컴퓨터가 한 대 있었다.

■ 나의 독해 점검표 ■

Step ❶ | 채점 결과 정리

1. 문장 삽입	O / X
2. 내용 일치	O / X
3. 서술형	O / X

• 나의 약점 유형은? __________

Step ❷ | 독해력 점검

□ 지문의 내용을 충분히 이해함
□ 지문의 내용을 대체로 이해함
□ 지문의 내용을 이해하지 못함

Step ❸ | 문제 해결력 점검

□ 정답과 오답의 근거를 모두 찾음
□ 정답과 오답의 근거를 대체로 찾음
□ 정답과 오답의 근거를 찾지 못함

기억을 잡아 두고 싶나요?

08-01

According to a new study, ______________________. Here's how: Are you a right-handed person? If so, tighten your right fist before taking in new information. Then tighten your left fist when you want to remember it later. This strange trick would work because making a fist activates the side of the brain that handles memory. For example, if you are a right-handed person, the left side of the brain is mainly responsible for storing information. On the other hand, the right side of the brain is responsible for remembering it. However, if you are left-handed, ㉠the opposite applies. Are you willing to make fists while studying for a test or an important speech? Just remember which hand you need to use.

제대로 독해법

어휘 Level Up

단어에 알맞은 우리말 뜻을 골라 그 기호를 빈칸에 쓰시오.
(뜻이 같은 단어에 한하여 중복 답 가능)

1 right-handed ....
2 tighten ....
3 fist ....
4 remember ....
5 later ....
6 strange ....
7 trick ....
8 activate ....
9 handle ....
10 brain ....
11 mainly ....
12 store ....
13 information ....
14 left-handed ....
15 apply ....

ⓐ (마음속에 떠올려서) 기억하다
ⓑ 나중에 ⓒ 뇌 ⓓ 다루다
ⓔ 오른손잡이의 ⓕ 왼손잡이의
ⓖ 요령 ⓗ 이상한
ⓘ 저장하다; 가게
ⓙ 적용되다, 적용하다 ⓚ 정보
ⓛ 주로, 대개 ⓜ 주먹
ⓝ 쥐다, 조이다 ⓞ 활성화시키다

▶ 해설편 p.15

빈칸 추론

1 이 글의 빈칸에 들어갈 말로 가장 적절한 것은?

① making a fist can improve your memory
② your brain is easily fooled by your feelings
③ people always try to use both brain equally
④ using both hands helps you to get better grades
⑤ right-handed people can remember information better

내용 일치

2 What is NOT true according to this passage?

① We need to use both hands to improve our memory.
② Our brain is linked to our hands.
③ Right-handed people remember better than left-handed ones.
④ The opposite side of the brain to the main hand stores information.
⑤ Making a fist can activate the brain.

3 밑줄 친 ㉠ the opposite이 의미하는 내용을 우리말로 쓰시오.

____

내신 Level Up

이 글의 내용과 일치하도록 빈칸에 알맞은 말을 쓰시오.

1. If you are a right-handed person, tighten your (1)______ fist to store information and tighten your (2)______ fist to recall memory.

2. If you are a left-handed person, tighten your (1)______ fist to store information and tighten your (2)______ fist to recall memory.

구문 Level Up

10~11행 Are you willing to make fists **while (you are)** studying for a test ~?

▶ 「~ 동안」을 나타낼 때 접속사 while과 전치사 during, for를 이용하여 표현할 수 있다.
① while+주어+동사: 접속사이므로 절과 함께 사용
② during / for+명사(구): 전치사이므로 명사(구)와 함께 사용

[확인 문제] 괄호 안에서 알맞은 것을 고르시오.

I went shopping (while / during) you were doing your homework.

네가 숙제를 하는 동안 나는 쇼핑을 갔다.

■ 나의 독해 점검표 ■

Step ❶ | 채점 결과 정리

1. 빈칸 추론	O / X
2. 내용 일치	O / X
3. 서술형	O / X

• 나의 약점 유형은? __________

Step ❷ | 독해력 점검

☐ 지문의 내용을 충분히 이해함
☐ 지문의 내용을 대체로 이해함
☐ 지문의 내용을 이해하지 못함

Step ❸ | 문제 해결력 점검

☐ 정답과 오답의 근거를 모두 찾음
☐ 정답과 오답의 근거를 대체로 찾음
☐ 정답과 오답의 근거를 찾지 못함

08-02

눈썹이 있는 이유

Look at yourself in the mirror. Short hairs are lined up on your forehead above your eyes. ⓐThey are eyebrows. Everybody has eyebrows above their eyes. Are you able to move ⓑthem up and down? Sure you can. But people don't have eyebrows just to move ⓒthem for fun. Eyebrows play an important role for people to express ⓓtheir emotions. Take a good look at your mom's eyebrows. You can easily know whether she is happy or not. But there is a more important reason why people have eyebrows. ⓔThey keep the eyes dry when sweating or walking around in the rain. The arch-shaped eyebrows send the raindrops or sweat on your forehead around to the side of your face.

*forehead 이마 **eyebrow 눈썹

제대로 독해법

어휘 Level Up

단어에 알맞은 우리말 뜻을 골라 그 기호를 빈칸에 쓰시오.
(뜻이 같은 단어에 한하여 중복 답 가능)

1 look at ....
2 mirror ....
3 line up ....
4 above ....
5 up and down ....
6 for fun ....
7 role ....
8 express ....
9 emotion ....
10 reason ....
11 sweat ....
12 arch-shaped ....
13 raindrop ....

ⓐ ~보다 위에 ⓑ ~을 보다[살펴보다] ⓒ 감정 ⓓ 거울 ⓔ 땀을 흘리다; 땀 ⓕ 빗방울 ⓖ 아치형의 ⓗ 역할 ⓘ 위아래로 ⓙ 이유 ⓚ 재미로 ⓛ 줄을 서다[이루다] ⓜ 표현하다

▶ 해설편 p.16

지칭 추론

1 밑줄 친 ⓐ~ⓔ 중에서 가리키는 대상이 나머지 넷과 다른 것은?

① ⓐ ② ⓑ ③ ⓒ ④ ⓓ ⑤ ⓔ

제목 추론

2 What is the best title for this passage?

① What Eyebrows Do for Us
② Eyebrows Protect You from Danger
③ Eyebrows Make Facial Expressions
④ How Are Eyes Linked to Eyebrows?
⑤ Eyebrows Express People's Emotions

서술형

3 눈썹의 역할을 본문에서 찾아 우리말로 쓰시오. (답 2개)

(1) ____________________

(2) ____________________

내신 Level Up

이 글의 내용과 일치하지 않는 것은?

① 눈썹은 짧은 모발이다.
② 사람들은 눈썹을 위아래로 움직일 수 있다.
③ 눈썹은 감정을 표현하는 데 중요한 역할을 한다.
④ 눈썹은 아치 모양이다.
⑤ 눈썹은 땀이나 빗방울이 얼굴에 고이게 한다.

구문 Level Up

첫번째 문장 Look at **yourself** in the mirror.

▶ 재귀대명사는 '~자신'이라는 뜻이며, 인칭대명사의 목적격 또는 소유격에 -self[selves]를 붙여서 만든다. 문장의 주어와 목적어가 같을 때 목적어 자리에 재귀대명사를 쓰는 것을 재귀 용법이라 하고, 주어, 목적어 뒤나 문장의 맨 마지막에 위치하여 주어나 목적어를 강조하는 것을 강조 용법이라고 한다. 재귀 용법으로 쓰일 때는 생략할 수 없고, 강조 용법으로 쓰일 때는 생략이 가능하다.

[확인 문제] **밑줄 친 재귀대명사의 용법으로 알맞은 것을 고르시오.**

Have yourselves a good time.

[재귀 용법 / 강조 용법]

즐거운 시간 보내.

■ 나의 독해 점검표 ■

Step ❶ | 채점 결과 정리

1. 지칭 추론	O / X
2. 제목 추론	O / X
3. 서술형	O / X

• 나의 약점 유형은? __________

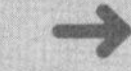

Step ❷ | 독해력 점검

□ 지문의 내용을 충분히 이해함
□ 지문의 내용을 대체로 이해함
□ 지문의 내용을 이해하지 못함

Step ❸ | 문제 해결력 점검

□ 정답과 오답의 근거를 모두 찾음
□ 정답과 오답의 근거를 대체로 찾음
□ 정답과 오답의 근거를 찾지 못함

▶ 해설편 p.16

어휘 테스트

A 사진을 보고, 빈칸에 알맞은 단어를 골라 쓰시오.

aisles	entrances	fist	lined up	mirror	percentages

1 It is usually placed on the opposite ends from the ________.

2 You have to walk passed all of the ________.

3 Blood type ________ vary among different countries.

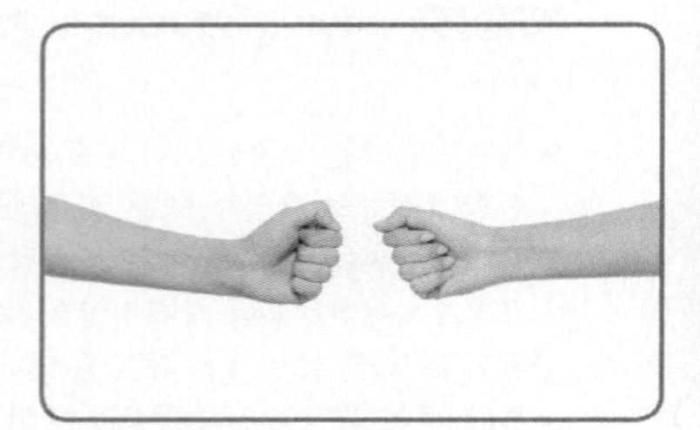

4 If so, tighten your right ________ before taking in new information.

5 Look at yourself in the ________.

6 Short hairs are ________ on your forehead.

B 다음 각 단어에 해당하는 의미를 짝지으시오.

1 wander •　　• ⓐ to cause something to start

2 activate •　　• ⓑ to walk around slowly without any clear purpose or direction

3 express •　　• ⓒ to show a feeling, opinion, or fact

영어 사전에 실린 한국어

hangul (한글)

the alphabetic script in which Korean is written
한국어가 쓰인 철자

kimchi (김치)

a vegetable pickle seasoned with garlic, red pepper, and ginger that is the national dish of Korea
(한국의 대표 음식으로 마늘, 고추, 생강으로 양념해 절인 채소)

soju (소주)

Korean vodca distilled usually from rice or sweet potato
쌀이나 고구마로 증류된 한국의 보드카

Chapter 5

Food 음식
★
Health 건강

내가 아는 단어는 몇 개?

▷▶ 다음 단어의 뜻을 추측해 보고, 알고 있는 단어에 ✔표시를 하시오.

☐ calorie

☐ order

☐ popcorn

☐ corn

☐ spinach

☐ kale

☐ blender

☐ survey

☐ score

다이어트를 돕는 메뉴판

09-01

New research shows that if restaurant menus show how much exercise is needed to burn off calories, it would be good for helping customers lose weight.

(A) Researchers say people do not really understand calories.

(B) For example, telling customers how many minutes they must walk to burn off the calories is helpful.

(C) When someone orders a hamburger, ㉠ the information is more effective than only showing how many calories the hamburger has.

Instead, they understand that they have to walk for 30 minutes. This new style of menu really helps people make healthier choices. One researcher said: "We are sure that it is possible to encourage people to order food with fewer calories by Ⓐ the new style of menu." Indeed, the people who had the menus with the exercise information tended to order food with the fewest calories.

제대로 독해법

어휘 Level Up

단어에 알맞은 우리말 뜻을 골라 그 기호를 빈칸에 쓰시오.
(뜻이 같은 단어에 한하여 중복 답 가능)

1 exercise ....
2 need ....
3 burn off ....
4 calorie ....
5 really ....
6 understand ....
7 helpful ....
8 instead ....
9 possible ....
10 encourage ....
11 order ....
12 indeed ....
13 tend ....

ⓐ (칼로리를) 태우다 ⓑ 가능한
ⓒ 경향이 있다 ⓓ 권장하다
ⓔ 대신에 ⓕ 도움이 되는 ⓖ 실제로
ⓗ 운동 ⓘ 이해하다
ⓙ 주문하다; 주문, 순서
ⓚ 칼로리, 열량 ⓛ 필요로 하다

▶ 해설편 p.17

밑줄 추론

1 밑줄 친 Ⓐthe new style of menu가 의미하는 바로 가장 적절한 것은?

① 음식의 칼로리를 명시한 메뉴
② 날씬한 배우들의 사진이 수록된 메뉴
③ 음식에 들어가는 모든 식재료가 표기된 메뉴
④ 살을 빼는 데 효과적인 운동 방법이 소개된 메뉴
⑤ 칼로리를 소비하는 데 필요한 운동 시간을 명시한 메뉴

순서 파악

2 What is the right order to read?

① (A) — (B) — (C)　② (A) — (C) — (B)　③ (B) — (C) — (A)
④ (C) — (A) — (B)　⑤ (C) — (B) — (A)

서술형

3 주어진 단어들 중에서 빈칸에 알맞은 말을 골라 이 글의 요약문을 완성하시오.

exercise　fewer　menu　order

New research says if a restaurant's (1) __________ shows how much (2) __________ is needed to burn off calories, people tend to (3) __________ food with (4) __________ calories.

내신 Level Up

밑줄 친 ㉠the information이 가리키는 것을 본문에서 찾아 의문문으로 바꿔 쓰시오. (11단어)

____
____

구문 Level Up

(B) For example, **telling** customers how many minutes they must walk to burn off the calories **is** helpful.

▶ telling은 「동사원형+-ing」의 형태로 문장의 주어 역할을 하는 동명사이다. 주어로 쓰이는 동명사는 단수 취급하므로 단수동사 is가 쓰였다.

[확인 문제] 우리말과 뜻이 같도록 동명사와 주어진 어구를 사용하여 문장을 완성하시오.

1. 다른 사람을 비난하는 것은 시간 낭비다. (blame others)
→ ______________________________ a waste of time.

2. 반 친구들과 어울리는 것은 중요하다. (get along with classmates)
→ ______________________________ important.

■ 나의 독해 점검표 ■

Step ❶ | 채점 결과 정리

1. 밑줄 추론	O / X
2. 순서 파악	O / X
3. 서술형	O / X

• 나의 약점 유형은? __________

Step ❷ | 독해력 점검

☐ 지문의 내용을 충분히 이해함
☐ 지문의 내용을 대체로 이해함
☐ 지문의 내용을 이해하지 못함

Step ❸ | 문제 해결력 점검

☐ 정답과 오답의 근거를 모두 찾음
☐ 정답과 오답의 근거를 대체로 찾음
☐ 정답과 오답의 근거를 찾지 못함

09-02

팝콘이 펑펑!

Popcorn is one of the most popular snacks in a movie theater. Many people enjoy eating popcorn during a movie. By the way, when we eat popcorn, we find some kernels of corn that don't pop. Why do you think this happens? (ⓐ) Popcorn is a small kernel before it pops. The kernel has a thin but very tight coat. (ⓑ) Inside of the coat, there is a little water. (ⓒ) The steam breaks through the kernel's coat. Pop! (ⓓ) The steam is released and popcorn is made. (ⓔ) But some kernels don't have enough water inside and that's why they don't pop.

*kernel 알갱이, 낟알

제대로 독해법

어휘 Level Up

단어에 알맞은 우리말 뜻을 골라 그 기호를 빈칸에 쓰시오.
(뜻이 같은 단어에 한하여 중복 답 가능)

1 popcorn ....
2 popular ....
3 snack ....
4 movie theater ....
5 enjoy ....
6 corn ....
7 pop ....
8 happen ....
9 thin ....
10 tight ....
11 coat ....
12 inside ....
13 steam ....
14 break through ....
15 release ....

ⓐ ~을 뚫고 나오다 ⓑ 간식
ⓒ 껍질, 외투[코트] ⓓ 내부에, 안에
ⓔ 단단한 ⓕ 팝콘 ⓖ 뿜어내다
ⓗ 생기다, 일어나다 ⓘ 얇은
ⓙ 영화관 ⓚ 옥수수, 곡식
ⓛ 인기 있는 ⓜ 즐기다 ⓝ 증기
ⓞ 터지다, 튀다; 펑하는 소리

▶ 해설편 p.18

1 이 글의 내용과 일치하지 않는 것은?

① 팝콘은 영화관에서 즐겨 먹는 간식이다.
② 옥수수 알갱이의 껍질은 얇지만 단단하다.
③ 열을 가하면 알갱이 속에 있는 수분이 증기로 바뀐다.
④ 증기가 껍질을 뚫고 나오면서 팝콘이 만들어진다.
⑤ 옥수수 알갱이 속에 수분이 적은 것이 잘 터진다.

문장 삽입

2 Where would the following sentence best fit?

When the kernel is heated up, the water inside the kernel turns to steam.

① ⓐ ② ⓑ ③ ⓒ ④ ⓓ ⑤ ⓔ

3 빈칸에 알맞은 말을 본문에서 찾아 이 글의 주제문을 완성하시오.

The reason some kernels of corn ________ ________

내신 Level Up

이 글을 읽고, 다음 질문에 대한 답을 완성하시오.

Why don't some kernels of corn pop?

→ Because they don't have enough ______ inside.

구문 Level Up

첫번째 문장 Popcorn is **one of the most popular snacks** in a movie theater.

▶ 「one of the 최상급+복수명사」는 '가장 ~한 것들 중의 하나'라는 의미를 가지며 단수 취급한다.

[확인 문제] **괄호 안에서 알맞은 것을 고르시오.**

1. Chuseok is one of the biggest national (holiday / holidays) in Korea.

   추석은 한국의 가장 큰 국경일 중 하나이다.

2. He is one of the (best / most) famous actors in Asia.

   그는 아시아에서 가장 유명한 배우들 중 한 명이다.

■ 나의 독해 점검표 ■

Step ❶ | 채점 결과 정리

1. 내용 일치	O / X
2. 문장 삽입	O / X
3. 서술형	O / X

• 나의 약점 유형은? ________

Step ❷ | 독해력 점검

□ 지문의 내용을 충분히 이해함
□ 지문의 내용을 대체로 이해함
□ 지문의 내용을 이해하지 못함

Step ❸ | 문제 해결력 점검

□ 정답과 오답의 근거를 모두 찾음
□ 정답과 오답의 근거를 대체로 찾음
□ 정답과 오답의 근거를 찾지 못함

10-01

건강한 그린 몬스터, 스무디

There is nothing in this smoothie except super-healthy fruits and vegetables! Don't let the green color scare you — it tastes fruity and delicious.

Ingredients: 1/2 cup of mango, 1/2 cup of pineapple, 1 banana, spinach, 1 kale leaf, 2/3 cup of water

Directions: Add mango, pineapple, and banana to the blender.

(A) Blend and enjoy! You'll have enough for two smoothies, and this one will last for up to two days in the fridge.

(B) Add in 2/3 cup of water, but you may need to add more or less, depending on how strong your blender is. Are you ready to blend them all?

(C) Add in one kale leaf and spinach. Spinach adds protein and it will keep you full! It changes the color, but not the taste, I promise!

*fridge 냉장고 **protein 단백질

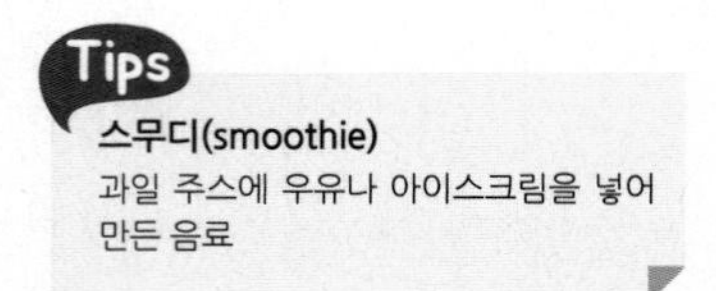

스무디(smoothie)
과일 주스에 우유나 아이스크림을 넣어 만든 음료

제대로 독해법

어휘 Level Up

단어에 알맞은 우리말 뜻을 골라 그 기호를 빈칸에 쓰시오.
(뜻이 같은 단어에 한하여 중복 답 가능)

1 except ....
2 vegetable ....
3 scare ....
4 taste ....
5 fruity ....
6 ingredient ....
7 mango ....
8 pineapple ....
9 spinach ....
10 kale ....
11 direction ....
12 add ....
13 blender ....
14 last ....
15 up to ....
16 promise ....

ⓐ ~까지 ⓑ 겁먹다, 겁주다
ⓒ 과일 맛이 나는 ⓓ 넣다, 더하다
ⓔ 맛이 나다 ⓕ 망고 ⓖ 믹서기
ⓗ 방법 ⓘ 시금치 ⓙ 약속하다
ⓚ 유지되다, 지속되다 ⓛ 재료
ⓜ 제외하고는 ⓝ 채소 ⓞ 케일
ⓟ 파인애플

▶ 해설편 p.19

1 주어진 글 다음에 이어질 글의 순서로 가장 적절한 것은?

① (A) — (B) — (C)
② (A) — (C) — (B)
③ (B) — (A) — (C)
④ (C) — (A) — (B)
⑤ (C) — (B) — (A)

목적 추론

2 What is the purpose of this passage?

① To recommend us to eat organic food
② To inform us of how to make green smoothie
③ To explain why green smoothies are good for health
④ To prove that green vegetables are easy to eat
⑤ To prevent us from eating junky foods

서술형

3 그린 스무디 속 시금치의 역할을 본문에서 찾아 우리말로 쓰시오. (답 2개)

(1) ______________________________

(2) ______________________________

내신 Level Up

이 글의 종류로 가장 적절한 것은?

① review
② diary
③ recipe
④ manual
⑤ prescription

구문 Level Up

2~3행 Don't **let the green color scare** you — it tastes fruity and delicious.

▶ 사역동사(make, have, let)는 목적어로 하여금 어떤 행동이나 동작을 하게 하는 동사이며, 목적격보어로 동사원형을 쓴다. 여기에서는 사역동사 let의 목적격보어로 동사원형 scare이 쓰였다.

[확인 문제] **괄호 안에서 알맞은 것을 고르시오.**

1. My wife had me (to wash / wash) the dishes.

내 아내가 나에게 설거지를 시켰다.

2. Terry let me (play / to play) with his cat.

Terry는 내가 그의 고양이와 함께 놀게 했다.

■ 나의 독해 점검표 ■

Step ❶ | **채점 결과 정리**

1. 순서 파악	O / X
2. 목적 추론	O / X
3. 서술형	O / X

• 나의 약점 유형은? __________

Step ❷ | **독해력 점검**

□ 지문의 내용을 충분히 이해함
□ 지문의 내용을 대체로 이해함
□ 지문의 내용을 이해하지 못함

Step ❸ | **문제 해결력 점검**

□ 정답과 오답의 근거를 모두 찾음
□ 정답과 오답의 근거를 대체로 찾음
□ 정답과 오답의 근거를 찾지 못함

잠의 중요성

10-02

Why is sleep important for children? ㉠A new study answers the question. In the study, the research team either added or subtracted one hour of sleep for healthy children. The goal was to see if small changes in the amount of sleep could affect a child's behavior. Before the survey began, students were asked to sleep the same amount of hours as they usually ㉡would. Their teachers were asked to score the children on emotional reactions. After five nights of the changed sleep pattern of the children, the teachers were asked to take the survey again. The result? Compared with their original scores, those who slept one hour less had worse behavior scores and those who were allowed to sleep an hour more had better behavior scores.

제대로 독해법

어휘 Level Up

단어에 알맞은 우리말 뜻을 골라 그 기호를 빈칸에 쓰시오.
(뜻이 같은 단어에 한하여 중복 답 가능)

1 answer ....
2 question ....
3 subtract ....
4 goal ....
5 amount ....
6 affect ....
7 behavior ....
8 survey ....
9 begin ....
(begin - began - begun)
10 score ....
11 emotional ....
12 reaction ....
13 result ....
14 compare ....

ⓐ (무엇의) 양 ⓑ 감정적인 ⓒ 결과
ⓓ 대답하다 ⓔ 목적 ⓕ 반응
ⓖ 비교하다 ⓗ 빼다 ⓘ 설문 조사
ⓙ 시작하다 ⓚ 영향을 미치다
ⓛ 점수를 매기다; 점수 ⓜ 질문
ⓝ 행동

▶ 해설편 p.20

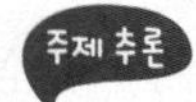

1 이 글의 주제로 가장 적절한 것은?

① 다양한 설문 조사 방법 소개
② 아이들에게 적절한 수면 시간
③ 아이들이 잠을 많이 자는 이유
④ 숙면이 학교 성적에 미치는 영향
⑤ 아이들이 잠을 충분히 자야 하는 이유

요약문 완성

2 What is the best choice for the blanks (A) and (B) according to this passage?

> Lack of ______(A)______ in days can make the children's ______(B)______ worse after all.

(A) (B)
① sleep ---- posture
② study ---- understanding
③ sleep ---- behavior
④ study ---- emotions
⑤ exercise ---- growth

3 밑줄 친 ㉠A new study의 목적과 과정을 본문에서 찾아 우리말로 쓰시오.

(1) 목적 : ______________________

(2) 과정 : (실험 전) ______________________

(실험 중) ______________________

(실험 후) ______________________

내신 Level Up

밑줄 친 ㉢would 뒤에 생략된 한 단어를 본문에서 찾아 쓰시오.

____

구문 Level Up

7~8행 Their teachers **were asked to score** the children on emotional reactions.

▶ 5형식 문장에서 목적격보어가 명사, 형용사, to부정사, 분사인 경우, 수동태로 바꾸면 2형식 문장이 되고 목적격보어를 주격보어로 그대로 쓴다.

[확인 문제] 두 문장의 뜻이 같도록 빈칸에 알맞은 말을 쓰시오.

> My mom allowed me to play the computer game for 30 minutes.
> = I ______ ______ ______ ______ the computer game for 30 minutes by my mom.

우리 엄마는 내가 30분 동안 컴퓨터 게임하는 것을 허락하셨다.(= 나는 우리 엄마에게 30분 동안 게임하는 것을 허락받았다.)

■ 나의 독해 점검표 ■

Step ❶ | 채점 결과 정리

1. 주제 추론	O / X
2. 요약문 완성	O / X
3. 서술형	O / X

• 나의 약점 유형은? ________

Step ❷ | 독해력 점검

□ 지문의 내용을 충분히 이해함
□ 지문의 내용을 대체로 이해함
□ 지문의 내용을 이해하지 못함

Step ❸ | 문제 해결력 점검

□ 정답과 오답의 근거를 모두 찾음
□ 정답과 오답의 근거를 대체로 찾음
□ 정답과 오답의 근거를 찾지 못함

▶ 해설편 p.20

어휘 테스트

A 사진을 보고, 빈칸에 알맞은 단어를 골라 쓰시오.

blender　calories　corn　popcorn　spinach　survey

1 Researchers say people do not really understand ________.

2 Many people enjoy eating ________ during a movie.

3 We find some kernels of ________ that don't pop.

4 Add in one kale leaf and ________.

5 Add mango, pineapple, and banana to the ________.

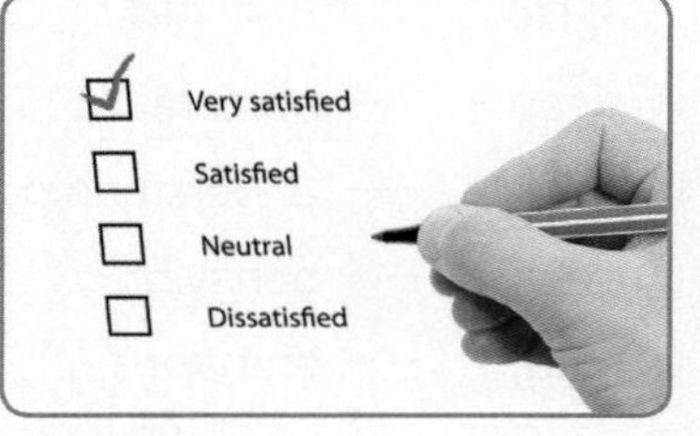

6 Before the ________ began, students were asked to sleep.

B 다음 각 단어에 해당하는 의미를 짝지으시오.

1 exercise •　　• ⓐ to tell someone that you will certainly do something

2 steam •　　• ⓑ physical activity that you do to make your body strong and healthy

3 promise •　　• ⓒ the hot gas that is produced when water boils

내 몸에 비타민은 충분한가?

피로감 없애는 Vitamin B (비타민 B)

비타민 B는 B1, B2, B3, B5, B6, B12, 엽산, 비오틴의 여러 개의 복합체로 이루어져 하나의 군으로 통칭해 부릅니다. 비타민 B군은 대표적인 활력 비타민이지만 체내에서는 만들어지지 않는 꼭 외부에서 섭취해야 하는 영양소입니다. 비타민 B군이 풍부한 식품으로는 녹황색 채소, 돼지고기, 달걀, 현미, 버섯, 유제품 등이 있습니다.

피로 회복에 좋은 Vitamin C (비타민 C)

우리는 비타민 C를 먹기 위해 과일과 채소를 먹는 경우가 많습니다. 특히 과일의 경우 비타민 C를 많이 함유하고 있을 뿐만 아니라, 향과 맛이 뛰어납니다. 비타민 C는 감귤류, 토마토, 딸기, 케일 등 대부분의 과일과 채소에 들어 있습니다.

뼈 건강에 중요한 Vitamin D (비타민 D)

비타민 D는 칼슘 흡수를 증가시켜 뼈를 튼튼하게 하고, 면역세포 생산을 도와주고, 체중 감소에 도움이 되며 암 발생을 줄여줍니다. 비타민 D를 보충하기 위해서는 일주일에 2~3회, 하루 10~20분 정도 햇볕을 쬐어야 하고, 비타민 D가 풍부한 생선, 달걀, 버섯 등의 식품을 섭취하고, 필요시 적절한 용량의 비타민 D 보충제를 복용해야 합니다.

Chapter 6

Animals 동물
★
Nature 자연

내가 아는 단어는 몇 개?

▷▶ 다음 단어의 뜻을 추측해 보고, 알고 있는 단어에 ✓표시를 하시오.

☐ cooperative

☐ planet

☐ attack

☐ cotton

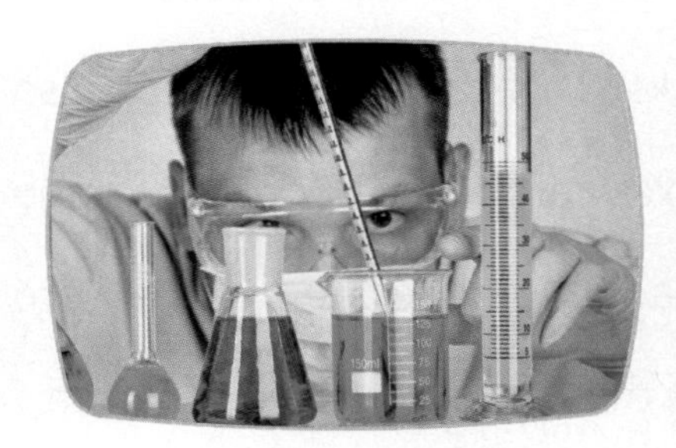

☐ chemical

☐ secret

☐ forest

☐ forest fire

☐ burn

11-01

갑자기 땅이 꺼지네!

You would think that a man could be safe in his house. Unfortunately for Jeffrey Bush, (A) [who / which] lived in Florida, that was not true. On a night when Mr. Bush was in bed, his bedroom just disappeared. How? It fell into a huge sinkhole under his home. Sinkholes are common in Florida. Why are these things called "sinkholes" or "snake holes?" Sometimes, if the rocks under the Earth's surface (B) [is / are] made up of some kinds of stone and the underground water keeps rising, it completely damages the rocks. This causes a sinkhole also known as a snake hole. Sinkholes can be small or really huge in size and can be formed gradually or suddenly. They are (C) [finding / found] throughout the world and even in Korea.

*sinkhole 싱크홀

Tips
싱크홀의 종류
지상에 생기면 싱크홀이라 하고, 바다에 생기면 블루홀이라고 한다.

제대로 독해법

어휘 Level Up

단어에 알맞은 우리말 뜻을 골라 그 기호를 빈칸에 쓰시오.
(뜻이 같은 단어에 한하여 중복 답 가능)

1 think ....
2 safe ....
3 unfortunately ....
4 disappear ....
5 fall into ....
6 huge ....
7 sometimes ....
8 surface ....
9 completely ....
10 damage ....
11 cause ....
12 form ....
13 gradually ....
14 suddenly ....

ⓐ ~로 빠지다 ⓑ ~을 야기하다; 원인
ⓒ 갑자기 ⓓ 거대한 ⓔ 때때로
ⓕ 불행하게도 ⓖ 사라지다
ⓗ 생각하다 ⓘ 서서히 ⓙ 안전한
ⓚ 완전히 ⓛ 손상시키다; 손상
ⓜ 표면 ⓝ 형성시키다; 유형

▶ 해설편 p.21

1 (A), (B), (C)의 각 네모 안에서 어법에 맞는 표현으로 가장 적절한 것은?

	(A)	(B)	(C)
①	which	are	found
②	who	is	finding
③	who	are	found
④	which	is	found
⑤	who	are	finding

내용 일치

2 Which is NOT true about sinkholes?

① They are often found in Florida.
② They are also called "snake holes."
③ They are sometimes caused by floods.
④ They can be formed all of a sudden.
⑤ They are found all over the world.

3 싱크홀이 만들어지는 원리를 본문에서 찾아 우리말로 쓰시오.

____

내신 Level Up

Bush 씨 집의 어느 부분이 싱크홀로 떨어졌는가?

① 서재 ② 주방 ③ 침실
④ 욕실 ⑤ 거실

구문 Level Up

3~4행 On *a night* **when** Mr. Bush was in bed, his bedroom just disappeared.

▶ 관계부사는 형용사절을 이끌며, 부사 역할을 한다. 여기에서는 시간을 나타내는 선행사 a night가 관계부사 when과 함께 쓰였다.
cf. 관계부사 vs. 관계대명사
「선행사+관계부사+완전한 문장」
「선행사+관계대명사+불완전한 문장」

[확인 문제] **다음 문장의 밑줄 친 부분을 바르게 고쳐 쓰시오.**

The day <u>which</u> I first met him was Valentine's Day.
→ ______________

내가 그를 처음 만났던 날은 밸런타인데이였다.

■ 나의 독해 점검표 ■

Step ❶ | 채점 결과 정리

1. 어법성 판단	O / X
2. 내용 일치	O / X
3. 서술형	O / X

• 나의 약점 유형은? __________

Step ❷ | 독해력 점검

□ 지문의 내용을 충분히 이해함
□ 지문의 내용을 대체로 이해함
□ 지문의 내용을 이해하지 못함

Step ❸ | 문제 해결력 점검

□ 정답과 오답의 근거를 모두 찾음
□ 정답과 오답의 근거를 대체로 찾음
□ 정답과 오답의 근거를 찾지 못함

개미가 주는 교훈

11-02

Ant colonies generally have at least one or more queens and the rest are worker ants. The worker ants' job is to get food, and take care of the queen. They collect the food, but they are not able to digest it. So they give the food to young ants. Then the young ants digest the food and give it back to worker ants. Isn't it really interesting? They are cooperative creatures. They have a nice support system. When a worker ant finds a good food source, he leaves a particular smell trail so that the others can find the source. Their unity has made them survive on our planet for a long time, about 100 million years. We can learn a lesson or two from them.

*colony 집단(*pl.* colonies)

제대로 독해법

어휘 Level Up

단어에 알맞은 우리말 뜻을 골라 그 기호를 빈칸에 쓰시오.
(뜻이 같은 단어에 한하여 중복 답 가능)

1 generally ....
2 at least ....
3 collect ....
4 digest ....
5 cooperative ....
6 support ....
7 source ....
8 leave ....
9 particular ....
10 trail ....
11 unity ....
12 survive ....
13 planet ....
14 million ....
15 lesson ....

ⓐ 100만 ⓑ 교훈
ⓒ 남기다, 떠나다 ⓓ 모으다
ⓔ 보통 ⓕ 살아남다
ⓖ 소화하다, 소화시키다 ⓗ 원천
ⓘ 적어도 ⓙ 지원; 지원하다
ⓚ 특별한, 특정한 ⓛ 행성
ⓜ 협동, 통합 ⓝ 협동하는 ⓞ 흔적

▶ 해설편 p.22

1 이 글의 내용과 일치하지 않는 것은?

① 여왕개미는 일개미의 보살핌을 받는다.
② 일개미는 식량을 구해 오는 역할을 한다.
③ 일개미는 음식물을 소화시키지 못한다.
④ 어린 개미는 여왕개미에게 식량을 공급한다.
⑤ 개미는 1억 년 이상 존재해 왔다.

2 What is the main idea for this passage?

① Why most ants live under the soil
② Ants: the toughest animal in the world
③ Cooperation makes ants survive for a long time
④ Lesson from ants: Diligence makes perfect
⑤ Ants can last longer than any other animal on Earth

서술형

3 일개미가 식량원을 찾았을 때 특별한 냄새를 남기는 이유를 우리말로 쓰시오.

____

내신 Level Up

이 글의 내용과 가장 잘 어울리는 속담은?

① The walls have ears.
② Look before you leap.
③ Practice makes perfect.
④ Blood is thicker than water.
⑤ Two heads are better than one.

구문 Level Up

4행 So they give the food **to** young ants.

▶ 4형식의 간접목적어 앞에 전치사(to, for, of)를 붙여 직접목적어 뒤에 두면 3형식이 된다.
(→ 4형식: So they give young ants the food.)
cf. 4형식을 3형식으로 바꾸는 문제는 자주 출제된다. 동사에 따라 사용하는 전치사는 다음과 같다.
of : ask 등
for : make, buy, cook, get, find 등
to : 그외 나머지 동사

[확인 문제] **다음 4형식 문장을 3형식 문장으로 바꿔 쓰시오.**

My brother gave me his book.
→ My brother ______________.

우리 형이 내게 자신의 책을 주었다.

■ 나의 독해 점검표 ■

Step ❶ | 채점 결과 정리

1. 내용 일치	O / X
2. 주제 추론	O / X
3. 서술형	O / X

• 나의 약점 유형은? __________

Step ❷ | 독해력 점검

□ 지문의 내용을 충분히 이해함
□ 지문의 내용을 대체로 이해함
□ 지문의 내용을 이해하지 못함

Step ❸ | 문제 해결력 점검

□ 정답과 오답의 근거를 모두 찾음
□ 정답과 오답의 근거를 대체로 찾음
□ 정답과 오답의 근거를 찾지 못함

12-01

보디가드 곤충

Plants must stand their ground even when plants are ⓐattacked by bad insects. There's simply no running away. But interestingly, some varieties of corn and cotton can call out for help and the helpers frequently come to help in ⓑresponse. Bodyguard insects eat the bad insects that attack the plants. So if the plants have enemies, then bodyguards are ⓒenemies of the plants' enemies. Of course, plants don't scream out to those helpers. Instead, they ⓓdetect chemicals, which easily turn from liquids into gases and travel on the winds. The smell of the gas makes insects or other helpers called "bodyguards" come to the plants. Scientists discovered this ⓔsecret signaling in 1988. This finding has helped farmers increase the amount of crops now.

제대로 독해법

어휘 Level Up

단어에 알맞은 우리말 뜻을 골라 그 기호를 빈칸에 쓰시오.
(뜻이 같은 단어에 한하여 중복 답 가능)

1 attack ....
2 simply ....
3 interestingly ....
4 variety ....
5 cotton ....
6 frequently ....
7 response ....
8 enemy ....
9 chemical ....
10 easily ....
11 liquid ....
12 discover ....
13 secret ....
14 signaling ....
15 finding ....
16 crop ....

ⓐ 공격하다; 공격
ⓑ 그야말로, 단순히 ⓒ 농작물
ⓓ 목화 ⓔ 발견,결과 ⓕ 발견하다
ⓖ 비밀의; 비밀 ⓗ 흥미롭게도
ⓘ 쉽게 ⓙ 신호 ⓚ 액체 ⓛ 응답
ⓜ 자주 ⓝ 적 ⓞ 품종, 다양성
ⓟ 화학 물질; 화학의

▶ 해설편 p.23

1 밑줄 친 ⓐ~ⓔ 중에서 문맥상 낱말의 쓰임이 적절하지 않은 것은?

① ⓐ ② ⓑ ③ ⓒ ④ ⓓ ⑤ ⓔ

요지 추론

2 What is this passage mainly about?

① Some plants can protect insects with their chemicals.
② Some insects may fight over their resources.
③ Some insects may save plants when they are attacked.
④ Different insects can help each other to survive.
⑤ Some plants are independent from their surroundings.

서술형

3 보디가드 곤충이 식물을 도와주는 방법을 본문에서 찾아 우리말로 쓰시오. (20자 이내)

____

내신 Level Up

이 글의 내용과 일치하도록 빈칸에 알맞은 말을 본문에서 찾아 쓰시오.

Plants produce (1)__________.

↓

They turn from liquids into (2)__________ and travel on the winds.

↓

The (3)__________ of the gas makes bodyguard insects come to the plants.

구문 Level Up

8~9행 ~ *chemicals*, **which** easily turn from liquids into gases and travel on the winds.

▶ 관계대명사의 계속적 용법은 관계대명사 앞에 콤마(,)를 붙이며 주로 선행사나 앞문장 전체에 대한 추가적인 정보를 제공할 때 쓴다. 관계대명사 that과 what은 계속적 용법으로 쓸 수 없다.

[확인 문제] 괄호 안에서 알맞은 것을 고르시오.

Our flight was delayed, (that / which) means we had to stay at the airport all night.

우리 비행기는 지연됐고, 그것은 우리가 밤새 공항에 머물러야 했다는 것을 의미한다.

■ 나의 독해 점검표 ■

Step ❶ | 채점 결과 정리

1. 어휘 파악	O / X
2. 요지 추론	O / X
3. 서술형	O / X

• 나의 약점 유형은? 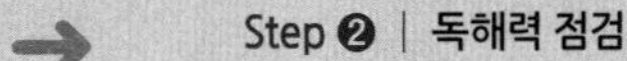

Step ❷ | 독해력 점검

□ 지문의 내용을 충분히 이해함
□ 지문의 내용을 대체로 이해함
□ 지문의 내용을 이해하지 못함

Step ❸ | 문제 해결력 점검

□ 정답과 오답의 근거를 모두 찾음
□ 정답과 오답의 근거를 대체로 찾음
□ 정답과 오답의 근거를 찾지 못함

12-02

세계에서 가장 큰 나무, 제너럴셔먼

In a deep forest in California, U.S.A, there is the largest tree in the world, General Sherman. Other trees may be taller, but not bigger than this. General Sherman is 31 meters around, and goes up to 84 meters in the sky. That is, its size is similar to a 25-story apartment building. In fact, General Sherman is the biggest living creature on the earth. ⓐIt has been standing in the woods for thousands of years. To our surprise, ⓑit is still growing. Many scientists are studying how this tree takes energy from the ground. Their explanation is that forest fires helped ⓒit grow. ⓓIt burnt other trees down around General Sherman, but ⓔit survived due to its thick skin. As a result, the tree could get nutrition from the ashes and ㉠grow bigger and bigger.

*ash 재

제대로 독해법

어휘 Level Up

단어에 알맞은 우리말 뜻을 골라 그 기호를 빈칸에 쓰시오.
(뜻이 같은 단어에 한하여 중복 답 가능)

1 deep ....
2 forest ....
3 around ....
4 similar ....
5 story ....
6 apartment ....
7 creature ....
8 woods ....
9 still ....
10 take ....
11 explanation ....
12 forest fire ....
13 burn ....
(burn - burnt - burnt)
14 survive ....
15 thick ....
16 nutrition ....

ⓐ (건물의) 층; 이야기 ⓑ 깊은
ⓒ 두꺼운 ⓓ 둘레가 ~인; ~ 주변에
ⓔ 비슷한 ⓕ 산불 ⓖ 살아남다
ⓗ 생명체, 생물 ⓘ 설명 ⓙ 숲
ⓚ 아파트 ⓛ 얻다 ⓜ 여전히; 고요한
ⓝ 영양분 ⓞ 태우다, 타다

▶ 해설편 p.24

지칭 추론

1 밑줄 친 ⓐ~ⓔ 중에서 가리키는 대상이 나머지 넷과 다른 것은?

① ⓐ ② ⓑ ③ ⓒ ④ ⓓ ⑤ ⓔ

2 Which is NOT true about General Sherman?

① It is located in California, USA.
② It is taller than any other tree.
③ It gets energy from the ground.
④ It is still alive.
⑤ It has thick skin.

서술형

3 General Sherman이 좁은 땅에서 충분한 영양분을 얻을 수 있었던 이유를 우리말로 쓰시오.

____

____

내신 Level Up

밑줄 친 ㉠grow 앞에 생략된 세 단어를 본문에서 찾아 쓰시오.

____

구문 Level Up

7~8행 To our surprise, it **is** still **growing**.

▶ is growing은 「be동사+-ing」 형태의 현재진행시제로 지금 진행 중인 동작을 나타내며 '~하고 있다'라는 뜻을 가진다.

[확인 문제] 괄호 안에 주어진 단어를 사용하여 문장을 완성하시오.

1. What ______ you ______ now? (do)

   너는 지금 무엇을 하고 있니?

2. I ______ ______ yoga classes these days. (take)

   나는 요즘 요가 수업을 듣고 있다.

■ 나의 독해 점검표 ■

Step ❶ | 채점 결과 정리

1. 지칭 추론	O / X
2. 내용 일치	O / X
3. 서술형	O / X

• 나의 약점 유형은? __________

Step ❷ | 독해력 점검

□ 지문의 내용을 충분히 이해함
□ 지문의 내용을 대체로 이해함
□ 지문의 내용을 이해하지 못함

Step ❸ | 문제 해결력 점검

□ 정답과 오답의 근거를 모두 찾음
□ 정답과 오답의 근거를 대체로 찾음
□ 정답과 오답의 근거를 찾지 못함

▶ 해설편 p.24

어휘 테스트

A 사진을 보고, 빈칸에 알맞은 단어를 골라 쓰시오.

burnt	chemicals	cooperative	cotton	forest fires	secret

1 They are __________ creatures.

2 Some varieties of corn and __________ can call out for help.

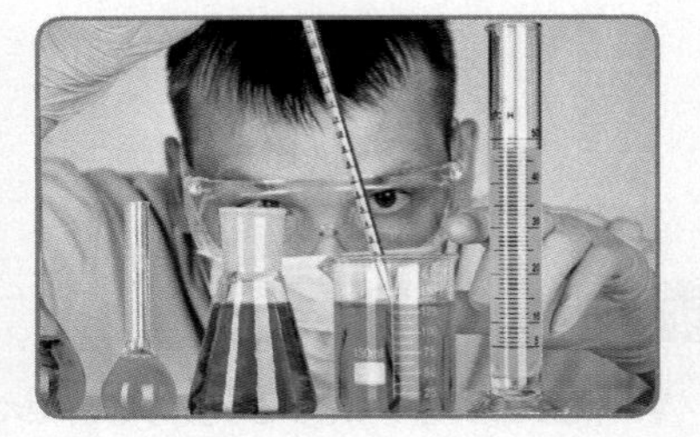

3 They produce __________.

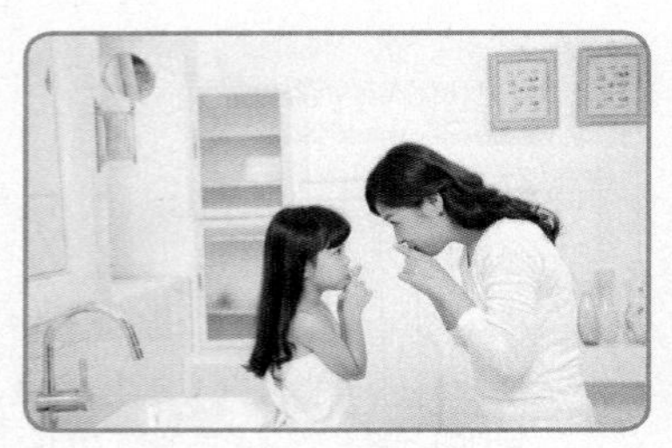

4 Scientists discovered this __________ signaling in 1988.

5 Their explanation is that __________ helped it grow.

6 It __________ other trees down around General Sherman.

B 다음 각 단어에 해당하는 의미를 짝지으시오.

1 huge •

2 collect •

3 explanation •

• ⓐ extremely large in size or amount

• ⓑ the details or reasons that someone gives to make something clear or easy to understand

• ⓒ to bring or gather together (a number of things)

도구를 사용할 줄 아는 동물들

8단계 문제를 풀어 먹이를 꺼내 먹은 '뉴칼레도니아 까마귀'

2014년 뉴질랜드 오클랜드 대학(University of Auckland)의 알렉산더 테일러(Alexander Taylor)는 나무 막대와 돌이 있는 '도구 상자' 과제를 뉴칼레도니아 까마귀(New Caledonian crows) 007에게 주었습니다. 이 실험에서 놀라운 것은 007이 도구를 사용해야 먹이를 먹을 수 있다는 사실뿐만 아니라 적절한 도구를 얻기 위해서는 다른 도구를 사용해야 한다는 사실도 알았다는 것입니다.

'돌고래'에게 거울을 줬더니 놀라운 일이 벌어졌다

최근 영국 BBC 다큐 전문채널 'BBC Earth'는 돌고래의 지능을 확인하기 위해 수족관 유리벽에 거울을 설치하고 반응을 살핀 영상을 재조명했습니다. 거울에 비친 자신의 외모에 관심을 보이며 자기애를 느끼는 돌고래의 놀라운 모습이 포착되었습니다.

돌을 깨서 도구를 만드는 '카푸친 원숭이'

영국 옥스퍼드 대학(University of Oxford)과 런던 대학(University of London), 브라질 상파울루 대학(University of São Paulo) 등 국제 공동 연구진은 브라질 세라다카피바라 국립공원(Serra da Capivara National Park)에 사는 카푸친 원숭이들(capuchin monkeys)이 구석기인처럼 돌을 깨서 석기를 만드는 것을 확인했다고 국제학술지 '네이처(Nature)'에 발표했습니다.

Chapter 7

Culture 문화
★
Psychology 심리

내가 아는 단어는 몇 개?

▷▶ 다음 단어의 뜻을 추측해 보고, 알고 있는 단어에 ✓표시를 하시오.

☐ shopping

☐ busy

☐ university

☐ professor

☐ serve

☐ India

☐ slide down

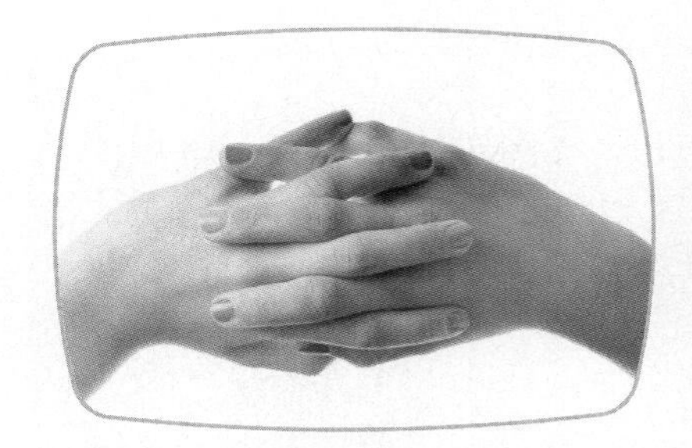

☐ nail

☐ serious

Day 13 Reading 01

블랙 프라이데이

13-01

Most Americans celebrate Thanksgiving. They share a meal, watch football, and enjoy talking to each other. (ⓐ) For some people, shopping is a big part of their Thanksgiving tradition as well. For many years, the day after Thanksgiving has been the busiest shopping day of the year. Many stores have sales on that day. (ⓑ) Many people go to the sales ㉠so that they can save money. (ⓒ) The shoppers are looking for bargains. This busy shopping day is called "Black Friday." (ⓓ) Recently, researchers have noticed another busy shopping day. This day is a little different. It is the busiest day of the year for online shopping. (ⓔ) On this day, more and more shoppers buy their holiday gifts online.

*bargain 싼 물건

제대로 독해법

어휘 Level Up

단어에 알맞은 우리말 뜻을 골라 그 기호를 빈칸에 쓰시오.
(뜻이 같은 단어에 한하여 중복 답 가능)

1 celebrate ....
2 share ....
3 enjoy ....
4 each other ....
5 shopping ....
6 tradition ....
7 as well ....
8 sale ....
9 busy ....
10 recently ....
11 notice ....
12 a little ....
13 different ....
14 online ....

ⓐ 기념하다 ⓑ 나누다 ⓒ 다른
ⓓ 바쁜 ⓔ 서로 ⓕ 세일, 판매
ⓖ 쇼핑 ⓗ 약간 ⓘ 역시, 또한
ⓙ 온라인의[으로] ⓚ 전통
ⓛ 주목하다 ⓜ 즐기다 ⓝ 최근에

▶ 해설편 p.25

1 **이 글의 흐름으로 보아, 주어진 문장이 들어가기에 가장 적절한 곳은?**

> The Monday after Thanksgiving has become known as "Cyber Monday."

① ⓐ　② ⓑ　③ ⓒ　④ ⓓ　⑤ ⓔ

2 **What is NOT true according to this passage?**

① On Thanksgiving, Americans share their food with others.
② Black Friday has something to do with Thanksgiving.
③ Black Friday is the best chance for shopping during the year.
④ Cyber Monday stands for the busiest day for department stores.
⑤ The online shoppers are increasing on Cyber Monday.

3 **밑줄 친 ㉠so that they can save money를 세 단어로 바꿔 쓰시오.**

____

내신 Level Up

이 글의 내용과 일치하도록 빈칸에 알맞은 말을 쓰시오.

Black Friday
the (1)__________ after Thanksgiving

Cyber Monday
the (2)__________ after Thanksgiving

구문 Level Up

6~7행 Many people go to the sales **so that** they can save money.

▶ so that은 '~하기 위하여, ~하도록'이라는 목적의 의미를 나타내는 접속사로 「so that + 주어 + can / could」의 형태로 쓴다. so that은 「in order that + 주어 + 동사」, (in order) to부정사, so as to부정사로 바꿔 쓸 수 있다.

[확인 문제] 괄호 안에서 알맞은 것을 고르시오.

> We stayed out for hours (so that / so as) we could watch shooting stars.

우리는 별똥별을 보기 위해서 몇 시간 동안 밖에 있었다.

■ 나의 독해 점검표 ■

Step ❶ | 채점 결과 정리

1. 문장 삽입	O / X
2. 내용 일치	O / X
3. 서술형	O / X

• 나의 약점 유형은? __________

Step ❷ | 독해력 점검

□ 지문의 내용을 충분히 이해함
□ 지문의 내용을 대체로 이해함
□ 지문의 내용을 이해하지 못함

Step ❸ | 문제 해결력 점검

□ 정답과 오답의 근거를 모두 찾음
□ 정답과 오답의 근거를 대체로 찾음
□ 정답과 오답의 근거를 찾지 못함

모자를 벗어주시겠습니까?

13-02

I teach science at a university in the United States. Students call me Professor Singh. One day, my wife and I went out for dinner. When we got to the restaurant, the manager asked me to take off my hat. I told him mine was not just a hat and I could not ㉠remove it. However, the manager didn't listen to me. He insisted that I remove my hat or he wouldn't serve us food. My wife and I left the restaurant right away.

In the United States, men take off their hats in restaurants. If they don't, it is considered rude. The manager wanted his customers to use good manners in his restaurant. However, Professor Singh is a Sikh from India. Sikh men wear a turban at all times. For a Sikh, a turban is a symbol of pride.

*Sikh 시크교도

제대로 독해법

어휘 Level Up

단어에 알맞은 우리말 뜻을 골라 그 기호를 빈칸에 쓰시오.
(뜻이 같은 단어에 한하여 중복 답 가능)

1 university ....
2 professor ....
3 manager ....
4 take off ....
5 remove ....
6 insist ....
7 serve ....
8 consider ....
9 rude ....
10 customer ....
11 India ....
12 wear ....
13 turban ....
14 symbol ....
15 pride ....

ⓐ (음식을) 내주다, 제공하다
ⓑ ~을 벗다 ⓒ 터번 ⓓ 교수
ⓔ 대학 ⓕ 무례한
ⓖ 벗다, 제거하다 ⓗ 상징 ⓘ 손님
ⓙ 쓰고[입고] 있다
ⓚ ~을 …로 여기다[생각하다]
ⓛ 인도 ⓜ 자존심
ⓝ 주장하다, 고집하다
ⓞ 지배인, 매니저

▶ 해설편 p.26

1 **Singh 교수에 관한 이 글의 내용과 일치하는 것은?**

① 대학에서 심리학을 가르친다.

② 아내와 함께 식당에 들어가면서 바로 모자를 벗었다.

③ 식당 지배인이 그에게 친절하게 대해 주었다.

④ 아내와 함께 식당에서 맛있는 식사를 했다.

⑤ 인도 출신이다.

주제 추론

2 **What is the main idea of this passage?**

① Table Manners in the USA

② The Popularity of Hats in India

③ The Manager's Misunderstanding

④ Many Kinds of Restaurants in the USA

⑤ Cultural Differences Between Countries

서술형

3 **다음 내용이 누구의 문화인지 본문에서 찾아 영어로 쓰시오.**

(1) "Wearing a hat in a restaurant can make other customers uncomfortable.":

____

(2) "Taking off a hat is a big shame on me.":

____

내신 Level Up

밑줄 친 ㉠remove와 같은 의미로 쓰인 표현을 본문에서 찾아 두 단어로 쓰시오.

____

구문 Level Up

6~7행 He **insisted that I remove** my hat or he wouldn't serve us food.

▶ 요구·주장·제안을 나타내는 동사 다음의 that절의 동사는 「(should)+동사원형」으로 나타낸다. 이때 should는 생략할 수 있다. 이 문장에서는 주장을 나타내는 동사 insist가 왔으므로 that절의 동사는 (should) remove가 쓰였다.

요구·주장·제안을 나타내는 동사
demand, insist, suggest 등

[확인 문제] 괄호 안에서 알맞은 것을 고르시오.

1. My wife suggested that we (have / had) dinner at a restaurant.

   내 아내는 레스토랑에서 저녁을 먹자고 제안했다.

2. The doctor suggested that I (take / took) a walk every morning.

   의사는 내가 매일 아침 산책을 해야 한다고 제안했다.

■ 나의 독해 점검표 ■

Step ❶ | 채점 결과 정리

1. 내용 일치	O / X
2. 주제 추론	O / X
3. 서술형	O / X

• 나의 약점 유형은? __________

Step ❷ | 독해력 점검

□ 지문의 내용을 충분히 이해함

□ 지문의 내용을 대체로 이해함

□ 지문의 내용을 이해하지 못함

Step ❸ | 문제 해결력 점검

□ 정답과 오답의 근거를 모두 찾음

□ 정답과 오답의 근거를 대체로 찾음

□ 정답과 오답의 근거를 찾지 못함

Day 14 Reading 01

시험 전 금기 사항

14-01

Superstitions can reduce anxiety in a number of situations. Some people believe that if a certain action is performed, some tragedy will occur. ⓐ Since Korean students are very concerned about test results, there are some superstitions for tests. For example, Korean students do not eat seaweed soup before the test. ⓑ Seaweed is slippery, so they think their test scores might slide down. Also, they don't cut their nails or get their hair cut before their test either. ⓒ Strong nails and hair tell how healthy you are. ⓓ They believe the knowledge will go out of their brains as their hair or nails get cut from their bodies. Although they know the superstitions don't have any direct effect, they continue to follow them. ⓔ The reason is that it helps them focus on their tests with a more positive mind.

*seaweed soup 미역국

제대로 독해법

어휘 Level Up

단어에 알맞은 우리말 뜻을 골라 그 기호를 빈칸에 쓰시오.
(뜻이 같은 단어에 한하여 중복 답 가능)

1 superstition ....
2 reduce ....
3 anxiety ....
4 situation ....
5 certain ....
6 perform ....
7 tragedy ....
8 occur ....
9 concerned ....
10 result ....
11 slippery ....
12 slide down ....
13 nail ....
14 knowledge ....
15 direct ....
16 effect ....
17 continue ....
18 focus on ....
19 positive ....

ⓐ ~에 집중하다 ⓑ 걱정하는
ⓒ 결과 ⓓ 계속하다 ⓔ 긍정적인
ⓕ 미끄러운 ⓖ 미끄러져 내려가다
ⓗ 미신 ⓘ 발생하다 ⓙ 불안(감)
ⓚ 비극 ⓛ 상황 ⓜ 손톱 ⓝ 영향
ⓞ 줄이다 ⓟ 지식 ⓠ 직접적인
ⓡ 특정한, 확실한
ⓢ (수)행하다, 공연하다

▶ 해설편 p.27

무관한 문장

1 ⓐ ~ ⓔ 중에서 글의 전체 흐름과 관계없는 문장은?

① ⓐ ② ⓑ ③ ⓒ ④ ⓓ ⑤ ⓔ

2 What is the best choice for the blanks (A) and (B) according to this passage?

Korean students don't do some ____(A)____ before a test due to ____(B)____.

	(A)		(B)
①	research	----	superstitions
②	action	----	knowledge
③	research	----	tragedy
④	action	----	superstitions
⑤	talking	----	knowledge

3 한국 학생들이 시험에 관해 가지고 있는 미신의 예를 본문에서 찾아 우리말로 쓰시오. (답 2개)

(1) ________________________________

(2) ________________________________

내신 Level Up

이 글의 내용과 일치하도록 빈칸에 알맞은 말을 본문에서 찾아 쓰시오.

Cause: Korean students think their test scores might slide (1)____________ because of (2)____________ seaweeds.

↓

Effect: They don't eat seaweed soup before a (3)____________.

구문 Level Up

11~12행 Although they know the superstitions don't have any direct effect, they **continue to follow** them.

▶ continue는 동명사와 to부정사 둘 다 목적어로 취하며 의미상 변화가 없다.

cf. 동명사와 to부정사를 둘 다 목적어로 취하며 의미 변화가 없는 동사
begin(시작하다), start(시작하다), continue(계속하다), love(사랑하다), like(좋아하다), hate(싫어하다) 등

[확인 문제] 우리말과 뜻이 같도록 주어진 단어를 사용하여 문장을 완성하시오.

그는 계속해서 그 소설을 읽고 있다. (continue, read)

→ He ________ ________ ________ the novel.

■ 나의 독해 점검표 ■

Step ❶ | 채점 결과 정리

1. 무관한 문장	O / X
2. 요약문 완성	O / X
3. 서술형	O / X

• 나의 약점 유형은? __________

Step ❷ | 독해력 점검

□ 지문의 내용을 충분히 이해함
□ 지문의 내용을 대체로 이해함
□ 지문의 내용을 이해하지 못함

Step ❸ | 문제 해결력 점검

□ 정답과 오답의 근거를 모두 찾음
□ 정답과 오답의 근거를 대체로 찾음
□ 정답과 오답의 근거를 찾지 못함

슬픈 음악은 심리 치료사

14-02

New research suggests listening to sad music can help overcome the sadness of an ended relationship. This is against our common sense that cheerful music is the best when feeling the blues. It might explain why people began singing the blues in ______________ times. Stephen Palmer, a researcher at the University of California, Berkeley, said, "Emotional experiences of art products are important to our happiness." When people experience serious emotional problems, they look for a way to replace their sadness. When people are in negative moods, they choose ㉠similar moods from sad music or dramas. Even when pleasant songs are available, they want to experience the similar feeling from music. In a similar way, sad movies and books provide comfort to them as well.

*common sense 상식

블루스
블루스는 19세기 중엽에 미국 흑인들 사이에서 발생한 장르의 음악으로 초기의 블루스에는 그 당시 해방은 되었으나 홀대받았던 흑인들의 비참함과 슬픔, 절망감 등이 녹아 있다.

제대로 독해법

어휘 Level Up

단어에 알맞은 우리말 뜻을 골라 그 기호를 빈칸에 쓰시오.
(뜻이 같은 단어에 한하여 중복 답 가능)

1 research ....
2 suggest ....
3 overcome ....
4 sadness ....
5 relationship ....
6 cheerful ....
7 emotional ....
8 experience ....
9 happiness ....
10 serious ....
11 replace ....
12 negative ....
13 mood ....
14 available ....
15 provide ....
16 comfort ....
17 as well ....

ⓐ ~도, 역시 ⓑ 감정, 기분
ⓒ 감정적인 ⓓ 경험 ⓔ 관계
ⓕ 구할[이용할] 수 있는 ⓖ 극복하다
ⓗ 대체[대신]하다 ⓘ 부정적인
ⓙ 슬픔 ⓚ 심각한, 진지한
ⓛ 연구 ⓜ 위안 ⓝ 제공하다
ⓞ 시사하다, 제안하다 ⓟ 즐거운
ⓠ 행복

▶ 해설편 p.28

내용 일치

1 이 글의 내용과 일치하지 않는 것은?

① 슬픈 음악이 실연당한 사람들의 슬픔을 달랠 수 있다.
② 많은 사람들이 우울할 때 즐거운 음악이 도움이 된다고 생각한다.
③ 예술 작품을 감정적으로 경험하는 것이 행복에 중요하다.
④ 슬픔을 느낄 때 사람들은 슬픈 음악을 듣고자 하는 경향이 있다.
⑤ 슬픈 책과 영화는 슬픈 음악만큼 감정 회복에 도움이 안 된다.

빈칸 추론

2 What is the best choice for the blank?

① happy and joyful
② excited and thrilled
③ painful and tough
④ boring and uninteresting
⑤ modern and fresh

서술형

3 밑줄 친 ㉠similar moods가 의미하는 바를 본문에서 찾아 한 단어로 쓰시오.

____

내신 Level Up

이 글의 내용에 따라 우울할 때 도움이 되는 것들을 아래에서 골라 쓰시오. (답 2개)

pleasant songs	sad dramas
tearful movies	funny novels

____

구문 Level Up

2~4행 This is against *our common sense* **that** cheerful music is the best when feeling the blues.

▶ 보통 news, fact, rumor, idea 등의 추상명사 뒤에 나오는 that절은 그 추상명사와 동격이다. 여기서 common sense와 that절은 동격 관계이다.

[확인 문제] **괄호 안에서 알맞은 것을 고르시오.**

I heard the news (that / which / who) an elephant escaped from the zoo.

나는 코끼리 한 마리가 동물원을 탈출했다는 뉴스를 들었다.

■ 나의 독해 점검표 ■

Step ❶ | 채점 결과 정리

1. 내용 일치	O / X
2. 빈칸 추론	O / X
3. 서술형	O / X

• 나의 약점 유형은? __________

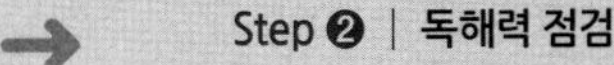

Step ❷ | 독해력 점검

□ 지문의 내용을 충분히 이해함
□ 지문의 내용을 대체로 이해함
□ 지문의 내용을 이해하지 못함

Step ❸ | 문제 해결력 점검

□ 정답과 오답의 근거를 모두 찾음
□ 정답과 오답의 근거를 대체로 찾음
□ 정답과 오답의 근거를 찾지 못함

어휘 테스트

A 사진을 보고, 빈칸에 알맞은 단어를 골라 쓰시오.

busiest　India　nails　serve　shopping　university

1 This busy __________ day is called “Black Friday.”

2 It is the __________ day of the year for online shopping.

3 I teach science at a __________.

4 He insisted that I remove my hat or he wouldn't __________ us food.

5 Professor Singh is a Sikh from __________.

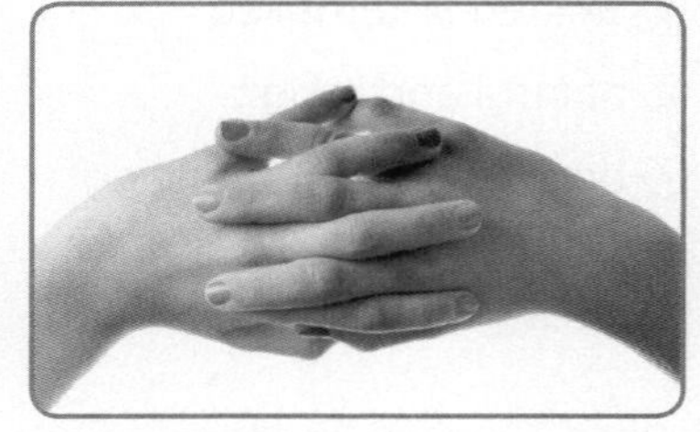

6 They don't cut their ______.

B 다음 각 단어에 해당하는 의미를 짝지으시오.

1 celebrate	•	• ⓐ belief that is not based on human reason or scientific knowledge
2 superstition	•	• ⓑ to show that an event or occasion is important by doing something special or enjoyable
3 available	•	• ⓒ able to be bought or used

인형을 통해 배우는 세계의 흥미로운 문화

닥종이 인형, 한국

우리나라의 전통 인형 중 하나인 닥종이 인형은 우리의 전통 종이인 닥종이를 여러 겹 정성스럽게 붙이고 말리는 과정을 반복해 만들어집니다. 닥종이 인형은 소박하지만 따뜻한 정이 묻어나면서, 한국의 정서를 가장 잘 표현해준다는 평을 받고 있습니다.

마리오네트 인형(Marionette), 체코(Czech)

체코의 문화에서 빼놓을 수 없는 것이 마리오네트 인형극입니다. 마리오네트는 소형 무대를 설치하고 조작하는 사람이 무대 상부에서 인형을 움직이는 것입니다. 18세기부터 체코어가 유일하게 허용된 장르는 인형극이었으며, 자국어를 지키고자 하는 체코인들은 마리오네트 인형극을 통해 지켰다고 합니다.

마트료시카(Matryoshka), 러시아(Russia)

큰 인형 속에 차례대로 다른 크기의 인형들이 들어 있는 마트료시카는 러시아의 전통 인형입니다. 러시아 사람들은 속 안에 또 다른 인형을 가지고 있는 이 마트료시카 인형을 일종의 수호신이라고 믿었다고 합니다. 또 비옥함과 다산의 의미를 내포하고 있어, 보통 이 인형을 부부 침대 위에 올려놓았다고 합니다.

Chapter 8

Science 과학 ★ Technology 기술

내가 아는 단어는 몇 개?

▷▶ 다음 단어의 뜻을 추측해 보고, 알고 있는 단어에 ✓표시를 하시오.

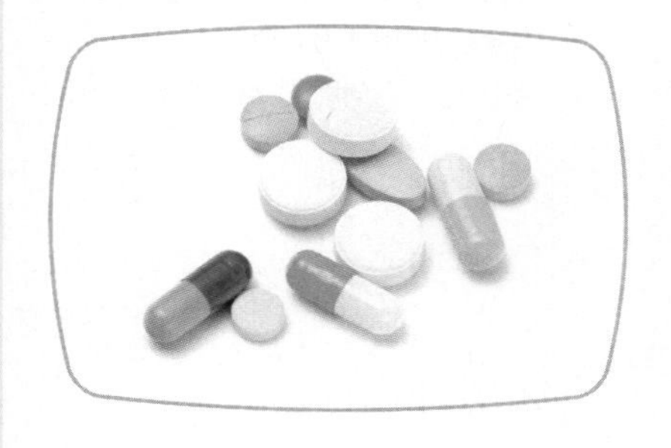

☐ pill

☐ confident

☐ hidden

☐ drop

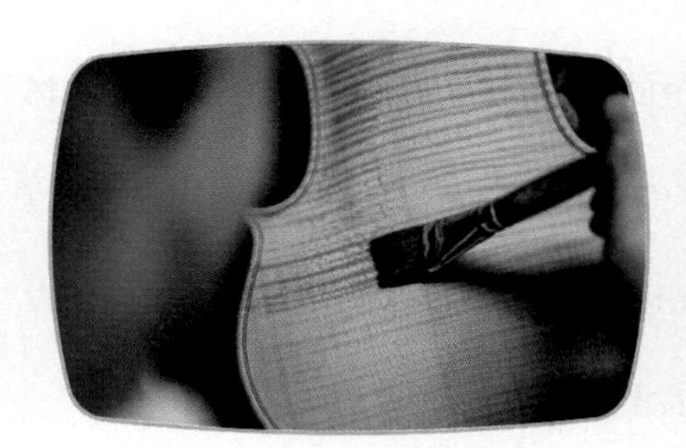

☐ brush

☐ light bulb

☐ detect

☐ train

☐ type

Day 15 Reading 01

캡슐 하나로 식사가 가능할까?

15-01

A meal in a tiny pill is not realistic. However, many scientists tried to make it. Actually, concerns for lack of food during the Cold War always pushed people ㉠뭔가 말도 안 되는 것을 발명하도록. American scientists needed to make a simple food to eat in case of emergency. They created TV dinners and became very confident to make "a meal pill." At that time, the U.S. president even promised that (A) people would put those meal pills in every pocket. The trouble, however, is that it is just impossible. After a long period of the research, scientists announced that pills are not enough for meals because they do not fill and satisfy our stomach physically. Today, we may take pills for vitamins and minerals, but ________________.

*Cold War (2차 대전 후 미국과 소련 간의) 냉전
**TV dinner 전자레인지에 돌려먹는 간편 식품 ***minerals 무기질

제대로 독해법

어휘 Level Up

단어에 알맞은 우리말 뜻을 골라 그 기호를 빈칸에 쓰시오.
(뜻이 같은 단어에 한하여 중복 답 가능)

1 pill ....
2 realistic ....
3 actually ....
4 concern ....
5 lack ....
6 emergency ....
7 confident ....
8 president ....
9 promise ....
10 impossible ....
11 announce ....
12 fill ....
13 satisfy ....
14 stomach ....
15 physically ....

ⓐ 대통령, 회장 ⓑ 만족시키다
ⓒ 물리적으로 ⓓ 현실적인
ⓔ 발표하다 ⓕ 부족 ⓖ 불가능한
ⓗ 비상사태 ⓘ 사실 ⓙ 알약
ⓚ 약속하다 ⓛ 염려 ⓜ 위(장)
ⓝ 자신감 있는 ⓞ 채우다

▶ 해설편 p.29

1 밑줄 친 (A) people would put those meal pills in every pocket이 의미하는 바로 가장 적절한 것은?

① People would not eat any food except meal pills.
② Meal pills would save people's lives.
③ Meal pills would be smaller than ever.
④ People would buy meal pills at a cheap price.
⑤ Meal pills would be supplied for everyone.

빈칸 추론

2 What is the best choice for the blank?

① they are dangerous
② we are still researching meal pills
③ they make our stomach full
④ we don't eat them as dinner
⑤ we can't buy them at a cheap price

서술형

3 meal pills가 식사를 대체할 수 없는 이유를 우리말로 쓰시오.

____

내신 Level Up

밑줄 친 ㉠의 우리말에 맞게 괄호 안에 주어진 단어들을 배열하시오.

㉠뭔가 말도 안 되는 것을 발명하도록
(crazy / invent / something / to)

→ ______________________

구문 Level Up

2~4행 Actually, concerns for lack of food during the Cold War **always** pushed people ~.

▶ always 같은 빈도부사는 어떤 일의 횟수나 정도를 나타내고 일반적으로 be동사나 조동사 뒤에, 일반동사 앞에 온다. 여기서는 일반동사 pushed 앞에 위치한다.

[확인 문제] 괄호 안에서 알맞은 것을 고르시오.

1. I (often wash / wash often) my father's car.
나는 자주 아버지의 차를 세차한다.

2. She (is sometimes late / is late sometimes) for school.
그녀는 가끔 학교에 지각한다.

■ 나의 독해 점검표 ■

Step ❶ | 채점 결과 정리

1. 밑줄 추론	O / X
2. 빈칸 추론	O / X
3. 서술형	O / X

• 나의 약점 유형은? ________

Step ❷ | 독해력 점검

□ 지문의 내용을 충분히 이해함
□ 지문의 내용을 대체로 이해함
□ 지문의 내용을 이해하지 못함

Step ❸ | 문제 해결력 점검

□ 정답과 오답의 근거를 모두 찾음
□ 정답과 오답의 근거를 대체로 찾음
□ 정답과 오답의 근거를 찾지 못함

15-02

비밀 편지 쓰기

Making ink that can't be seen ⓐis lots of fun. You can act as if you are a secret agent as you keep all your secret codes and messages ⓑhidden from others. You only need some household objects such as cups and bowls and a little lemon juice.

1. Drop some lemon juice into the bowl and add a few ⓒdrops of water.
2. Mix the water and lemon juice with the spoon.
3. Dip a brush in the mixture.
4. Write a message onto the white paper with the brush.
5. Wait for the juice to dry so that it becomes ⓓcompletely unseen.

All done. When you are ready to read your secret message or ⓔshows it to someone else, heat the paper by holding it close to a light bulb. Then the hidden message will turn brown.

*secret agent 첩보원 **dip 적시다, (살짝) 담그다

제대로 독해법

어휘 Level Up

단어에 알맞은 우리말 뜻을 골라 그 기호를 빈칸에 쓰시오.
(뜻이 같은 단어에 한하여 중복 답 가능)

1 ink ....
2 secret ....
3 code ....
4 hidden ....
5 household ....
6 object ....
7 bowl ....
8 drop ....
9 brush ....
10 mixture ....
11 completely ....
12 hold ....
13 light bulb ....
14 turn ....
15 brown ....

ⓐ 가정의, 가사의 ⓑ 갈색; 갈색의
ⓒ 숨겨진 ⓓ 그릇 ⓔ 물건, 대상
ⓕ 떨어뜨리다; 방울
ⓖ 변하다, 바꾸다 ⓗ 붓, 솔
ⓘ 비밀의; 비밀 ⓙ 암호, 부호
ⓚ 완전히 ⓛ 잉크 ⓜ 잡고 있다
ⓝ 전구 ⓞ 혼합물

▶ 해설편 p.30

1 밑줄 친 ⓐ ~ ⓔ 중에서 어법상 틀린 것은?

① ⓐ ② ⓑ ③ ⓒ ④ ⓓ ⑤ ⓔ

2 What is the purpose of this passage?

① to teach readers how to create hidden message notes
② to recommend readers to take lemon juice regularly
③ to make readers handwrite letters better
④ to help readers draw pictures better
⑤ to explain how to erase ink letters on paper

서술형

3 비밀 쪽지를 만드는 데 필요한 재료를 본문에서 모두 찾아 우리말로 쓰시오. (답 6개)

____

내신 Level Up

다음 중 비밀 잉크로 쓴 메시지를 볼 수 있는 사람은? (답 2개)

① 범균: 나는 종이를 다림질했어.
② 소라: 나는 종이를 물에 담갔어.
③ 태현: 나는 종이를 냉동실에 넣어두었어.
④ 민지: 나는 종이를 선풍기 바람에 말렸어.
⑤ 영준: 나는 종이를 전구 가까이에 대고 있었어.

구문 Level Up

6~7행 1. Drop some lemon juice into the bowl and add **a few drops** of water.

▶ 「(a) few + 셀 수 있는 복수명사」, 「(a) little + 셀 수 없는 명사」의 형태로 쓴다.

[확인 문제] 괄호 안에서 알맞은 것을 고르시오.

1. He put (a few / a little) things into a bag.

그는 몇 가지 물건들을 가방에 넣었다.

2. He has (few / little) friends. He spends most of his time alone.

그는 친구가 거의 없다. 그는 대부분의 시간을 혼자 보낸다.

■ 나의 독해 점검표 ■

Step ❶ | 채점 결과 정리

1. 어법성 판단	O / X
2. 목적 추론	O / X
3. 서술형	O / X

• 나의 약점 유형은? ________

Step ❷ | 독해력 점검

□ 지문의 내용을 충분히 이해함
□ 지문의 내용을 대체로 이해함
□ 지문의 내용을 이해하지 못함

Step ❸ | 문제 해결력 점검

□ 정답과 오답의 근거를 모두 찾음
□ 정답과 오답의 근거를 대체로 찾음
□ 정답과 오답의 근거를 찾지 못함

Day 16 Reading 01

왜 여름엔 덥고, 겨울엔 추울까?

16-01

In summer, we wear shorts because of the heat. But in winter, we wear a coat because of the cold. Why is it hot in summer and cold in winter? Many people think that it is hot because the Earth is closer to the Sun in summer and it is cold because the Earth is farther from the Sun in winter. However, the answer lies in ___________________. In summer, the sunrays hit the Earth at a ㉠sharp angle. This is because the Earth's axis is tilted. ⓐ The light does not spread out very much. ⓑ So, the Sun shines more strongly on certain places. ⓒ But in winter, the Sun shines on the Earth at a gentle angle. ⓓ The sunray to the Earth gets weaker if the Sun goes farther from it. ⓔ The light spreads out more and it reduces the amount of energy that hits on certain places.

*sunray 태양 광선

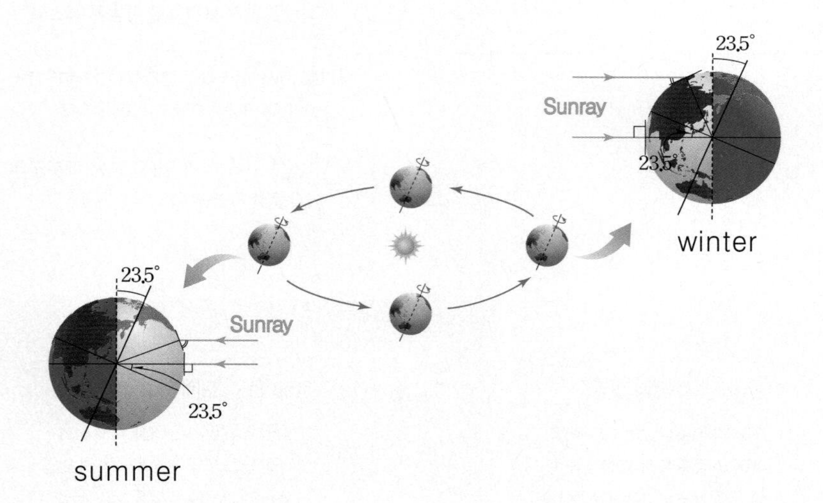

제대로 독해법

어휘 Level Up

단어에 알맞은 우리말 뜻을 골라 그 기호를 빈칸에 쓰시오.
(뜻이 같은 단어에 한하여 중복 답 가능)

1 wear ....
2 heat ....
3 farther ....
4 answer ....
5 lie ....
6 sharp ....
7 angle ....
8 axis ....
9 tilt ....
10 strongly ....
11 certain ....
12 gentle ....
13 reduce ....

ⓐ [천문] 지축 ⓑ 가파른, 급격한
ⓒ 각도 ⓓ 강하게 ⓔ 기울다
ⓕ 더 멀리 ⓖ 더위, 열
ⓗ 완만한, 부드러운 ⓘ 입고 있다
ⓙ 있다, 눕다 ⓚ 정답, 대답
ⓛ 줄이다 ⓜ 특정한, 확실한

▶ 해설편 p.31

1 **ⓐ ~ ⓔ 중에서 글의 전체 흐름과 관계없는 문장은?**

① ⓐ ② ⓑ ③ ⓒ ④ ⓓ ⑤ ⓔ

2 **What is the best choice for the blank?**

① distance between the Earth and the Sun
② the types of light from the Sun
③ the amount of air in the sky
④ the temperature of the Sun
⑤ the angle of the sunray

서술형

3 **태양 광선이 여름과 겨울에 지구에 다른 각도로 들어오는 이유를 본문에서 찾아 우리말로 쓰시오.**

____

내신 Level Up

밑줄 친 ㉠sharp와 반대되는 말을 본문에서 찾아 한 단어로 쓰시오.

____

구문 Level Up

첫 번째 문장 In summer, we wear shorts **because of** the heat.

▶ because of는 '~ 때문에'의 뜻을 가지고 명사(구)와 함께 쓴다. 절(주어+동사)과 함께 쓰이는 접속사 because와 구별해서 쓰도록 주의한다.

[확인 문제] **괄호 안에서 알맞은 것을 고르시오.**

1. I closed the window (because / because of) it got cold.

나는 날씨가 추워져서 창문을 닫았다.

2. I studied hard yesterday (because / because of) my English test.

나는 내 영어 시험 때문에 어제 열심히 공부했다.

■ 나의 독해 점검표 ■

Step ❶ | 채점 결과 정리

1. 무관한 문장	O / X
2. 빈칸 추론	O / X
3. 서술형	O / X

• 나의 약점 유형은? ________

Step ❷ | 독해력 점검

□ 지문의 내용을 충분히 이해함
□ 지문의 내용을 대체로 이해함
□ 지문의 내용을 이해하지 못함

Step ❸ | 문제 해결력 점검

□ 정답과 오답의 근거를 모두 찾음
□ 정답과 오답의 근거를 대체로 찾음
□ 정답과 오답의 근거를 찾지 못함

고양이 발을 감지해 드립니다

16-02

Have you ever had issues with your cat walking on your computer keyboard and deleting data when you are sending emails? Well in Tucson, Arizona, there is a man (A) [that/who/which] can help you out with this. He is the inventor of "PawSense." It is a software program especially (B) [designed/designing] to detect when your cats are running across your computer keyboard. Also, it can help train your cat to stay off the computer keyboard. If a cat gets on the keyboard, PawSense detects the cat typing. Then it will disable any inputs from the keyboard. At the same time it makes a sound that ______________. This teaches your cat that getting on the keyboard is bad even if humans aren't watching.

제대로 독해법

어휘 Level Up

단어에 알맞은 우리말 뜻을 골라 그 기호를 빈칸에 쓰시오.
(뜻이 같은 단어에 한하여 중복 답 가능)

1 issue ....
2 delete ....
3 data ....
4 send ....
5 inventor ....
6 software ....
7 especially ....
8 detect ....
9 train ....
10 stay off ....
11 type ....
12 disable ....
13 input ....

ⓐ 감지하다 ⓑ 멀리 있다
ⓒ 못하게 하다 ⓓ 문제, 주제
ⓔ 발명가 ⓕ 보내다 ⓖ 삭제하다
ⓗ 소프트웨어 ⓘ 입력; 입력하다
ⓙ 자료 ⓚ 훈련시키다
ⓛ 키보드를 치다; 유형
ⓜ 특히, 특별하게

▶ 해설편 p.32

1 (A), (B)의 각 네모 안에서 어법에 맞는 표현으로 가장 적절한 것은?

	(A)		(B)
①	that	----	designing
②	who	----	designing
③	who	----	designed
④	which	----	designed
⑤	which	----	designing

2 What is the best choice for the blank?

① attracts cats
② calls for help
③ annoys cats
④ is similar to cat's sound
⑤ blocks errors

서술형

3 PawSense의 기능을 본문에서 찾아 우리말로 쓰시오. (답 2개)

(1) ____________________

(2) ____________________

내신 Level Up

주어진 단어들 중에서 빈칸에 알맞은 말을 골라 PawSense를 설명하는 문장을 완성하시오.

stay off, train, disable, keyboard

"PawSense" is a software program that can be used to (1)______ any inputs from the cat typing and (2)______ the cat to (3)______ the computer keyboard.

구문 Level Up

첫번째 문장 **Have you *ever* had** issues with your cat walking on your computer keyboard and deleting data when you are sending emails?

▶ 「Have/Has+주어+p.p. ~?」 형태의 현재완료 의문문으로 '~ 해본 적 있니?'라는 의미를 나타낸다. 부사 ever(이제[지금]까지)가 쓰인 것으로 보아 현재완료의 경험 용법이다.

[확인 문제] 우리말과 뜻이 같도록 주어진 단어를 사용하여 문장을 완성하시오.

너는 태국 음식을 먹어 본 적이 있니? (eat)

→ ________ you ever ________ Thai food?

■ 나의 독해 점검표 ■

Step ❶ | 채점 결과 정리

1. 어법성 판단	O / X
2. 빈칸 추론	O / X
3. 서술형	O / X

• 나의 약점 유형은? ________

Step ❷ | 독해력 점검

□ 지문의 내용을 충분히 이해함
□ 지문의 내용을 대체로 이해함
□ 지문의 내용을 이해하지 못함

Step ❸ | 문제 해결력 점검

□ 정답과 오답의 근거를 모두 찾음
□ 정답과 오답의 근거를 대체로 찾음
□ 정답과 오답의 근거를 찾지 못함

▶ 해설편 p.32

어휘 테스트

A 사진을 보고, 빈칸에 알맞은 단어를 골라 쓰시오.

brush confident detects hidden pill train

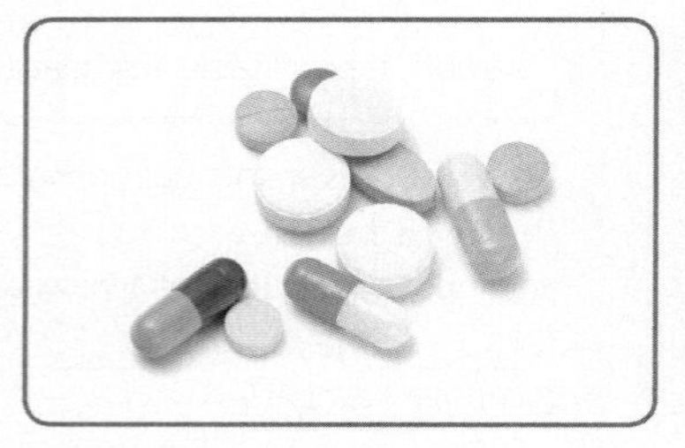

1 A meal in a tiny ________ is not realistic.

2 They became very ________ to make "a meal pill."

3 The ________ message will turn brown.

4 Dip a ________ in the mixture.

5 It ________ the cat typing.

6 It can help ________ your cat.

B 다음 각 단어에 해당하는 의미를 짝지으시오.

1 concern	•	• ⓐ to make something known or tell people about something officially
2 announce	•	• ⓑ a subject or problem that people are thinking and talking about
3 issue	•	• ⓒ a worried or nervous feeling about something

5G 이후 세상은 어떻게 변할까?

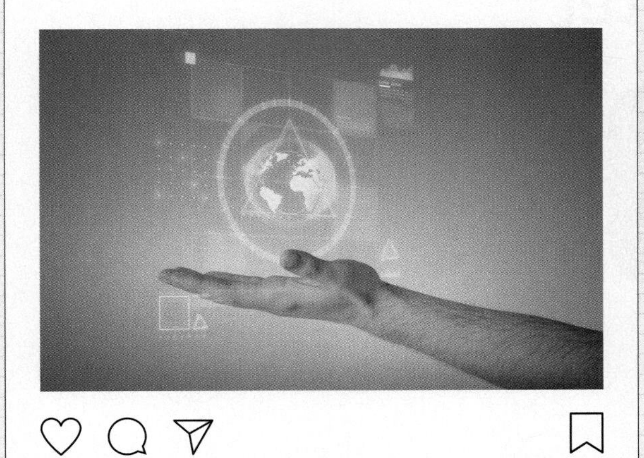

가상현실(VR) 또는 증강현실(AR)을 구현하다

5G는 대용량 데이터의 실시간 고속 전송을 특징으로 하는 통신 시스템으로서, 고화질 영화 한 편을 2~3초 안에 다운로드 받을 수 있습니다. 5G를 통해 앞으로 가상현실(VR)과 증강현실(AR), 홀로그램 3D 입체영상을 즐길 수 있습니다.

선이 필요 없는 '와이어리스(wireless)' 세상

5G 상용화 서비스가 시작되면 가정이나 사무실에 자리 잡고 있는 랜선, 광케이블, TV 케이블이 사라질 전망입니다. 5G 네트워크가 유선 케이블을 대체할 정도로 빠르기 때문입니다.

스마트 의료, 자율주행차

안정성이 필수적인 커넥티드카, 스마트 의료 등 기존 네트워크 환경에서는 제한적이었던 기술과 서비스가 발전됩니다. 이로 인해 자율주행차, 원격의료, 원격로봇이 가능하며 인공지능 비서, 지능형 로봇이 가능해집니다.

Chapter 9

Jobs 직업
★
People 사람들

내가 아는 단어는 몇 개?

▷▶ 다음 단어의 뜻을 추측해 보고, 알고 있는 단어에 ✔표시를 하시오.

☐ taste

☐ film

☐ palace

☐ fountain

☐ fall asleep

☐ cook

☐ lamb

☐ hardboiled

☐ reporter

Day 17 Reading 01

인터넷 콘텐츠 크리에이터는 괜찮은 직업일까?

17-01

Once you connect to the Internet, you will find lots of new videos. These videos are generally fun and interesting and usually ⓐexclude advertisements. A number of people make a huge income from ㉠them, so people think creating these videos for a living is a successful job. However, it doesn't seem to be ⓑpositive for two reasons. First of all, the field is very ⓒcompetitive. Anyone can do this job with simple skills. Even if you had a big talent for this and became ⓓsuccessful, there would be new challengers with bigger passion and better ability. Second, it is not ⓔsure that they get paid every day. Most of media creators earn money from advertisements. But if the Internet site goes broke and nobody reaches your contents, you will get nothing.

*go broke 파산하다

제대로 독해법

어휘 Level Up

단어에 알맞은 우리말 뜻을 골라 그 기호를 빈칸에 쓰시오.
(뜻이 같은 단어에 한하여 중복 답 가능)

1 connect ....
2 generally ....
3 exclude ....
4 advertisement ....
5 income ....
6 create ....
7 positive ....
8 reason ....
9 field ....
10 competitive ....
11 challenger ....
12 passion ....
13 ability ....
14 creator ....
15 contents ....

ⓐ ~을 만들어 내다 ⓑ 경쟁적인
ⓒ 광고 ⓓ 긍정적인 ⓔ 능력
ⓕ 도전자 ⓖ 분야, 밭 ⓗ 소득, 수입
ⓘ 열정 ⓙ 이유 ⓚ 일반적으로
ⓛ 접속하다, 연결하다 ⓜ 제외하다
ⓝ 창작자 ⓞ (인터넷상의) 콘텐츠, 정보

주제 추론

1 이 글의 주제로 가장 적절한 것은?

① Negative points of being an Internet contents creator as a job
② How to join the contents creating market
③ The amount of money on advertisements
④ Hot trends of Internet contents
⑤ The side effect of Internet contents

어휘 파악

2 Which is NOT a suitable word in ⓐ ~ ⓔ?

① ⓐ ② ⓑ  ③ ⓒ ④ ⓓ  ⑤ ⓔ

서술형

3 Internet contents creator에 대한 글쓴이의 전망과 그 이유를 우리말로 쓰시오.

전망: ______________________

이유: (1) ______________________

(2) ______________________

내신 Level Up

밑줄 친 ㉠them이 가리키는 것을 본문에서 찾아 한 단어로 쓰시오.

____

구문 Level Up

11행 **Most of** media creators **earn** money from advertisements.

▶ 「most[half, part, 분수] of + 단수명사」는 단수 취급하고, 「most[half, part, 분수] of + 복수명사」는 복수 취급한다. 여기에서는 Most of 뒤에 media creators(복수명사)가 왔으므로 복수동사 earn이 쓰였다.

[확인 문제] 괄호 안에서 알맞은 것을 고르시오.

1. Half of the houses in the village (was / were) burnt down.

그 마을에 있는 집들의 절반이 타버렸다.

2. Most of the students (does / do) not know his name.

대부분의 학생들이 그의 이름을 모른다.

■ 나의 독해 점검표 ■

Step ❶ | 채점 결과 정리

1. 주제 추론	O / X
2. 어휘 파악	O / X
3. 서술형	O / X

• 나의 약점 유형은? __________

Step ❷ | 독해력 점검

□ 지문의 내용을 충분히 이해함
□ 지문의 내용을 대체로 이해함
□ 지문의 내용을 이해하지 못함

Step ❸ | 문제 해결력 점검

□ 정답과 오답의 근거를 모두 찾음
□ 정답과 오답의 근거를 대체로 찾음
□ 정답과 오답의 근거를 찾지 못함

17-02

특이한 직업들

There are various, unique jobs as well as commonly heard of jobs such as teachers, doctors, and police officers. Here are two examples. (ⓐ) You might have heard of a sommelier, someone who is in charge of wines at a restaurant. (ⓑ) In the past few years, however, some restaurants have been employing experts to taste various mineral waters. (ⓒ) A "water sommelier" recommends which type of mineral water tastes best with a particular food. (ⓓ) A location manager is someone who works for movie companies. It is his job to find the best sites for filming scenes outside the studio. Once he has found the appropriate places, he has to make a schedule. (ⓔ) Though the efforts of location managers are often unknown, depending on the type of the movie, it can be a really interesting job.

*sommelier 소믈리에 **mineral water 생수, 광천수

제대로 독해법

어휘 Level Up

단어에 알맞은 우리말 뜻을 골라 그 기호를 빈칸에 쓰시오.
(뜻이 같은 단어에 한하여 중복 답 가능)

1 various ....
2 unique ....
3 as well as ....
4 commonly ....
5 employ ....
6 expert ....
7 taste ....
8 recommend ....
9 type ....
10 particular ....
11 location ....
12 company ....
13 film ....
14 appropriate ....

ⓐ ~뿐만 아니라 ⓑ 고용하다
ⓒ 다양한 ⓓ 독특한
ⓔ 로케이션, 야외 촬영지
ⓕ 맛보다; 맛 ⓖ 흔히
ⓗ 적합한, 적절한 ⓘ 전문가
ⓙ 종류, 유형 ⓚ 촬영하다; 영화
ⓛ 추천하다 ⓜ 특정한 ⓝ 회사

▶ 해설편 p.34

목적 추론

1 이 글의 목적으로 가장 적절한 것은?

① 독특한 직업을 소개하려고
② 직업 선택의 중요성을 강조하려고
③ 획일적인 직업 선택을 비판하려고
④ 새로 나온 영화 제작 방법을 설명하려고
⑤ 많은 직업이 사라지고 있는 것에 대해 경고하려고

문장 삽입

2 Where would the following sentence best fit?

> Another unique job is a location manager.

① ⓐ ② ⓑ ③ ⓒ ④ ⓓ ⑤ ⓔ

3 다음 직업이 하는 일을 본문에서 찾아 우리말로 쓰시오.

(1) A water sommelier : ______________________

(2) A location manager : ______________________

내신 Level Up

이 글에서 사용된 글의 서술 방식으로 가장 적절한 것은?

① 예시 ② 비교 ③ 대조
④ 인과 ⑤ 분석

구문 Level Up

3~4행 You **might have heard** of a sommelier, someone who is in charge of wines at a restaurant.

▶ 「조동사+have+p.p.」는 반드시 외워야 하는 중요 표현이다.

should have p.p.	~했어야 했는데 (하지 않았다)
might have p.p.	~했을지도 모른다
must have p.p.	~했음에 틀림없다
cannot have p.p.	~했을 리가 없다

[확인 문제] 괄호 안에서 알맞은 것을 고르시오.

> He (should / cannot) have done such a thing. He is always kind to everyone.

그가 그런 일을 했을 리가 없다. 그는 언제나 모두에게 친절하다.

■ 나의 독해 점검표 ■

Step ❶ | 채점 결과 정리

1. 목적 추론	O / X
2. 문장 삽입	O / X
3. 서술형	O / X

• 나의 약점 유형은? ________

Step ❷ | 독해력 점검

□ 지문의 내용을 충분히 이해함
□ 지문의 내용을 대체로 이해함
□ 지문의 내용을 이해하지 못함

Step ❸ | 문제 해결력 점검

□ 정답과 오답의 근거를 모두 찾음
□ 정답과 오답의 근거를 대체로 찾음
□ 정답과 오답의 근거를 찾지 못함

일하는 백만장자

18-01

Most people want to earn much money, so they work hard. If you became a millionaire, or if you had very rich parents, would you want to keep working hard? Maybe not. Here is a story about a Chinese millionaire. This 53-year-old Chinese millionaire, Yu Youzhen, works very hard. She has worked hard for about 40 years as a farmer, cook, driver, and street cleaner. Being a diligent woman, she finally became very rich. However, she keeps working. These days, she works as a street cleaner six days a week. A reporter asked her why she keeps working so hard. She said that this is because of her son. She didn't want her son to be lazy because of her wealth, so she wanted to be her son's role model. It reminds us of the saying, '__________________________.' She is not only a great worker, but also a wise mother.

제대로 독해법

어휘 Level Up

단어에 알맞은 우리말 뜻을 골라 그 기호를 빈칸에 쓰시오.
(뜻이 같은 단어에 한하여 중복 답 가능)

1 earn ....
2 millionaire ....
3 Chinese ....
4 diligent ....
5 finally ....
6 reporter ....
7 lazy ....
8 wealth ....
9 role model ....
10 remind ....
11 saying ....
12 great ....
13 wise ....

ⓐ (돈을) 벌다 ⓑ 게으른 ⓒ 근면한
ⓓ 리포터 ⓔ 마침내 ⓕ 백만장자
ⓖ 생각나게 하다 ⓗ 속담
ⓘ 역할 모델 ⓙ 재산, 부유함
ⓚ 중국(인)의; 중국인 ⓛ 지혜로운
ⓜ 훌륭한

▶ 해설편 p.35

1 이 글의 목적으로 가장 적절한 것은?

① to introduce various jobs in China
② to give tips about becoming wealthy
③ to give a lesson about working hard
④ to teach workers how to make money
⑤ to warn people about dangerous jobs

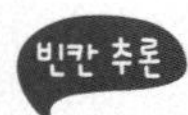

2 What is the best choice for the blank?

① Two heads are better than one.
② Examples are better than precepts.
③ A bad workman always blames his tools.
④ A bird in the hand is worth two in the bush.
⑤ All work and no play makes Jack a dull boy.

3 Yu Youzhen이 아들에게 전하고자 한 교훈이 무엇인지 생각해보고 다음 빈칸에 들어갈 한 단어를 본문에서 찾아 문장을 완성하시오.

Yu Youzhen wanted her son to be ________________.

내신 Level Up

이 글의 내용과 일치하도록 빈칸에 알맞은 말을 본문에서 찾아 쓰시오.

The name of the millionaire: (1) ______ Youzhen
The age of the millionaire: (2) ______ years old
The nationality of the millionaire: China
The period of her working experience: (3) ______ years
Her jobs(from past to present): farmer, (4) ______, driver, and street cleaner

구문 Level Up

7~8행 Being a diligent woman, she finally became very rich.

▶ Being a diligent woman은 이유를 나타내는 분사구문으로 Because she was a diligent woman으로 바꾸어 쓸 수 있다.

[확인 문제] 다음 두 문장의 뜻이 같도록 분사구문을 사용하여 문장을 완성하시오.

When I have spare time, I usually surf the Internet.
→ ______________, I usually surf the Internet.

여가 시간이 있을 때, 나는 보통 인터넷 서핑을 한다.

■ 나의 독해 점검표 ■

Step ❶ | 채점 결과 정리

1. 목적 추론	O / X
2. 빈칸 추론	O / X
3. 서술형	O / X

• 나의 약점 유형은? ________

Step ❷ | 독해력 점검

□ 지문의 내용을 충분히 이해함
□ 지문의 내용을 대체로 이해함
□ 지문의 내용을 이해하지 못함

Step ❸ | 문제 해결력 점검

□ 정답과 오답의 근거를 모두 찾음
□ 정답과 오답의 근거를 대체로 찾음
□ 정답과 오답의 근거를 찾지 못함

18-02

괴짜 왕 루이 14세

Louis XIV built a huge palace at Versailles. The gardens of the palace had 1,400 fountains. (ⓐ) The fountains used water, but Louis himself ㉠did not! (ⓑ) He hated to wash. He washed only one part of his body — the tip of his nose. Louis had other unusual habits. He liked being watched by many people when he got dressed. (ⓒ) Also, only the king and queen were allowed to sit on chairs with arms. Louis had problems sleeping. (ⓓ) He went from one bed to another until he fell asleep. But he had a good appetite. (ⓔ) His cook served him plenty of food. A normal dinner was four bowls of soup, two whole chickens, ham, lamb, a salad, cakes, fruit, and hardboiled eggs. According to records, his stomach was two times the size of a normal stomach.

제대로 독해법

어휘 Level Up

단어에 알맞은 우리말 뜻을 골라 그 기호를 빈칸에 쓰시오.
(뜻이 같은 단어에 한하여 중복 답 가능)

1 palace ....
2 fountain ....
3 hate ....
4 tip ....
5 unusual ....
6 habit ....
7 get dressed ....
8 fall asleep ....
9 appetite ....
10 cook ....
11 plenty of ....
12 normal ....
13 lamb ....
14 hardboiled ....
15 stomach ....

ⓐ 궁전 ⓑ (뾰족한) 끝, (실용적인) 조언
ⓒ 많은 ⓓ 잠들다 ⓔ 버릇
ⓕ 특이한 ⓖ 보통의 ⓗ 분수
ⓘ 삶은, 달걀이 완숙된 ⓙ 식욕
ⓚ 싫어하다 ⓛ 어린[새끼] 양, 양고기
ⓜ 옷을 입다 ⓝ 요리사; 요리하다
ⓞ 위(장), 배

▶ 해설편 p.36

내용 일치

1 루이 14세에 관한 이 글의 내용과 일치하지 않는 것은?

① 씻기를 싫어했다.
② 옷을 입을 때 자신을 내보였다.
③ 팔걸이가 없는 의자를 선호했다.
④ 많은 침대를 옮겨 다니며 잠을 잤다.
⑤ 대식가였다.

문장 삽입

2 Where would the following sentence best fit?

He had 413 beds.

① ⓐ　② ⓑ　 ③ ⓒ　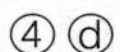 ④ ⓓ　⑤ ⓔ

서술형

3 루이 14세가 살았던 베르사유 궁전 내부의 모습을 두 가지 이상 본문에서 찾아 우리말로 쓰시오.

____

____

내신 Level Up

밑줄 친 ㉠did not 뒤에 생략된 두 단어를 쓰시오.

____

구문 Level Up

2~3행 The fountains used water, but Louis **himself** did not!

▶ himself는 재귀대명사로 주어인 Louis를 강조한다. 이처럼, 재귀대명사가 주어 또는 목적어와 동격으로 쓰여 의미를 강조하는 것을 강조 용법이라고 한다. 이 때 재귀대명사는 강조하고자 하는 단어의 바로 뒤나 문장의 맨 마지막에 오고 생략이 가능하다. 또한 재귀대명사는 강조하고자 하는 단어의 인칭과 수에 주의하며 표현한다.

[확인 문제] 우리말과 뜻이 같도록 빈칸에 알맞은 재귀대명사를 쓰시오.

1. 그녀가 직접 그 소설을 썼다.
→ She ________ wrote the novel.

2. Mia는 바로 그 보고서를 썼다.
→ Mia wrote the report ________.

■ 나의 독해 점검표 ■

Step ❶ | 채점 결과 정리

1. 내용 일치	O / X
2. 문장 삽입	O / X
3. 서술형	O / X

• 나의 약점 유형은? ________

Step ❷ | 독해력 점검

☐ 지문의 내용을 충분히 이해함
☐ 지문의 내용을 대체로 이해함
☐ 지문의 내용을 이해하지 못함

Step ❸ | 문제 해결력 점검

☐ 정답과 오답의 근거를 모두 찾음
☐ 정답과 오답의 근거를 대체로 찾음
☐ 정답과 오답의 근거를 찾지 못함

▶ 해설편 p.36

어휘 테스트

A 사진을 보고, 빈칸에 알맞은 단어를 골라 쓰시오.

cook fell asleep filming fountains palace reporter

1 It is his job to find the best sites for ____________ scenes.

2 Louis XIV built a huge ____________ at Versailles.

3 The gardens of the palace had 1,400 ____________.

4 He went from one bed to another until he __________.

5 His ____________ served him plenty of food.

6 A ____________ asked her why she keeps working so hard.

B 다음 각 단어에 해당하는 의미를 짝지으시오.

1 income •

2 appetite •

3 remind •

• ⓐ money that is earned from doing work or received from investments

• ⓑ to make someone think of something they have forgotten or might have forgotten

• ⓒ the feeling that you want to eat food

10대들의 진로 고민 Q&A

꿈이 자주 바뀌면 안 되는 건가요?

장래 희망을 딱 한 개의 직업으로 고수할 필요는 없습니다. 10대 때는 일 년에도 몇 번씩 하고 싶은 일이 바뀔 수 있습니다. 그리고 꿈이 없는 것보다는 꿈이 여러 번 바뀌는 편이 앞으로 하고 싶은 일을 찾는 데 도움이 됩니다. 단, 원하는 직업에 대해 알아보려고 노력한다면 말입니다. 그 과정에서 내가 이 직업에 어울리는지 살펴보게 되고, 실제 일하는 모습도 상상해 보면서 진짜 원하는 꿈을 찾을 수 있습니다.

좋아하는 것과 잘하는 것, 어떤 걸 선택해야 하나요?

어떤 사람들은 좋아하는 걸 선택하면 열정을 가지고 재밌게 일할 수 있고, 좋아서 하다 보면 결국 잘할 수 있다고 말합니다. 또 어떤 사람들은 자기가 잘하는 일을 하면 재밌을 수밖에 없고, 남들보다 더 잘하니까 자신감이 넘쳐 신이 난다고 말합니다. 최고로 좋은 건 좋아하는 일을 잘하는 것이겠지만, 좋아하는 것을 선택하든 잘하는 것을 선택하든 아직은 배우고 노력할 게 많다는 점에서 마찬가지입니다. 지금 둘 중 하나를 선택했다는 것은 단지 원하는 방향으로 한 발자국을 더 뗀 것이라고 할 수 있습니다. 결국 무엇을 선택하든 열심히 하겠다는 강한 의지가 더 중요합니다.

원하는 직업이 내 성격과 맞지 않으면 어떡하나요?

"이 직업엔, 이런 성격!"이라고 정해져 있는 기준은 없습니다. 어딜 가도 '그런' 사람들이 꼭 있는 것처럼, 한 직업에도 굉장히 다양한 성격의 사람들이 존재합니다. 자유분방한 디자인 회사에도 계획적으로 일하는 사람이 있고, 모두 점잖고 근엄할 것 같은 교수님 중에도 개그맨 못지않게 웃긴 분들이 있습니다. 물론 직업에 따라 장점이 되는 성격은 있습니다. 경찰관으로서 정직하고 정의로운 성격은 일을 하는 데 큰 힘이 됩니다. 결국 일을 하는 데 좀 더 도움이 되는 성격은 있어도 직업 선택에 걸림돌이 되는 성격은 없다고 봐도 좋습니다.

Chapter 10

Stories 이야기
★
Origins 유래

내가 아는 단어는 몇 개?

▷▶ 다음 단어의 뜻을 추측해 보고, 알고 있는 단어에 ✔표시를 하시오.

☐ candle

☐ garage

☐ junk

☐ street

☐ penguin

☐ amusement park

☐ pirate

☐ sail

☐ skull

Day 19 Reading 01

생일 때 촛불을 끄는 이유

19-01

Once a year, you celebrate the day when you were born. It's your ________. Everybody sings the Happy Birthday song with candles burning. When the song finishes, it's time ⓐfor you to make a wish and blow out the candles. By the way, have you ever ⓑwonder why you blow out the candles on your birthday? (A) A long time ago, people believed that their wishes could reach God better with smoke. (B) The greater the amount of smoke was, ⓒthe better it was. (C) To make a wish come true, people started to blow candles all at the same time on birthdays. (D) Now, when you blow your candles on your birthday this year, take a deep breath and ⓓblow out all the candles at once to make the biggest smoke ever. (E) Tell God your wish and make it ⓔspecial among all the other wishes you've made so far.

제대로 독해법

어휘 Level Up

단어에 알맞은 우리말 뜻을 골라 그 기호를 빈칸에 쓰시오.
(뜻이 같은 단어에 한하여 중복 답 가능)

1 celebrate ....
2 candle ....
3 burn ....
4 make a wish ....
5 blow out ....
6 by the way ....
7 wonder ....
8 believe ....
9 reach ....
10 smoke ....
11 come true ....
12 breath ....
13 at once ....
14 special ....
15 among ....
16 so far ....

ⓐ (불어서) 끄다 ⓑ (불에) 타다
ⓒ ~ 중에서 ⓓ ~에 닿다
ⓔ 궁금해 하다 ⓕ 그런데
ⓖ 기념하다, 축하하다 ⓗ 믿다
ⓘ 소원을 빌다 ⓙ 숨 ⓚ 양초, 초
ⓛ 연기 ⓜ 이루어지다
ⓝ 지금까지 ⓞ 특별한
ⓟ 한 번에, 즉시

▶ 해설편 p.37

1 밑줄 친 ⓐ~ⓔ 중에서 어법상 틀린 것은?

① ⓐ ② ⓑ ③ ⓒ ④ ⓓ ⑤ ⓔ

2 Where would the following sentence best fit?

Therefore, blowing out all the candles at once was the best way to make a wish.

① (A) ② (B) ③ (C) ④ (D) ⑤ (E)

3 이 글의 빈칸에 들어갈 말을 본문에서 찾아 한 단어로 쓰시오.

____

내신 Level Up

이 글의 내용과 일치하면 T, 일치하지 않으면 F에 ✓ 표시를 하시오.

(1) T F
In the past, people thought smoke helped their wishes to be heard by God.

(2) T F
When the amount of smoke was greater, it was thought to be better.

(3) T F
Blowing out all the candles at once was considered bad luck.

구문 Level Up

7~8행 **The greater** the amount of smoke was, **the better** it was.

▶ 「The 비교급(+주어+동사), the 비교급(+주어+동사)」는 '~하면 할수록 점점 더 …하다'의 의미이다.

[확인 문제] 괄호 안에서 알맞은 것을 고르시오.

The more we have, the (many / much / more) we want.

우리는 많이 가지면 가질수록, 더 많이 원한다.

■ 나의 독해 점검표 ■

Step ❶ | 채점 결과 정리

1. 어법성 판단	O / X
2. 문장 삽입	O / X
3. 서술형	O / X

• 나의 약점 유형은? __________

Step ❷ | 독해력 점검

□ 지문의 내용을 충분히 이해함
□ 지문의 내용을 대체로 이해함
□ 지문의 내용을 이해하지 못함

Step ❸ | 문제 해결력 점검

□ 정답과 오답의 근거를 모두 찾음
□ 정답과 오답의 근거를 대체로 찾음
□ 정답과 오답의 근거를 찾지 못함

19-02

애물단지 '흰 코끼리'

"Every time you go to a garage sale, you come home with another white elephant!" This is what my mom yelled at my father yesterday. You might see people selling "white elephants" at a flea market or school fair. ㉠Don't look for any white-colored animals. "White elephants" are just some junk that people don't want anymore and would like to sell to you. A long time ago in Thailand, a white elephant was a holy animal. When the king of Thailand was angry at someone, he gave that person a white elephant as a "present." The white elephant could never be made to work. It would live only in comfortable and luxurious condition, so its new owner would run out of money caring for it. This is why we call __________ stuff a "white elephant."

*luxurious 호화로운

제대로 독해법

어휘 Level Up

단어에 알맞은 우리말 뜻을 골라 그 기호를 빈칸에 쓰시오.
(뜻이 같은 단어에 한하여 중복 답 가능)

1 garage ....
2 yell ....
3 flea market ....
4 fair ....
5 junk ....
6 Thailand ....
7 holy ....
8 comfortable ....
9 condition ....
10 owner ....
11 run out of ....
12 care for ....
13 stuff ....

ⓐ ~을 다 써버리다 ⓑ ~을 돌보다
ⓒ 것, 물건 ⓓ 고물, 폐물
ⓔ 벼룩시장 ⓕ 상태 ⓖ 성스러운
ⓗ 외치다 ⓘ 장터; 공정한 ⓙ 주인
ⓚ 차고, 주차장 ⓛ 태국 ⓜ 편안한

▶ 해설편 p.38

밑줄 추론

1 밑줄 친 ㉠ Don't look for any white-colored animals.의 이유로 가장 적절한 것은?

① 엄마가 원하는 동물이 아니므로
② 흰 코끼리는 성스럽지 못하므로
③ 벼룩시장에는 회색 코끼리만 있으므로
④ 실제 흰 코끼리를 의미하는 게 아니므로
⑤ 태국의 왕이 화가 나서 선물로 주었으므로

빈칸 추론

2 What is the best choice for the blank?

① light ② useless ③ precious
④ luxurious ⑤ important

서술형

3 이 글의 내용과 일치하도록 빈칸에 알맞은 말을 주어진 단어들 중에서 골라 쓰시오.

sell money junk present

Once upon a time, if the king of Thailand was angry at someone, he gave that person a white elephant as a (1) __________. It would live only in comfortable and luxurious condition, so the new owner would run out of (2) __________ to take care of it. Today, the expression a "white elephant" refers to (3) __________ that people don't need and would like to (4) __________.

내신 Level Up

'흰 코끼리'와 같은 의미를 가진 한 단어를 본문에서 찾아 쓰시오.

____

구문 Level Up

9~10행 The white elephant could never **be made to work**.

▶ 사역동사 make의 목적격보어는 능동태에서는 동사원형이지만, 수동태에서는 to부정사로 바뀐다. 이처럼 사역동사의 수동태는 「be동사+p.p.+to부정사」 형태로 나타낸다.
(→ He could never **make** the white elephant **work**.)

[확인 문제] 다음 문장을 수동태로 쓸 때, 빈칸에 알맞은 말을 쓰시오.

She made the builder fix her kitchen last month.
→ The builder ______________ her kitchen last month by her.

그녀는 지난달에 건축업자가 그녀의 주방을 수리하게 했다.
→ 건축업자는 그녀에 의해 지난달에 그녀의 주방을 수리하게 되었다.

■ 나의 독해 점검표 ■

Step ❶ | 채점 결과 정리

1. 밑줄 추론	O / X
2. 빈칸 추론	O / X
3. 서술형	O / X

• 나의 약점 유형은? __________

Step ❷ | 독해력 점검

□ 지문의 내용을 충분히 이해함
□ 지문의 내용을 대체로 이해함
□ 지문의 내용을 이해하지 못함

Step ❸ | 문제 해결력 점검

□ 정답과 오답의 근거를 모두 찾음
□ 정답과 오답의 근거를 대체로 찾음
□ 정답과 오답의 근거를 찾지 못함

남자와 펭귄

20-01

One day, a police officer was walking down the street. As he was walking, he saw a man with a penguin following him.

(A) "You should take it to the zoo," the officer said. "That's a good idea," the man said, and he went off with the penguin.

(B) The next day, the police officer saw the man on the street again, with the penguin still behind him. "I thought I told you to take the penguin to the zoo," the officer said. "Oh, I did," the man replied, "and today I'm taking it to the amusement park."

(C) "What are you doing with that penguin?" the police officer asked. "Well, I don't know. I saw the penguin on the street and then it started following me," the man answered.

제대로 독해법

어휘 Level Up

단어에 알맞은 우리말 뜻을 골라 그 기호를 빈칸에 쓰시오.
(뜻이 같은 단어에 한하여 중복 답 가능)

1 one day ....
2 police officer ....
3 walk ....
4 street ....
5 penguin ....
6 follow ....
7 take ....
8 zoo ....
9 again ....
10 still ....
11 behind ....
12 reply ....
13 amusement park ....
14 ask ....
15 answer ....

ⓐ 거리 ⓑ 걷다 ⓒ 경찰관
ⓓ 놀이공원 ⓔ 다시 ⓕ 대답하다
ⓖ 데려가다 ⓗ 동물원 ⓘ 뒤에
ⓙ 따라가다 ⓚ 묻다, 요청하다
ⓛ 어느 날 ⓜ 여전히 ⓝ 펭귄

▶ 해설편 p.39

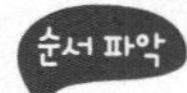

1 주어진 글 다음에 이어질 글의 순서로 가장 적절한 것은?

① (A) — (B) — (C)　② (A) — (C) — (B)　③ (B) — (A) — (C)
④ (C) — (A) — (B)　⑤ (C) — (B) — (A)

내용 일치

2 Which is TRUE according to this passage?

① The police officer saw a penguin following a man.
② The police officer advised a man to play with a penguin.
③ A man saw a penguin in the street and then he started following it.
④ A man returned a penguin to the zoo.
⑤ The penguin was the man's pet.

서술형

3 경찰관이 말한 "You should take it to the zoo,"가 각자에게 의미한 바를 쓰시오.

(1) 경찰관: ______________________

(2) 펭귄을 데리고 다닌 남자: ______________________

내신 Level Up

이 글의 내용과 가장 잘 어울리는 속담은?

① Talking to the wall.
② Bad news travels fast.
③ Every dog has his day.
④ Honesty is the best policy.
⑤ Gather roses while you may.

구문 Level Up

첫 번째 문장 One day, a police officer **was walking** down the street.

▶ was walking은 「was/were+-ing」 형태의 과거진행시제이다. 과거진행시제는 과거의 특정 시점에 진행 중이던 동작을 나타내며 '~하고 있었다'라는 의미를 나타내며, 과거시제처럼 과거를 나타내는 부사(구)와 함께 쓰인다.

[확인 문제] 괄호 안에서 알맞은 것을 고르시오.

Tony and Tom (was eating / were eating) cheeseburgers.

Tony와 Tom은 치즈버거를 먹고 있었다.

■ 나의 독해 점검표 ■

Step ❶ | 채점 결과 정리

1. 순서 파악	O / X
2. 내용 일치	O / X
3. 서술형	O / X

• 나의 약점 유형은? ________

Step ❷ | 독해력 점검

□ 지문의 내용을 충분히 이해함
□ 지문의 내용을 대체로 이해함
□ 지문의 내용을 이해하지 못함

Step ❸ | 문제 해결력 점검

□ 정답과 오답의 근거를 모두 찾음
□ 정답과 오답의 근거를 대체로 찾음
□ 정답과 오답의 근거를 찾지 못함

🎧 20-02

가짜 깃발, 진짜 깃발!

Have you ever heard the old expression, "㉠to sail under false colors?" Linguists say that it was born more than two hundred and fifty years ago. At that time, pirates sailed the seas, attacking trade ships. ⓐThey flew the flag of a friendly country, (A) [sail / to sail / sailing] toward other ships. ⓑThey sailed under the false flag until ⓒthey were close enough to attack the ships. When the time came, the pirates pulled down the false flag, showing ⓓtheir true flag. As you can imagine, there was a skull and cross bones in their true flag. Today, the expression is applied to a person, not a ship. Such people pretend to be nice with their true colors (B) [hiding / hidden]. ⓔThey may try to get something from you. If you are careful, however, you will soon see their ____________.

*false colors 가짜 국기 **linguist 언어학자

제대로 독해법

어휘 Level Up

단어에 알맞은 우리말 뜻을 골라 그 기호를 빈칸에 쓰시오.
(뜻이 같은 단어에 한하여 중복 답 가능)

1 expression ....
2 pirate ....
3 sail ....
4 attack ....
5 trade ....
6 fly ....
7 flag ....
8 friendly ....
9 toward ....
10 false ....
11 pull down ....
12 imagine ....
13 skull ....
14 apply ....
15 pretend ....
16 hide ....
17 careful ....

ⓐ (깃발을) 달다, 날다 ⓑ ~을 내리다
ⓒ ~을 향하여 ⓓ ~인 척하다
ⓔ 가짜의, 틀린 ⓕ 공격하다; 공격
ⓖ 깃발 ⓗ 무역; 거래하다
ⓘ 상상하다 ⓙ 숨기다
ⓚ 우호적인, 친근한
ⓛ 적용하다, 지원하다
ⓜ 조심하는, 주의 깊은 ⓝ 표현
ⓞ 항해하다 ⓟ 해골, 두개골
ⓠ 해적

▶ 해설편 p.40

밑줄 추론

1 밑줄 친 ㉠ to sail under false colors가 의미하는 바로 가장 적절한 것은?

① 공격하다
② 실수하다
③ 이익을 얻다
④ 본색을 감추다
⑤ 헌신적으로 돕다

어법성 판단

2 What is the grammatically correct one in each box (A) and (B)?

	(A)		(B)
①	sail	----	hiding
②	to sail	----	hiding
③	sailing	----	hiding
④	to sail	----	hidden
⑤	sailing	----	hidden

서술형

3 이 글의 빈칸에 들어갈 말을 본문에서 찾아 두 단어로 쓰시오.

____

내신 Level Up

밑줄 친 ⓐ~ⓔ 중에서 가리키는 대상이 나머지 넷과 다른 것은?

① ⓐ ② ⓑ ③ ⓒ
④ ⓓ ⑤ ⓔ

구문 Level Up

3~4행 At that time, pirates sailed the seas, **attacking** trade ships.

▶ 사건이나 동작이 연속해서 일어나는 것을 나타낼 때 분사구문을 사용할 수 있다. attacking은 연속동작을 나타내는 분사구문으로 and (they) attacked으로 바꾸어 쓸 수 있다.
(→ At that time, pirates sailed the seas, **and (they) attacked** trade ships.)

[확인 문제] **다음 두 문장의 뜻이 같도록 분사구문을 사용하여 빈칸을 완성하시오.**

A ball flew into the room, and it broke the vase on the desk.
→ A ball flew into the room, __________ the vase on the desk.

공이 방으로 날아와서, 책상 위에 있는 꽃병을 깨뜨렸다.

■ 나의 독해 점검표 ■

Step ❶ | 채점 결과 정리

1. 밑줄 추론	O / X
2. 어법성 판단	O / X
3. 서술형	O / X

• 나의 약점 유형은? __________

Step ❷ | 독해력 점검

□ 지문의 내용을 충분히 이해함
□ 지문의 내용을 대체로 이해함
□ 지문의 내용을 이해하지 못함

Step ❸ | 문제 해결력 점검

□ 정답과 오답의 근거를 모두 찾음
□ 정답과 오답의 근거를 대체로 찾음
□ 정답과 오답의 근거를 찾지 못함

▶ 해설편 p.40

어휘 테스트

A 사진을 보고, 빈칸에 알맞은 단어를 골라 쓰시오.

amusement park	penguin	pirates	sailed	skull	street

1 A police officer was walking down the ____________.

2 I saw a ____________ in the street.

3 I'm taking the penguin to the ____________.

4 At that time, ____________ sailed the seas, attacking trade ships.

5 They ____________ under the false flag.

6 There was a ____________ and cross bones in their true flag.

B 다음 각 단어에 해당하는 의미를 짝지으시오.

1 breath •
2 flea market •
3 attack •

• ⓐ a market where old or used goods are sold cheaply
• ⓑ the air that goes into and out of your lungs
• ⓒ to try to hurt or defeat using violence

흥미로운 영어 어원

roll out: (신제품 등)을 출시하다

roll out이 '신제품을 출시하다'라는 의미를 갖게 된 이유는 무엇일까요? 실크 판매상이 동그랗게 말린 실크 두루마리를 펼쳐 보이며, 실크를 판매하는 모습에서 유래하였습니다. 시간이 흘러 은유적 표현으로 변화되어 '신제품을 출시하다'라는 의미로 사용하게 되었습니다.

cap off: (일 등을) 끝마치다, 완료하다

cap은 '모자'이고, off는 '무언가를 멀리 떨어뜨리는' 것을 의미합니다. cap off는 문자 그대로 '쓰고 있던 모자를 벗어서 멀리 놓아두다'라는 의미입니다. 작업을 모두 마친 공사장 노동자가 안전모를 벗어 놓고 퇴근하는 장면, 대학교 졸업식이 끝나자 졸업생들이 학사모를 하늘로 던지는 장면에서처럼 '모자'가 작업 전체를 의미하는 비유법으로 사용되어 '모자를 벗다'라는 의미가 '작업을 끝마쳤다'라는 의미로 사용되었습니다.

kick off: (경기, 사업, 일 등)을 시작하다

kick off는 축구 경기에서 유래한 표현입니다. 축구는 심판의 호각 소리와 함께 선수가 공을 발로 차는 행위로부터 경기가 시작됩니다. 여기서 '발로 차다'라는 의미의 동사 kick과 '시작하다'라는 의미의 off가 만나 kick off '(경기, 사업, 일 등)을 시작하다'라는 표현이 만들어 졌습니다.

Chapter	Day	Reading	Grammar
Chapter 1	Day 01	Reading 01	가주어, 진주어(to부정사)
		Reading 02	가정법 과거
	Day 02	Reading 01	병렬구조
		Reading 02	5형식 문장
Chapter 2	Day 03	Reading 01	접속사 that
		Reading 02	stop+-ing, stop+to부정사
	Day 04	Reading 01	비교급 비교
		Reading 02	even if
Chapter 3	Day 05	Reading 01	there is/are
		Reading 02	주격 관계대명사
	Day 06	Reading 01	가주어, 진주어(that절)
		Reading 02	if 조건절
Chapter 4	Day 07	Reading 01	의문사가 있는 간접의문문
		Reading 02	도치
	Day 08	Reading 01	while vs. during, for
		Reading 02	재귀대명사(재귀 용법)
Chapter 5	Day 09	Reading 01	동명사(주어)
		Reading 02	one of the 최상급+복수명사
	Day 10	Reading 01	사역동사
		Reading 02	5형식 문장의 수동태
Chapter 6	Day 11	Reading 01	관계부사절(시간)
		Reading 02	4형식 문장의 3형식 전환
	Day 12	Reading 01	계속적용법의 관계대명사
		Reading 02	현재진행시제
Chapter 7	Day 13	Reading 01	접속사 so that
		Reading 02	요구·주장·제안 동사+that+주어+should
	Day 14	Reading 01	동명사와 to부정사를 모두 목적어로 쓰는 동사
		Reading 02	동격의 that절
Chapter 8	Day 15	Reading 01	빈도부사 위치
		Reading 02	(a) few+셀 수 있는 명사
	Day 16	Reading 01	because vs. because of
		Reading 02	현재완료(경험)
Chapter 9	Day 17	Reading 01	most[half, part, 분수] of+단수명사
		Reading 02	조동사+have p.p.
	Day 18	Reading 01	분사구문
		Reading 02	재귀대명사(강조 용법)
Chapter 10	Day 19	Reading 01	the 비교급(+주어+동사), the 비교급(+주어+동사)
		Reading 02	사역동사의 수동태
	Day 20	Reading 01	과거진행시제
		Reading 02	분사구문(연속동작)

#READING

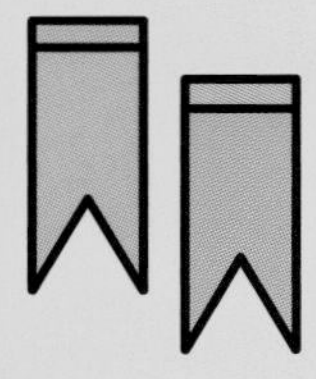

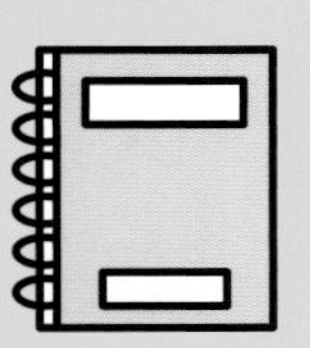

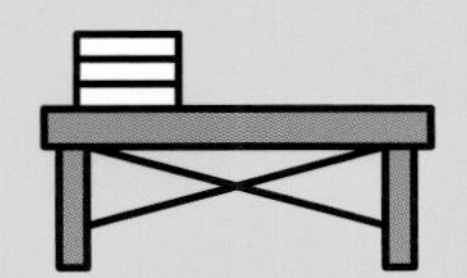

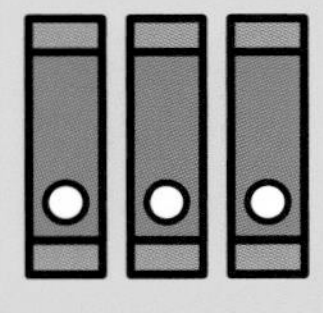

적중! 영어독해 중2

Workbook

Word List
&
Word Test

▷▶ **Word Test의 정답은 Word List에서 확인할 수 있습니다.**

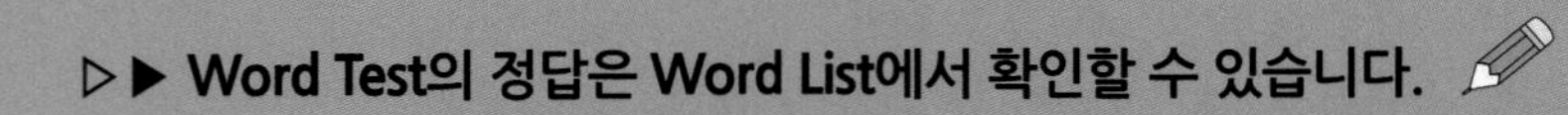

Word List

Chapter 1

DAY 01

Reading 01

- □ 01 outdoor 형 야외의
- □ 02 indoor 형 실내의
- □ 03 rubber 명 고무
- □ 04 fail 동 실패하다
- □ 05 move 동 움직이다
- □ 06 quickly 부 빠르게
- □ 07 demand 명 부담, 요구

Reading 02

- □ 08 determine 동 결정하다
- □ 09 force 명 힘
- □ 10 fast 형 빠른 부 빠르게
- □ 11 lose 동 잃다
- □ 12 balance 명 균형
- □ 13 such as ~와 같은
- □ 14 forward 부 앞으로
- □ 15 important 형 중요한

DAY 02

Reading 01

- □ 16 escape 명 탈출 동 탈출하다
- □ 17 exit 명 출구
- □ 18 gather 동 모으다
- □ 19 solve 동 풀다, 해결하다
- □ 20 for example 예를 들어
- □ 21 invisible 형 눈에 보이지 않는
- □ 22 password 명 암호

Reading 02

- □ 23 several 형 여러 가지의
- □ 24 kind 명 종류 형 친절한
- □ 25 mean 동 의미하다
- □ 26 roll 동 굴리다
- □ 27 knock down 넘어뜨리다
- □ 28 in a row 연속으로
- □ 29 meat 명 고기
- □ 30 decide 동 결정하다

Word Test

Chapter 1

A 영어는 우리말로, 우리말은 영어로 쓰시오.

01	outdoor	______	11	잃다	______
02	indoor	______	12	균형	______
03	rubber	______	13	~와 같은	______
04	fail	______	14	앞으로	______
05	move	______	15	중요한	______
06	quickly	______	16	탈출; 탈출하다	______
07	demand	______	17	출구	______
08	determine	______	18	모으다	______
09	force	______	19	풀다, 해결하다	______
10	fast	______	20	예를 들어	______

B 다음 각 단어에 해당하는 의미를 짝지으시오.

21	invisible	•	• 결정하다
22	password	•	• 고기
23	several	•	• 굴리다
24	kind	•	• 넘어뜨리다
25	mean	•	• 눈에 보이지 않는
26	roll	•	• 암호
27	knock down	•	• 여러 가지의
28	in a row	•	• 연속으로
29	meat	•	• 의미하다
30	decide	•	• 종류; 친절한

Word List

Chapter 2

DAY 03

Reading 01

□ 01	argue	동 논쟁하다
□ 02	climate	명 기후
□ 03	due to	~ 때문에
□ 04	activity	명 활동
□ 05	satellite	명 위성
□ 06	development	명 발전
□ 07	connect	동 연관 짓다, 연결하다

Reading 02

□ 08	plastic	명 플라스틱
□ 09	concentration	명 농축물, 집중
□ 10	recycle	동 재활용하다
□ 11	fisherman	명 어부
□ 12	piece	명 조각
□ 13	sink	동 가라앉다
□ 14	plankton	명 플랑크톤
□ 15	absorb	동 흡수하다

DAY 04

Reading 01

□ 16	invent	동 개발하다, 발명하다
□ 17	a lot of	많은
□ 18	economy	명 경제
□ 19	local	형 지역의
□ 20	prefer	동 선호하다
□ 21	seed	명 종자, 씨앗
□ 22	supply	명 공급

Reading 02

□ 23	freezing	형 엄청[몹시] 추운
□ 24	contain	동 포함하다
□ 25	feather	명 깃털
□ 26	pull	동 (새 등의) 털을 뽑다
□ 27	fur	명 모피, 털
□ 28	colorful	형 다채로운
□ 29	collar	명 옷깃
□ 30	careful	형 신중한

Word Test

Chapter 2

A 영어는 우리말로, 우리말은 영어로 쓰시오.

01	argue	______	11	어부	______
02	climate	______	12	조각	______
03	due to	______	13	가라앉다	______
04	activity	______	14	플랑크톤	______
05	satellite	______	15	흡수하다	______
06	development	______	16	개발하다, 발명하다	______
07	connect	______	17	많은	______
08	plastic	______	18	경제	______
09	concentration	______	19	지역의	______
10	recycle	______	20	선호하다	______

B 다음 각 단어에 해당하는 의미를 짝지으시오.

21	seed	•	• (새 등의) 털을 뽑다
22	supply	•	• 공급
23	freezing	•	• 깃털
24	contain	•	• 다채로운
25	feather	•	• 모피, 털
26	pull	•	• 신중한
27	fur	•	• 엄청[몹시] 추운
28	colorful	•	• 옷깃
29	collar	•	• 종자, 씨앗
30	careful	•	• 포함하다

Word List

Chapter 3

DAY 05

Reading 01

- □ 01 tropical fish 명 열대어
- □ 02 octopus 명 문어
- □ 03 squid 명 오징어
- □ 04 seasonal 형 계절의
- □ 05 movement 명 이동
- □ 06 aquarium 명 아쿠아리움, 수족관
- □ 07 disappointed 형 실망한

Reading 02

- □ 08 traveler 명 여행자
- □ 09 travel 동 여행하다
- □ 10 journey 명 여행
- □ 11 plan 동 계획하다
- □ 12 vacation 명 휴가, 방학
- □ 13 mountain-climbing 명 등산
- □ 14 scuba-diving 명 스쿠버 다이빙
- □ 15 athlete 명 운동선수

DAY 06

Reading 01

- □ 16 degree 명 (온도 단위인) 도
- □ 17 freeze 동 얼다, 얼리다
- □ 18 successfully 부 성공적으로
- □ 19 coastline 명 해안선
- □ 20 wide 형 넓은
- □ 21 record 명 기록 동 기록하다
- □ 22 at the same time 동시에

Reading 02

- □ 23 measure 동 측정하다
- □ 24 flat 형 납작한
- □ 25 amazing 형 엄청난, 놀라운
- □ 26 pressure 명 압력
- □ 27 adventurer 명 모험가
- □ 28 dive 동 뛰어들다
- □ 29 hurt 동 다치게 하다 형 다친
- □ 30 technology 명 기술

Word Test

Chapter 3

A 영어는 우리말로, 우리말은 영어로 쓰시오.

01 tropical fish ____________
02 octopus ____________
03 squid ____________
04 seasonal ____________
05 movement ____________
06 aquarium ____________
07 disappointed ____________
08 traveler ____________
09 travel ____________
10 journey ____________
11 계획하다 ____________
12 휴가, 방학 ____________
13 등산 ____________
14 스쿠버 다이빙 ____________
15 운동선수 ____________
16 (온도 단위인) 도 ____________
17 얼다, 얼리다 ____________
18 성공적으로 ____________
19 해안선 ____________
20 넓은 ____________

B 다음 각 단어에 해당하는 의미를 짝지으시오.

21 record •	• 기록; 기록하다
22 at the same time •	• 기술
23 measure •	• 납작한
24 flat •	• 다치게 하다; 다친
25 amazing •	• 동시에
26 pressure •	• 뛰어들다
27 adventurer •	• 모험가
28 dive •	• 압력
29 hurt •	• 엄청난, 놀라운
30 technology •	• 측정하다

Word List

Chapter 4

DAY 07

Reading 01

□ 01	probably	부 아마
□ 02	strategy	명 전략
□ 03	entrance	명 출입구
□ 04	aisle	명 통로
□ 05	display	명 진열 동 진열하다
□ 06	wander	동 돌아다니다
□ 07	pay	동 (돈을) 지불하다

Reading 02

□ 08	ratio	명 비율
□ 09	common	형 흔한
□ 10	population	명 인구
□ 11	rare	형 드문
□ 12	vary	동 다르다
□ 13	among	전 ~ 사이에
□ 14	emergency	명 응급, 비상
□ 15	receive	동 받다

DAY 08

Reading 01

□ 16	tighten	동 죄다, 조이다
□ 17	remember	동 기억하다
□ 18	trick	명 요령
□ 19	activate	동 활성화시키다
□ 20	handle	동 다루다
□ 21	mainly	부 주로, 대개
□ 22	information	명 정보

Reading 02

□ 23	mirror	명 거울
□ 24	role	명 역할
□ 25	express	동 표현하다
□ 26	emotion	명 감정
□ 27	reason	명 이유
□ 28	sweat	동 땀을 흘리다 명 땀
□ 29	arch-shaped	형 아치형의
□ 30	raindrop	명 빗방울

Word Test

Chapter 4

A 영어는 우리말로, 우리말은 영어로 쓰시오.

01	probably	__________	11	드문	__________
02	strategy	__________	12	다르다	__________
03	entrance	__________	13	~ 사이에	__________
04	aisle	__________	14	응급, 비상	__________
05	display	__________	15	받다	__________
06	wander	__________	16	쥐다, 조이다	__________
07	pay	__________	17	기억하다	__________
08	ratio	__________	18	요령	__________
09	common	__________	19	활성화시키다	__________
10	population	__________	20	다루다	__________

B 다음 각 단어에 해당하는 의미를 짝지으시오.

21	mainly	•	• 감정
22	information	•	• 거울
23	mirror	•	• 땀을 흘리다; 땀
24	role	•	• 빗방울
25	express	•	• 아치형의
26	emotion	•	• 역할
27	reason	•	• 이유
28	sweat	•	• 정보
29	arch-shaped	•	• 주로, 대개
30	raindrop	•	• 표현하다

Word List

Chapter 5

DAY 09

Reading 01

□ 01	exercise	명 운동
□ 02	need	동 필요로 하다
□ 03	understand	동 이해하다
□ 04	helpful	형 도움이 되는
□ 05	order	동 주문하다 명 주문, 순서
□ 06	indeed	부 실제로
□ 07	tend	동 경향이 있다

Reading 02

□ 08	popular	형 인기 있는
□ 09	happen	동 생기다, 일어나다
□ 10	thin	형 얇은
□ 11	tight	형 단단한
□ 12	coat	명 껍질, 외투[코트]
□ 13	inside	부 내부에, 안에
□ 14	steam	명 증기
□ 15	release	동 뿜어내다

DAY 10

Reading 01

□ 16	except	제외하고는
□ 17	scare	겁먹다, 겁주다
□ 18	ingredient	재료
□ 19	spinach	시금치
□ 20	direction	방법
□ 21	add	넣다, 더하다
□ 22	blender	믹서기

Reading 02

□ 23	subtract	동 빼다
□ 24	affect	동 영향을 미치다
□ 25	behavior	명 행동
□ 26	survey	명 설문 조사
□ 27	begin	동 시작하다
□ 28	emotional	형 감정적인
□ 29	reaction	명 반응
□ 30	compare	동 비교하다

Word Test

Chapter 5

A 영어는 우리말로, 우리말은 영어로 쓰시오.

01 exercise ______
02 need ______
03 understand ______
04 helpful ______
05 order ______
06 indeed ______
07 tend ______
08 popular ______
09 happen ______
10 thin ______
11 단단한 ______
12 껍질, 외투[코트] ______
13 내부에, 안에 ______
14 증기 ______
15 뿜어내다 ______
16 제외하고는 ______
17 겁먹다, 겁주다 ______
18 재료 ______
19 시금치 ______
20 방법 ______

B 다음 각 단어에 해당하는 의미를 짝지으시오.

21 add •	• 감정적인
22 blender •	• 넣다, 더하다
23 subtract •	• 믹서기
24 affect •	• 반응
25 behavior •	• 비교하다
26 survey •	• 빼다
27 begin •	• 설문 조사
28 emotional •	• 시작하다
29 reaction •	• 영향을 미치다
30 compare •	• 행동

Chapter 6

DAY 11

Reading 01

- □ 01 unfortunately 부 불행하게도
- □ 02 disappear 동 사라지다
- □ 03 surface 명 표면
- □ 04 damage 동 손상시키다 명 손상
- □ 05 form 동 형성시키다 명 유형
- □ 06 gradually 부 서서히
- □ 07 suddenly 부 갑자기

Reading 02

- □ 08 at least 적어도
- □ 09 collect 동 모으다
- □ 10 digest 동 소화하다, 소화시키다
- □ 11 cooperative 형 협동하는
- □ 12 particular 형 특별한, 특정한
- □ 13 trail 명 흔적
- □ 14 unity 명 협동, 통합
- □ 15 survive 동 살아남다

DAY 12

Reading 01

- □ 16 attack 동 공격하다 명 공격
- □ 17 frequently 부 자주
- □ 18 response 명 응답
- □ 19 chemical 명 화학 물질 형 화학의
- □ 20 easily 부 쉽게
- □ 21 liquid 명 액체
- □ 22 discover 동 발견하다

Reading 02

- □ 23 deep 형 깊은
- □ 24 forest 명 숲
- □ 25 similar 형 비슷한
- □ 26 explanation 명 설명
- □ 27 forest fire 산불
- □ 28 burn 동 태우다, 타다
- □ 29 thick 형 두꺼운
- □ 30 nutrition 명 영양분

Word Test

Chapter 6

A 영어는 우리말로, 우리말은 영어로 쓰시오.

01 unfortunately ____________
02 disappear ____________
03 surface ____________
04 damage ____________
05 form ____________
06 gradually ____________
07 suddenly ____________
08 at least ____________
09 collect ____________
10 digest ____________
11 협동하는 ____________
12 특별한, 특정한 ____________
13 흔적 ____________
14 협동, 통합 ____________
15 살아남다 ____________
16 공격하다; 공격 ____________
17 자주 ____________
18 응답 ____________
19 화학 물질; 화학의 ____________
20 쉽게 ____________

B 다음 각 단어에 해당하는 의미를 짝지으시오.

21 liquid	•	• 깊은
22 discover	•	• 두꺼운
23 deep	•	• 발견하다
24 forest	•	• 비슷한
25 similar	•	• 산불
26 explanation	•	• 설명
27 forest fire	•	• 숲
28 burn	•	• 액체
29 thick	•	• 영양분
30 nutrition	•	• 태우다, 타다

Word List

Chapter 7

DAY 13

Reading 01

- □ 01 celebrate 통 기념하다
- □ 02 share 통 나누다
- □ 03 tradition 명 전통
- □ 04 as well 역시, 또한
- □ 05 recently 부 최근에
- □ 06 notice 통 주목하다
- □ 07 different 형 다른

Reading 02

- □ 08 university 명 대학
- □ 09 professor 명 교수
- □ 10 take off ~을 벗다
- □ 11 remove 통 벗다, 제거하다
- □ 12 insist 통 주장하다, 고집하다
- □ 13 consider 통 ~을 …로 여기다
- □ 14 rude 형 무례한
- □ 15 customer 명 손님

DAY 14

Reading 01

- □ 16 superstition 명 미신
- □ 17 anxiety 명 불안(감)
- □ 18 perform 통 (수)행하다, 공연하다
- □ 19 tragedy 명 비극
- □ 20 occur 통 발생하다
- □ 21 slippery 형 미끄러운
- □ 22 continue 통 계속하다

Reading 02

- □ 23 overcome 통 극복하다
- □ 24 sadness 명 슬픔
- □ 25 relationship 명 관계
- □ 26 cheerful 형 즐거운
- □ 27 experience 명 경험
- □ 28 happiness 명 행복
- □ 29 replace 통 대체[대신]하다
- □ 30 negative 형 부정적인

Word Test

Chapter 7

A 영어는 우리말로, 우리말은 영어로 쓰시오.

01	celebrate	________	11	벗다, 제거하다	________
02	share	________	12	주장하다, 고집하다	________
03	tradition	________	13	~을 …로 여기다	________
04	as well	________	14	무례한	________
05	recently	________	15	손님	________
06	notice	________	16	미신	________
07	different	________	17	불안(감)	________
08	university	________	18	(수)행하다, 공연하다	________
09	professor	________	19	비극	________
10	take off	________	20	발생하다	________

B 다음 각 단어에 해당하는 의미를 짝지으시오.

21	slippery	•	• 경험
22	continue	•	• 계속하다
23	overcome	•	• 관계
24	sadness	•	• 극복하다
25	relationship	•	• 대체[대신]하다
26	cheerful	•	• 미끄러운
27	experience	•	• 부정적인
28	happiness	•	• 슬픔
29	replace	•	• 즐거운
30	negative	•	• 행복

Word List

Chapter 8

DAY 15

Reading 01

□ 01	pill	명 알약
□ 02	realistic	형 현실적인
□ 03	concern	명 염려
□ 04	lack	명 부족
□ 05	confident	형 자신감 있는
□ 06	impossible	형 불가능한
□ 07	announce	동 발표하다

Reading 02

□ 08	hidden	형 숨겨진
□ 09	household	형 가정의, 가사의
□ 10	object	명 물건, 대상
□ 11	bowl	명 그릇
□ 12	drop	동 떨어뜨리다 명 방울
□ 13	mixture	명 혼합물
□ 14	hold	동 잡고 있다
□ 15	light bulb	전구

DAY 16

Reading 01

□ 16	heat	명 더위, 열
□ 17	sharp	형 가파른, 급격한
□ 18	angle	명 각도
□ 19	axis	명 [천문] 지축
□ 20	tilt	동 기울다
□ 21	strongly	부 강하게
□ 22	gentle	형 완만한, 부드러운

Reading 02

□ 23	issue	명 문제, 주제
□ 24	delete	동 삭제하다
□ 25	inventor	명 발명가
□ 26	especially	부 특히, 특별하게
□ 27	detect	동 감지하다
□ 28	stay off	멀리 있다
□ 29	disable	동 못하게 하다
□ 30	input	명 입력 동 입력하다

Word Test

Chapter 8

A 영어는 우리말로, 우리말은 영어로 쓰시오.

01	pill	________	11	그릇	________
02	realistic	________	12	떨어뜨리다; 방울	________
03	concern	________	13	혼합물	________
04	lack	________	14	잡고 있다	________
05	confident	________	15	전구	________
06	impossible	________	16	더위, 열	________
07	announce	________	17	가파른, 급격한	________
08	hidden	________	18	각도	________
09	household	________	19	[천문] 지축	________
10	object	________	20	기울다	________

B 다음 각 단어에 해당하는 의미를 짝지으시오.

21	strongly	•	• 감지하다
22	gentle	•	• 강하게
23	issue	•	• 멀리 있다
24	delete	•	• 못하게 하다
25	inventor	•	• 문제, 주제
26	especially	•	• 발명가
27	detect	•	• 삭제하다
28	stay off	•	• 완만한, 부드러운
29	disable	•	• 입력; 입력하다
30	input	•	• 특히, 특별하게

Word List

Chapter 9

DAY 17

Reading 01

- □ 01 exclude 동 제외하다
- □ 02 advertisement 명 광고
- □ 03 income 명 소득, 수입
- □ 04 competitive 형 경쟁적인
- □ 05 challenger 명 도전자
- □ 06 passion 명 열정
- □ 07 ability 명 능력

Reading 02

- □ 08 various 형 다양한
- □ 09 unique 형 독특한
- □ 10 commonly 부 흔히
- □ 11 employ 동 고용하다
- □ 12 expert 명 전문가
- □ 13 recommend 동 추천하다
- □ 14 location 명 로케이션, 야외 촬영지
- □ 15 appropriate 형 적합한, 적절한

DAY 18

Reading 01

- □ 16 earn 동 (돈을) 벌다
- □ 17 diligent 형 근면한
- □ 18 finally 부 마침내
- □ 19 lazy 형 게으른
- □ 20 wealth 명 재산, 부유함
- □ 21 remind 동 생각나게 하다
- □ 22 wise 형 지혜로운

Reading 02

- □ 23 palace 명 궁전
- □ 24 fountain 명 분수
- □ 25 hate 동 싫어하다
- □ 26 unusual 형 특이한
- □ 27 habit 명 버릇
- □ 28 appetite 명 식욕
- □ 29 normal 형 보통의
- □ 30 hardboiled 형 삶은, 달걀이 완숙된

Word Test

Chapter 9

A 영어는 우리말로, 우리말은 영어로 쓰시오.

01 exclude ____________
02 advertisement ____________
03 income ____________
04 competitive ____________
05 challenger ____________
06 passion ____________
07 ability ____________
08 various ____________
09 unique ____________
10 commonly ____________
11 고용하다 ____________
12 전문가 ____________
13 추천하다 ____________
14 로케이션, 야외 촬영지 ____________
15 적합한, 적절한 ____________
16 (돈을) 벌다 ____________
17 근면한 ____________
18 마침내 ____________
19 게으른 ____________
20 재산, 부유함 ____________

B 다음 각 단어에 해당하는 의미를 짝지으시오.

21 remind •	• 궁전
22 wise •	• 버릇
23 palace •	• 보통의
24 fountain •	• 분수
25 hate •	• 삶은, 달걀이 완숙된
26 unusual •	• 생각나게 하다
27 habit •	• 식욕
28 appetite •	• 싫어하다
29 normal •	• 지혜로운
30 hardboiled •	• 특이한

Word List Chapter 10

DAY 19

Reading 01

□ 01	candle	명 양초, 초
□ 02	by the way	그런데
□ 03	wonder	통 궁금해 하다
□ 04	believe	통 믿다
□ 05	reach	통 ~에 닿다
□ 06	come true	이루어지다
□ 07	breath	명 숨

Reading 02

□ 08	garage	명 차고, 주차장
□ 09	yell	통 외치다
□ 10	fair	명 장터 형 공정한
□ 11	junk	명 고물, 폐물
□ 12	Thailand	명 태국
□ 13	holy	형 성스러운
□ 14	comfortable	형 편안한
□ 15	care for	~을 돌보다

DAY 20

Reading 01

□ 16	police officer	명 경찰관
□ 17	follow	통 따라가다
□ 18	behind	전 부 뒤에
□ 19	reply	통 대답하다
□ 20	amusement park	명 놀이공원
□ 21	ask	통 묻다, 요청하다
□ 22	answer	통 대답하다

Reading 02

□ 23	expression	명 표현
□ 24	pirate	명 해적
□ 25	sail	통 항해하다
□ 26	trade	명 무역 통 거래하다
□ 27	flag	명 깃발
□ 28	friendly	형 우호적인, 친근한
□ 29	imagine	통 상상하다
□ 30	pretend	통 ~인 척하다

Word Test Chapter 10

A 영어는 우리말로, 우리말은 영어로 쓰시오.

01	candle	______	11	고물, 폐물	______
02	by the way	______	12	태국	______
03	wonder	______	13	성스러운	______
04	believe	______	14	편안한	______
05	reach	______	15	~을 돌보다	______
06	come true	______	16	경찰관	______
07	breath	______	17	따라가다	______
08	garage	______	18	뒤에	______
09	yell	______	19	대답하다	______
10	fair	______	20	놀이공원	______

B 다음 각 단어에 해당하는 의미를 짝지으시오.

21	ask	•	• ~인 척하다
22	answer	•	• 깃발
23	expression	•	• 대답하다
24	pirate	•	• 무역; 거래하다
25	sail	•	• 묻다, 요청하다
26	trade	•	• 상상하다
27	flag	•	• 우호적인, 친근한
28	friendly	•	• 표현
29	imagine	•	• 항해하다
30	pretend	•	• 해적

적중! 영어독해 중2

Workbook

Writing Test & 정답

Writing Test

Chapter 1

○ 우리말에 맞게 주어진 단어들을 배열하시오. (대·소문자 변화 가능)

▶ 정답 p.45

DAY 01

Reading 01 언제나 재밌게 즐기는 실내 스포츠, 탁구

1 겨울에는 야외 스포츠를 즐기는 것이 쉽지 않다.
(in winter, / outdoor sports / to enjoy / it / easy / is not / .)

→ ______________________________

2 실내 스포츠로서 탁구를 해보는 것이 어떨까?
(an indoor sport / as / table tennis / try / why don't you / ?)

→ ______________________________

3 한 선수가 15점을 먼저 따면, 그 사람이 이긴다.
(one player / 15 points / gets / first, / If / he or she / wins / .)

→ ______________________________

Reading 02 왜 인간은 100m를 9초대 이하로 못 뛸까?

1 속도는 다리 힘에 의해 결정된다.
(speed / by the legs' force / is determined / .)

→ ______________________________

2 더 빨리 달리기 위한 두 가지 방법이 있다.
(faster / to run / two ways / there are / .)

→ ______________________________

3 치타 같은 빠른 동물들은 첫 번째 방법을 사용한다.
(cheetahs / such as / fast animals / the first method / use / .)

→ ______________________________

▶ 정답 p.45

DAY 02

Reading 01 요즘 유행하는 방탈출 게임 해봤니?

1 방탈출 게임하는 것을 좋아하는가?
(room escape games / playing / like / do / you / ?)

→ ______________________________

2 설명이나 출구가 전혀 없다.
(explanation / exit / at all / no / and / there is / no / .)

→ ______________________________

3 그것은 보통 출구를 찾기 위한 퍼즐들을 제공한다.
(it / usually / an exit / to find / some puzzles / provides / .)

→ ______________________________

Reading 02 볼링과 터키의 관계는?

1 이것은 새의 한 종류일 수도 있고, 유럽에 있는 나라일 수도 있다.
(It / bird / a kind of / may / be / or / in Europe / a country / .)

→ ______________________________

2 당신은 가능한 한 많은 핀을 넘어뜨리기 위해 공을 굴려야 한다.
(you / possible / as many pins as / to knock down / the ball / roll / have to / .)

→ ______________________________

3 연속으로 그것을 세 번하면, 당신은 그것을 터키라고 부른다.
(in a row, / if you do this / you / it / a turkey / call / three times / .)

→ ______________________________

Writing Test

Chapter 2

○ 우리말에 맞게 주어진 단어들을 배열하시오. (대·소문자 변화 가능)

▶ 정답 p.45

DAY 03

Reading 01 기후 변화의 원인에 대한 논쟁

1 자동차에서 나오는 화석 연료 가스가 지구의 온도를 올리고 있다.
(from cars / fossil fuel gas / of the Earth / the temperature / is raising / .)

→ ______________________________

2 기후 변화와 특정 날씨 발생을 연관 짓기가 어렵다.
(climate change / certain weather events / it / to connect / is difficult / and / .)

→ ______________________________

3 여름이 전 세계적으로 점점 더 더워지고 있다.
(the summer / around the world / hotter and hotter / is getting / .)

→ ______________________________

Reading 02 우리는 매일 플라스틱을 먹고 있다

1 우리는 이것이 우리에게 돌아오는지 신경을 안 쓴다.
(we / it / to us / returns / whether / don't care / .)

→ ______________________________

2 과학자들은 우리가 플라스틱 제품을 사용하는 것을 멈춰야 한다고 제안한다.
(scientists / we / plastic products / using / stop / that / suggest / .)

→ ______________________________

3 그것들은 우리 건강에 좋아 보이지 않는다.
(they / for our health / good / do not seem / .)

→ ______________________________

▶ 정답 p.45

DAY 04

Reading 01 아보카도는 과연 좋기만 할까?

1 아보카도는 버터와 같은 맛이 나지만, 진짜 버터보다 훨씬 더 건강하다.
(avocados / butter, / like / taste / but / real butter / healthier than / are / much / .)

→ ______________________________

2 이 녹색 과일에는 문제가 있다.
(this green fruit / problems / there are / about / .)

→ ______________________________

3 이것이 멕시코 땅을 사막처럼 점점 더 메마르게 만든다.
(it / the land of Mexico / the desert / drier and drier / makes / like / .)

→ ______________________________

Reading 02 따뜻한 롱패딩을 위해 죽어 가는 동물들

1 그것들은 날씨가 엄청 춥더라도 우리를 따뜻하게 해준다.
(they / the weather / is freezing / even if / us / can make / warm / .)

→ ______________________________

2 상당히 많은 동물들이 이 유행 때문에 죽고 있다.
(are killed / animals / for this trend / quite a few / .)

→ ______________________________

3 소비자들은 이러한 사실들을 알아야 한다.
(these facts / should / consumers / be aware of / .)

→ ______________________________

○ 우리말에 맞게 주어진 단어들을 배열하시오. (대·소문자 변화 가능)

▶ 정답 p.45

DAY 05

Reading 01 몰디브에서 볼 수 있는 동물은?

1 해파리, 문어, 오징어 그리고 조개와 같은 해양 생물들 또한 흔하다.
(and clams / like / squid, / jellyfish, / octopus, / sea creatures / are also common / .)

→ ______________________________

2 만약 동물원을 찾는다면, 당신은 실망할지도 모른다.
(if / zoos, / are looking for / you / disappointed / may / you / be / .)

→ ______________________________

3 육지 동물이 거의 없다.
(very few / land animals / there are / .)

→ ______________________________

Reading 02 당신은 어떤 유형의 여행자인가요?

1 당신은 어떤 유형의 여행자인지 읽고 확인해라.
(you are / what type of / read and check / traveler / .)

→ ______________________________

2 그들은 운동 중심으로 휴가를 계획하는 것을 좋아한다.
(sports / vacations / they / plan / like to / around / .)

→ ______________________________

3 그들은 운동선수형 여행자와 거의 반대이다.
(the athlete travelers / almost / they / the opposite of / are / .)

→ ______________________________

▶ 정답 pp.45~46

DAY 06

Reading 01 미국의 가장 특이한 주, 알래스카

1 알래스카 전체가 겨울 동안 얼어붙는 것은 사실이다.
(that / Alaska / during wintertime / freezes all over / it is true / .)

→ ______________________________

2 그 땅은 또 다른 흥미로운 점이 있다.
(another / point / the land / interesting / has / .)

→ ______________________________

3 알래스카는 그 나라에서 가장 적은 인구를 가지고 있다.
(in the country / Alaska / the smallest / has / population / .)

→ ______________________________

Reading 02 세계에서 가장 깊은 곳, 마리아나 해구

1 마리아나 해구는 지구의 바다에서 가장 깊은 장소이다.
(in the Earth's oceans / Mariana Trench / the deepest place / is / .)

→ ______________________________

2 미국 연구자들은 이곳이 얼마나 깊은지 측정했다.
(how deep / measured / it / American researchers / is / .)

→ ______________________________

3 전 세계의 모험가들이 이곳 지면으로 뛰어들려고 노력했다.
(of this point / tried / adventurers / to dive into the ground / around the world / .)

→ ______________________________

Writing Test

Chapter 4

○ 우리말에 맞게 주어진 단어들을 배열하시오. (대·소문자 변화 가능)

▶ 정답 p.46

DAY 07

Reading 01 슈퍼마켓에 이런 전략이!

1 당신은 아마 사려고 계획하지 않았던 것들을 살지 모른다.
(which / you / may / didn't plan / buy / you / to / items / .)

→ ______________________________

2 우리는 더 많이 돌아다닐수록 더 많이 물건을 사기 쉽다.
(wander, / the more / we / the more likely / are to buy items / we / .)

→ ______________________________

3 그들은 돈을 지불하려고 줄을 서서 기다리고 있다.
(to pay / they / in line / are waiting / .)

→ ______________________________

Reading 02 혈액형 이야기

1 당신의 혈액형은 무엇인가?
(your / what's / blood type / ?)

→ ______________________________

2 대략 세계 인구의 40~60%가 이 혈액형을 가지고 있다.
(about / this blood type / has / of the world's population / 40 to 60% / .)

→ ______________________________

3 O형이 대부분의 나라들에서 가장 흔하다.
(is / the most common / type O / in most countries / .)

→ ______________________________

▶ 정답 p.46

DAY 08

Reading 01 기억을 잡아 두고 싶나요?

1 당신은 오른손잡이인가?
(you / a right-handed person / are / ?)

→ ______________________________

2 주먹을 쥐는 것이 기억을 다루는 쪽의 뇌를 활성화시킨다.
(activates / the side of the brain / handles / memory / making a fist / that / .)

→ ______________________________

3 어떤 손을 사용해야 할지만 기억해라.
(which hand / you / just remember / need to use / .)

→ ______________________________

Reading 02 눈썹이 있는 이유

1 거울 속의 당신을 들여다보라.
(yourself / look at / in the mirror / .)

→ ______________________________

2 당신은 눈썹을 위아래로 움직일 수 있는가?
(move / up and down / are / able to / them / you / ?)

→ ______________________________

3 사람들에게 눈썹이 있는 더 중요한 이유가 있다.
(why / have / people / there is / eyebrows / a more important reason / .)

→ ______________________________

Writing Test

Chapter 5

○ 우리말에 맞게 주어진 단어들을 배열하시오. (대·소문자 변화 가능)

▶ 정답 p.46

DAY 09

Reading 01 다이어트를 돕는 메뉴판

1 그것은 고객들이 살을 빼는 것을 도와주는 데 좋을 것이다.
(be good for / it / customers / would / lose weight / helping / .)

→ ______________________________

2 대신에 그들은 30분간 걸어야 한다는 것은 이해한다.
(that / have to / instead, / they / for 30 minutes / understand / walk / they / .)

→ ______________________________

3 이런 새로운 스타일의 메뉴는 정말 사람들로 하여금 더 건강한 선택을 하도록 돕는다.
(helps / this new style of menu / healthier / really / make / choices / people / .)

→ ______________________________

Reading 02 팝콘이 펑펑!

1 많은 사람들이 영화를 보는 동안 팝콘 먹는 것을 즐긴다.
(enjoy / popcorn / many people / eating / during a movie / .)

→ ______________________________

2 우리는 터지지 않은 옥수수 알갱이들을 보게 된다.
(that / some kernels of corn / find / we / don't pop / .)

→ ______________________________

3 이런 일이 왜 생긴다고 생각하는가?
(do you think / why / happens / this / ?)

→ ______________________________

▶ 정답 p.46

DAY 10

Reading 01 건강한 그린 몬스터, 스무디

1 초록색에 겁먹지 마라.
(don't / you / the green color / let / scare / .)

→ ______________________________

2 그것들 모두를 갈 준비가 되었는가?
(blend / ready to / them all / you / are / ?)

→ ______________________________

3 시금치가 단백질을 첨가하고 당신을 배부르게 유지시켜줄 것이다!
(spinach / protein / adds / and it / you / will / keep / full / !)

→ ______________________________

Reading 02 잠의 중요성

1 아이들에게 잠이 왜 중요할까?
(important / children / why / sleep / is / for / ?)

→ ______________________________

2 연구팀은 건강한 아이들의 수면 시간을 1시간 더하거나 줄였다.
(for healthy children / the research team / either added / or subtracted / one hour of sleep / .)

→ ______________________________

3 1시간을 덜 잔 아이들은 더 나쁜 행동 점수를 받았다.
(behavior scores / slept / children / who / worse / one hour less / had / .)

→ ______________________________

Writing Test

Chapter 6

○ **우리말에 맞게 주어진 단어들을 배열하시오. (대·소문자 변화 가능)**

▶ 정답 pp.46~47

DAY 11

Reading 01 갑자기 땅이 꺼지네!

1 여러분은 사람은 집에서 안전할 것이라고 생각할 것이다.
(could be safe / you / that / would think / a man / in his house / .)

→ ______________________________

2 그것이 그의 집 아래에 있던 거대한 싱크홀로 빠졌다.
(it / under his home / a huge sinkhole / fell into / .)

→ ______________________________

3 이것이 스네이크홀이라고도 알려진 싱크홀을 야기한다.
(this / a sinkhole / also / a snake hole / known / causes / as / .)

→ ______________________________

Reading 02 개미가 주는 교훈

1 그들은 그 식량을 어린 개미들에게 준다.
(young ants / they / the food / give / to / .)

→ ______________________________

2 그는 다른 일개미들이 그것을 찾을 수 있도록 특별한 냄새 흔적을 남긴다.
(so that / the source / he / leaves / the others / a particular smell trail / can find / .)

→ ______________________________

3 그들의 협동이 그들을 긴 시간 동안 지구에서 살아남게 했다.
(has made / survive / their unity / for a long time / them / on our planet / .)

→ ______________________________

▶ 정답 p.47

DAY 12

Reading 01 보디가드 곤충

1 도우미들이 자주 (그에 대한) 응답으로 도와주러 온다.
(in response / to help / the helpers / come / frequently / .)

→ ______________________________

2 보디가드 곤충들은 그 식물을 공격하는 해충들을 잡아먹는다.
(that / bodyguard insects / eat / the plants / the bad insects / attack / .)

→ ______________________________

3 이 발견이 지금은 농부들이 농작물의 양을 증가시키는 데 도움이 되고 있다.
(increase / this finding / farmers / the amount of crops / has helped / now / .)

→ ______________________________

Reading 02 세계에서 가장 큰 나무, 제너럴셔먼

1 다른 나무들이 키가 더 클 수도 있지만, 이것보다 더 (부피가) 크진 않다.
(may / but / be / other trees / taller, / this / not bigger than / .)

→ ______________________________

2 이것의 크기는 25층 아파트 건물 높이와 비슷하다.
(its size / a 25-story apartment building / is similar to / .)

→ ______________________________

3 많은 과학자들은 어떻게 이 나무가 땅으로부터 에너지를 얻는지 연구하고 있다.
(how / from the ground / many scientists / this tree / are studying / takes energy / .)

→ ______________________________

Writing Test

Chapter 7

○ 우리말에 맞게 주어진 단어들을 배열하시오. (대·소문자 변화 가능)

▶ 정답 p.47

DAY 13

Reading 01 블랙 프라이데이

1 많은 사람들이 돈을 절약하기 위해 세일하는 곳에 간다.
(so that / many people / money / they / go to the sales / can save / .)

→ ______________________________

2 그것은 온라인 쇼핑을 위한 일 년 중 가장 바쁜 날이다.
(it / for online shopping / the busiest day of the year / is / .)

→ ______________________________

3 점점 더 많은 쇼핑객들이 온라인에서 명절 선물을 구입한다.
(online / more and more shoppers / their holiday gifts / buy / .)

→ ______________________________

Reading 02 모자를 벗어주시겠습니까?

1 학생들은 나를 Singh(싱) 교수라고 부른다.
(call / Professor Singh / students / me / .)

→ ______________________________

2 그 지배인은 그의 손님이 식당에서 좋은 예의를 갖춰 주기를 원했다.
(his customers / the manager / good manners / wanted / to use / in his restaurant / .)

→ ______________________________

3 시크교도에게 터번은 자존심의 상징이다.
(a symbol of pride / is / for a Sikh, / a turban / .)

→ ______________________________

▶ 정답 p.47

DAY 14

Reading 01 시험 전 금기사항

1 미신은 많은 상황에서 불안감을 줄일 수 있다.
(a number of / anxiety / superstitions / can / in / reduce / situations / .)

→ ______________________________

2 튼튼한 손톱과 모발은 당신이 얼마나 건강한지 알려준다.
(how healthy / strong nails and hair / you / tell / are / .)

→ ______________________________

3 그들은 계속해서 미신을 따른다.
(continue / the superstitions / they / to follow / .)

→ ______________________________

Reading 02 슬픈 음악은 심리 치료사

1 슬픈 음악을 듣는 것이 슬픔을 극복하도록 도울 수 있다.
(the sadness / listening to sad music / overcome / can help / .)

→ ______________________________

2 그들은 그들의 슬픔을 대체할 방법을 찾는다.
(to replace / they / a way / their sadness / look for / .)

→ ______________________________

3 그들은 음악에서 비슷한 감정을 경험하길 원한다.
(the similar feeling / want / from music / they / to experience / .)

→ ______________________________

Writing Test

Chapter 8

○ 우리말에 맞게 주어진 단어들을 배열하시오. (대·소문자 변화 가능)

▶ 정답 p.47

DAY 15

Reading 01 캡슐 하나로 식사가 가능할까?

1 작은 알약에 든 식사는 현실적이지 않다.
(realistic / a meal / is not / in a tiny pill / .)

→ ______________________________

2 문제는 이것이 그냥 불가능하다는 것이다.
(that / is / just / the trouble / impossible / is / it / .)

→ ______________________________

3 알약이 물리적으로 우리의 배(위장)를 채우지 못하고 만족시키지 못한다.
(our stomach / do not / pills / fill and satisfy / physically / .)

→ ______________________________

Reading 02 비밀편지 쓰기

1 보이지 않는 잉크를 만드는 것은 아주 재미있다.
(that / is / making ink / lots of fun / can't be seen / .)

→ ______________________________

2 당신은 마치 첩보원인 것처럼 행동할 수 있다.
(you / as if / a secret agent / you are / can act / .)

→ ______________________________

3 약간의 레몬주스를 그릇에 떨어뜨리고 물을 몇 방울 넣어라.
(a few drops of water / and / drop / into the bowl / some lemon juice / add / .)

→ ______________________________

▶ 정답 pp.47~48

DAY 16

Reading 01 왜 여름엔 덥고, 겨울엔 추울까?

1 우리는 더위 때문에 반바지를 입는다.
(because of / we / shorts / the heat / wear / .)

→ ______________________________

2 이것은 지축이 기울어져 있기 때문이다.
(is tilted / this is / the Earth's axis / because / .)

→ ______________________________

3 태양이 특정 지역에 더 강하게 비친다.
(more strongly / the Sun / on certain places / shines / .)

→ ______________________________

Reading 02 고양이 발을 감지해 드립니다

1 당신은 고양이가 컴퓨터 키보드 위를 걸어 다니는 문제를 겪은 적이 있는가?
(have you ever / on your computer keyboard / your cat walking / had issues with / ?)

→ ______________________________

2 그것은 당신의 고양이가 컴퓨터 키보드에서 멀리 있도록 훈련시키는 것도 도와줄 수 있다.
(it / to stay off / train / the computer keyboard / can help / your cat / .)

→ ______________________________

3 그것은 고양이를 짜증나게 하는 소리를 낸다.
(that / it / cats / makes a sound / annoys / .)

→ ______________________________

Writing Test

Chapter 9

○ 우리말에 맞게 주어진 단어들을 배열하시오. (대·소문자 변화 가능)

▶ 정답 p.48

DAY 17

Reading 01 인터넷 콘텐츠 크리에이터는 괜찮은 직업일까?

1 사람들은 생계 수단으로 이러한 영상을 만드는 것을 성공적인 직업으로 여긴다.
(creating these videos / people / is / think / for a living / a successful job / .)

→ ______________________________

2 그것은 두 가지 이유로 긍정적으로 보이지 않는다.
(to be positive / it / for two reasons / doesn't seem / .)

→ ______________________________

3 돈을 매일 벌 수 있을지 확실하지 않다.
(get paid / it / sure that / is not / they / every day / .)

→ ______________________________

Reading 02 특이한 직업들

1 흔히 들어본 직업들뿐만 아니라 다양하고 독특한 직업들이 있다.
(as well as / there are / commonly heard of jobs / various, unique jobs / .)

→ ______________________________

2 몇몇 레스토랑이 다양한 생수를 맛보는 전문가들을 고용하고 있다.
(to taste / some restaurants / various mineral waters / experts / are employing / .)

→ ______________________________

3 일단 그가 적합한 장소를 찾으면, 그는 스케줄을 짜야 한다.
(has to / once / he / the appropriate places, / make a schedule / has found / he / .)

→ ______________________________

▶ 정답 p.48

DAY 18

Reading 01 일하는 백만장자

1 대다수의 사람들은 돈을 많이 벌기를 원한다.
(to earn / people / much money / most / want / .)

→ ______________________________

2 그녀는 약 40년간 열심히 일해 왔다.
(she / for about 40 years / hard / has worked / .)

→ ______________________________

3 근면한 여성이었기 때문에, 그녀는 마침내 매우 부유해졌다.
(she / being / finally / became / a diligent woman, / very rich / .)

→ ______________________________

Reading 02 괴짜왕 루이 14세

1 루이는 다른 특이한 버릇들도 있었다.
(unusual / had / Louis / other / habits / .)

→ ______________________________

2 그는 그가 옷을 입을 때 많은 사람들에게 보여지는 것을 좋아했다.
(when / he / liked / by many people / he / got dressed / being watched / .)

→ ______________________________

3 그는 잠이 들 때까지 한 침대에서 또 다른 침대로 옮겨 다녔다.
(until / he / went / to another / he / from one bed / fell asleep / .)

→ ______________________________

Writing Test

Chapter 10

○ 우리말에 맞게 주어진 단어들을 배열하시오. (대·소문자 변화 가능)

▶ 정답 p.48

DAY 19

Reading 01 생일 때 촛불을 끄는 이유

1 당신은 당신이 태어난 날을 기념한다.
(were born / you / the day / when / celebrate / you / .)

→ ______________________________

2 연기의 양이 많을수록, 더 좋았다.
(was, / the better / the greater / it / the amount of smoke / was / .)

→ ______________________________

3 사람들은 생일에 초를 모두 동시에 불기 시작했다.
(to blow / on birthdays / started / candles all / people / at the same time / .)

→ ______________________________

Reading 02 애물단지 '흰 코끼리'

1 이것은 어제 엄마가 아빠에게 외친 말이다.
(yesterday / what / my mom / my father / this is / yelled at / .)

→ ______________________________

2 흰색의 동물을 찾지 마라.
(any / look for / white-colored animals / don't / .)

→ ______________________________

3 흰 코끼리는 일하도록 시킬 수가 없었다.
(be made / to work / could / the white elephant / never / .)

→ ______________________________

▶ 정답 p.48

DAY 20

Reading 01 남자와 펭귄

1 당신은 그것을 동물원에 데려가야 합니다.
(take / you / it / the zoo / should / to / .)

→ ______________________________

2 제가 그 펭귄을 동물원에 데려가라고 말했던 것 같은데요.
(to take / I / the penguin / to the zoo / thought / I / told / you / .)

→ ______________________________

3 펭귄이랑 뭘 하는 겁니까?
(doing / what / are / with that penguin / you / ?)

→ ______________________________

Reading 02 가짜 깃발, 진짜 깃발!

1 해적들은 바다를 항해하면서 무역선들을 공격했다.
(attacking / sailed / pirates / trade ships / the seas, / .)

→ ______________________________

2 해적들은 가짜 깃발을 내리고 그들의 진짜 깃발을 드러냈다.
(the false flag, / their true flag / the pirates / showing / pulled down / .)

→ ______________________________

3 그들의 진짜 깃발에는 해골과 엇갈린 뼈가 있었다.
(their true flag / a skull and cross bones / there was / in / .)

→ ______________________________

Writing Test 정답

Chapter 1

DAY 01

Reading 01 언제나 재밌게 즐기는 실내 스포츠, 탁구

1 In winter, it is not easy to enjoy outdoor sports.
2 Why don't you try table tennis as an indoor sport?
3 If one player gets 15 points first, he or she wins.

Reading 02 왜 인간은 100m를 9초대 이하로 못 뛸까?

1 Speed is determined by the legs' force.
2 There are two ways to run faster.
3 Fast animals such as cheetahs use the first method.

DAY 02

Reading 01 요즘 유행하는 방탈출 게임 해봤니?

1 Do you like playing room escape games?
2 There is no explanation and no exit at all.
3 It usually provides some puzzles to find an exit.

Reading 02 볼링과 터키의 관계는?

1 It may be a kind of bird or a country in Europe.
2 You have to roll the ball to knock down as many pins as possible.
3 If you do this three times in a row, you call it a turkey.

Chapter 2

DAY 03

Reading 01 기후 변화의 원인에 대한 논쟁

1 Fossil fuel gas from cars is raising the temperature of the Earth.
2 It is difficult to connect climate change and certain weather events.
3 The summer is getting hotter and hotter around the world.

Reading 02 우리는 매일 플라스틱을 먹고 있다

1 We don't care whether it returns to us.
2 Scientists suggest that we stop using plastic products.
3 They do not seem good for our health.

DAY 04

Reading 01 아보카도는 과연 좋기만 할까?

1 Avocados taste like butter, but are much healthier than real butter.
2 There are problems about this green fruit.
3 It makes the land of Mexico drier and drier like the desert.

Reading 02 따뜻한 롱패딩을 위해 죽어 가는 동물들

1 They can make us warm even if the weather is freezing.
2 Quite a few animals are killed for this trend.
3 Consumers should be aware of these facts.

Chapter 3

DAY 05

Reading 01 몰디브에서 볼 수 있는 동물은?

1 Sea creatures like jellyfish, octopus, squid, and clams are also common.
2 If you are looking for zoos, you may be disappointed.
3 There are very few land animals.

Reading 02 당신은 어떤 유형의 여행자인가요?

1 Read and check what type of traveler you are.
2 They like to plan vacations around sports.
3 They are almost the opposite of the athlete travelers.

DAY 06

Reading 01 미국의 가장 특이한 주, 알래스카

1 It is true that Alaska freezes all over during wintertime.
2 The land has another interesting point.
3 Alaska has the smallest population in the country.

Reading 02 세계에서 가장 깊은 곳, 마리아나 해구

1 Mariana Trench is the deepest place in the Earth's oceans.
2 American researchers measured how deep it is.
3 Adventurers around the world tried to dive into the ground of this point.

Chapter 4

Reading 01 슈퍼마켓에 이런 전략이!

1 You may buy items which you didn't plan to.
2 The more we wander, the more likely we are to buy items.
3 They are waiting in line to pay.

Reading 02 혈액형 이야기

1 What's your blood type?
2 About 40 to 60% of the world's population has this blood type.
3 Type O is the most common in most countries.

DAY 08

Reading 01 기억을 잡아 두고 싶나요?

1 Are you a right-handed person?
2 Making a fist activates the side of the brain that handles memory.
3 Just remember which hand you need to use.

Reading 02 눈썹이 있는 이유

1 Look at yourself in the mirror.
2 Are you able to move them up and down?
3 There is a more important reason why people have eyebrows.

Chapter 5

Reading 01 다이어트를 돕는 메뉴판

1 It would be good for helping customers lose weight.
2 Instead, they understand that they have to walk for 30 minutes.
3 This new style of menu really helps people make healthier choices.

Reading 02 팝콘이 펑펑!

1 Many people enjoy eating popcorn during a movie.
2 We find some kernels of corn that don't pop.
3 Why do you think this happens?

DAY 10

Reading 01 건강한 그린 몬스터, 스무디

1 Don't let the green color scare you.
2 Are you ready to blend them all?
3 Spinach adds protein and it will keep you full!

Reading 02 잠의 중요성

1 Why is sleep important for children?
2 The research team either added or subtracted one hour of sleep for healthy children.
3 Children who slept one hour less had worse behavior scores.

Chapter 6

Reading 01 갑자기 땅이 꺼지네!

1 You would think that a man could be safe in his house.
2 It fell into a huge sinkhole under his home.
3 This causes a sinkhole also known as a snake hole.

Reading 02 개미가 주는 교훈

1 They give the food to young ants.
2 He leaves a particular smell trail so that the others can find the source.
3 Their unity has made them survive on our planet for a long time.

Reading 01 보디가드 곤충

1 The helpers frequently come to help in response.
2 Bodyguard insects eat the bad insects that attack the plants.
3 This finding has helped farmers increase the amount of crops now.

Reading 02 세계에서 가장 큰 나무, 제너럴셔먼

1 Other trees may be taller, but not bigger than this.
2 Its size is similar to a 25-story apartment building.
3 Many scientists are studying how this tree takes energy from the ground.

Chapter 7

Reading 01 블랙 프라이데이

1 Many people go to the sales so that they can save money.
2 It is the busiest day of the year for online shopping.
3 More and more shoppers buy their holiday gifts online.

Reading 02 모자를 벗어주시겠습니까?

1 Students call me Professor Singh.
2 The manager wanted his customers to use good manners in his restaurant.
3 For a Sikh, a turban is a symbol of pride.

DAY 14

Reading 01 시험 전 금기사항

1 Superstitions can reduce anxiety in a number of situations.
2 Strong nails and hair tell how healthy you are.
3 They continue to follow the superstitions.

Reading 02 슬픈 음악은 심리 치료사

1 Listening to sad music can help overcome the sadness.
2 They look for a way to replace their sadness.
3 They want to experience the similar feeling from music.

Chapter 8

Reading 01 캡슐 하나로 식사가 가능할까?

1 A meal in a tiny pill is not realistic.
2 The trouble is that it is just impossible.
3 Pills do not fill and satisfy our stomach physically.

Reading 02 비밀편지 쓰기

1 Making ink that can't be seen is lots of fun.
2 You can act as if you are a secret agent.
3 Drop some lemon juice into the bowl and add a few drops of water.

DAY 16

Reading 01 왜 여름엔 덥고, 겨울엔 추울까?

1 We wear shorts because of the heat.
2 This is because the Earth's axis is tilted.
3 The Sun shines more strongly on certain places.

Reading 02 고양이 발을 감지해 드립니다

1 Have you ever had issues with your cat walking on your computer keyboard?
2 It can help train your cat to stay off the computer keyboard.
3 It makes a sound that annoys cats.

Chapter 9

Reading 01 인터넷 콘텐츠 크리에이터는 괜찮은 직업일까?

1 People think creating these videos for a living is a successful job.
2 It doesn't seem to be positive for two reasons.
3 It is not sure that they get paid every day.

Reading 02 특이한 직업들

1 There are various, unique jobs as well as commonly heard of jobs.
2 Some restaurants are employing experts to taste various mineral waters.
3 Once he has found the appropriate places, he has to make a schedule.

DAY 18

Reading 01 일하는 백만장자

1 Most people want to earn much money.
2 She has worked hard for about 40 years.
3 Being a diligent woman, she finally became very rich.

Reading 02 괴짜왕 루이 14세

1 Louis had other unusual habits.
2 He liked being watched by many people when he got dressed.
3 He went from one bed to another until he fell asleep.

Chapter 10

Reading 01 생일 때 촛불을 끄는 이유

1 You celebrate the day when you were born.
2 The greater the amount of smoke was, the better it was.
3 People started to blow candles all at the same time on birthdays.

Reading 02 애물단지 '흰 코끼리'

1 This is what my mom yelled at my father yesterday.
2 Don't look for any white-colored animals.
3 The white elephant could never be made to work.

Reading 01 남자와 펭귄

1 You should take it to the zoo.
2 I thought I told you to take the penguin to the zoo.
3 What are you doing with that penguin?

Reading 02 가짜 깃발, 진짜 깃발!

1 Pirates sailed the seas, attacking trade ships.
2 The pirates pulled down the false flag, showing their true flag.
3 There was a skull and cross bones in their true flag.

중등 2

처음 수능 공부를 시작하는 고등학생이라면 반드시!!!

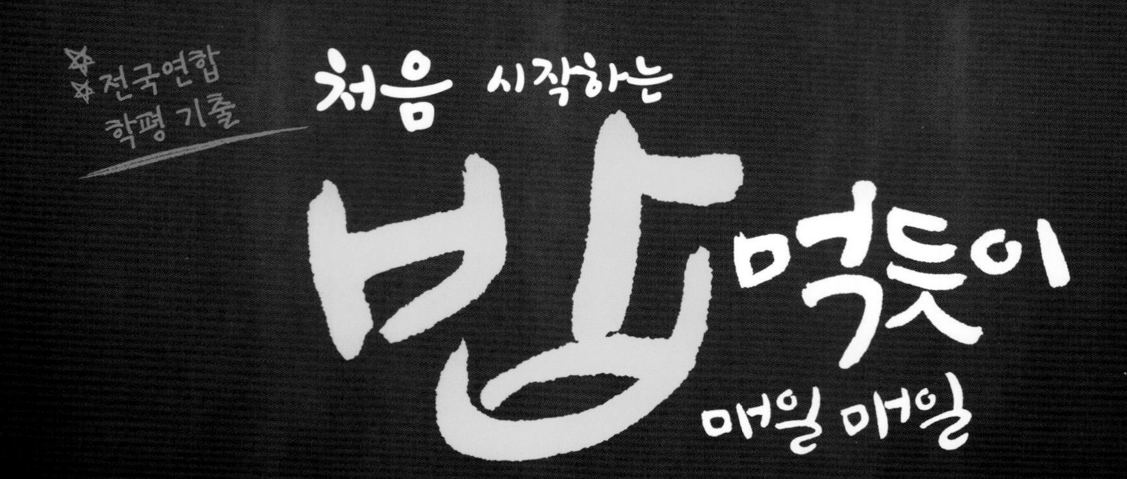

[비문학 독서] [영어 독해]

밥 먹듯이 **매일매일** 공부하면 **수능 국어, 수능 영어**가 쉬워집니다!

01 **3단계 3독 3해** 학습법으로 완성하는 자기 주도 문제 해결 능력과 자기 주도 공부 습관

02 **〈제대로 접근법〉**과 **〈제대로 독해법〉**으로 제대로 된 지문 분석과 문제 풀이 능력 완성

03 **수능 국어와 수능 영어** 유형에 따라 매일 2~4개 지문으로 학평 기출 국어 및 영어 독해 4주 완성

04 **지문 분석 시간 단축**과 **문제 해결력 향상**이 가능한 선과 도형을 활용한 지문 분석

국어와 영어 학습에 최적화된 **"3독 3해 학습법"**을 통해

4주 완성 집중 학습 ➡ 수능 국어, 수능 영어 1등급 달성!

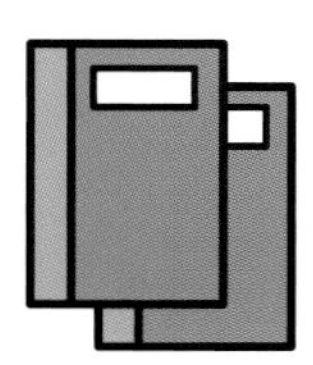

#READING

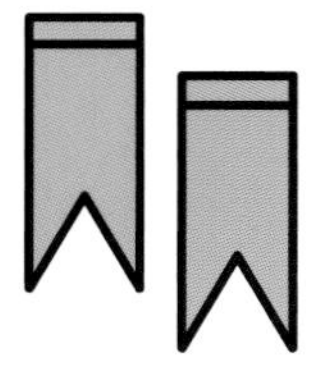

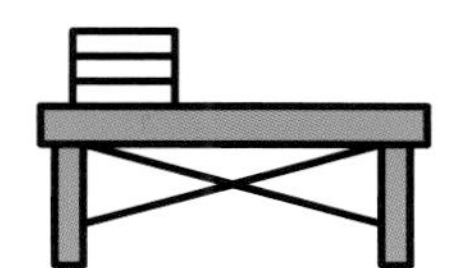

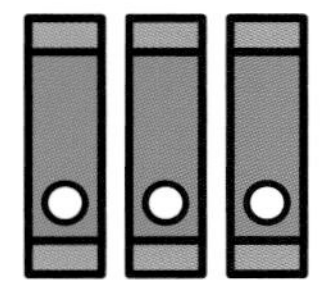

[정답과 해설]

Sports · Leisure

▸ pp.10~11

언제나 재밌게 즐기는 실내 스포츠, 탁구

지문 분석

❶ In winter, it is not easy to enjoy outdoor sports. ❷ Then, why don't you try table tennis as an indoor sport? ❸ [Table tennis, or ping-pong], only needs [a table with a net in the center, rubber rackets, and a tiny ball]. ❹ The rules are also simple. ❺ You just hit the ball over the net, and bounce it to the other player. ❻ If one misses or fails to return the ball, one score goes to the other player. ❼ If one player gets 15 points first, he or she wins. ❽ You have to move quickly because the ball speed is very fast. ❾ However, ㉠it doesn't give you much stress or physical demands, but it gives you good health. ❿ If you want to spend winter time playing sports with your friends, table tennis is a good option.

(it: 가주어 / to enjoy outdoor sports: 진주어(to부정사구) / why don't you ~: ~하는 게 어떨까? / as: 전 ~로서 / Table tennis, or ping-pong: 주어 / needs: 동사 / a table ~ ball: 목적어 / A, B, and C 병렬구조 / hit: 동사 1 / over: 전 ~위로 / bounce: 동사 2 / to: 전 ~에게 / If: 접 ~라면(조건) / to return: to부정사(목적어) / to: 전 ~에게 / If: 접 ~라면(조건) / have to: ~해야 한다(= must) / because: 접 ~ 때문에(이유) / However: 그러나 / not A but B: A가 아니라 B / If: 접 ~라면(조건) / spend+시간+-ing: ~하는 데 (시간)을 보내다)

지문 해석

❶ 겨울에는 야외 스포츠를 즐기는 것이 쉽지 않다. ❷ 그렇다면 실내 스포츠로서 탁구를 해보는 것이 어떨까? ❸ 탁구는 중앙에 네트가 있는 테이블, 고무 라켓, 그리고 작은 공만 필요로 한다. ❹ 규칙도 또한 단순하다. ❺ 단지 공을 네트 위로 쳐서 상대 선수에게 튀긴다. ❻ 한 사람이 공을 놓치거나 받아치는 것을 실패하면 1점이 상대 선수에게 간다. ❼ 한 선수가 15점을 먼저 따면, 그 사람이 이긴다. ❽ 공이 매우 빠르기 때문에 당신은 빠르게 움직여야 한다. ❾ 그러나 그것(탁구)은 당신에게 많은 스트레스나 신체적 부담이 아니라 건강을 준다. ❿ 당신이 친구들과 함께 운동을 하며 겨울을 보내고 싶다면, 탁구는 좋은 선택이다.

정답인 이유

1 빈칸 추론

정답 ①

해설 문맥상 탁구로 얻을 수 있는 것은 건강으로 볼 수 있으므로 ①이 정답이다.

해석

① 건강 ② 아픈 부상 ③ 많은 돈 ④ 큰 소음 ⑤ 높은 지능

2 제목 추론

정답 ④

해설 이 글의 전체 내용은 겨울에 쉽고 재미있게 할 수 있는 운동으로 탁구를 추천하는 내용이다. 따라서 ④ '겨울에 좋은 실내 스포츠: 탁구'가 제목으로 가장 적절하다.

해석 이 글의 제목으로 가장 적절한 것은?

① 겨울에는 운동하지 마라

② 탁구에서 빨리 움직일 수 있는 방법

③ 탁구는 어렵지만 재미있다

④ 겨울에 좋은 실내 스포츠: 탁구

⑤ 야외 스포츠 vs. 실내 스포츠

3 서술형

정답

(1) 겨울에도 운동할 수 있다.

(2) 실내에서 즐길 수 있다.

(3) 비교적 장비가 간단하다.

(4) 규칙이 간단하다.

(5) 건강에 좋다.

(6) 친구랑 좋은 시간을 보내게 해준다.

해설 겨울 운동, 실내 운동, 간단한 장비, 간단한 규칙, 건강, 친구 관계의 단어가 언급되면 정답으로 인정한다.

제대로 독해법

어휘 Level Up

1 ① 2 ⓝ 3 ⓘ 4 ⓑ 5 ⓚ 6 ⓒ 7 ⓙ 8 ⓓ 9 ⓜ 10 ⓕ 11 ⓗ 12 ⓔ 13 ⓐ 14 ⓖ

내신 Level Up

정답 table tennis

해설 밑줄 친 it은 table tennis(탁구)를 가리킨다.

구문 Level Up

정답

1. It is his dream to become an actor.
2. It is dangerous to walk against the traffic light.

해설

1, 2. to부정사구가 주어로 쓰인 경우, 주어 자리에 가주어 it을 쓰고 to부정사구를 뒤로 보낸다.

▸ pp.12~13

왜 인간은 100m를 9초대 이하로 못 뛸까?

지문 분석

❶ For most runners, speed is determined by the legs' force. ❷ So, there are two ways to run faster: jump and stay in the air longer, or kick the ground harder.
(For most runners: 전치사구 / speed: 주어 / is determined: 수동태(be동사+p.p.) / by: ~에 의해 / to run: to부정사(two ways 수식) / longer: long의 비교급 / harder: hard의 비교급)

(B) ❸ Fast animals such as cheetahs use the first method. ❹ They run with four legs to jump and to stay in the air longer. ❺ They can move forward much faster when they are in the air.
(Fast animals: 주어 / such as: ~와 같은 / use: 동사 / to jump and to stay in: to부정사(결과) / much: 비교급 강조 / when: 접 ~할 때(시간))

(A) ❻ However, people cannot do this because they run with two legs and it's easy to lose their balance in the air. ❼ So the second way is the only option for humans to run faster.
(However: 그러나 / because: 접 ~ 때문에(이유) / to lose: to부정사(easy 수식) / only: 유일한 / for humans: 의미상 주어 / to run: to부정사(option 수식))

(C) ❽ In that way, it is important to hit the ground ㉠harder. ❾ The fastest runner in the world hits the ground 2.5 times stronger than his body weight. ❿ If we made the power stronger, it would break the world's record.
(it: 가주어 / to hit the ground: 진주어(to부정사구) / The fastest runner: 주어 / in the world: 전치사구 / hits: 동사 / 2.5 times stronger than: 배수사+비교급+than: …보다 ~배 -한 / If we made ~ would break: 가정법 과거: If+주어+동사의 과거형 ~, 주어+would+동사원형)

지문 해석

❶ 대부분의 달리기 선수들에게 있어서 속도는 다리 힘에 의해 결정된다. ❷ 그래서 더 빨리 달리기 위한 두 가지 방법이 있다. 뛰어서 공중에 더 오래 머물러 있거나 땅을 더 힘차게 차는 것이다. (B) ❸ 치타 같은 빠른 동물들은 첫 번째 방법을 사용한다. ❹ 그들은 네 다리로 달려서 점프해 공중에 더 오래 머무른다. ❺ 그것들이 공중에 있을 때는 앞으로 훨씬 더 빠르게 움직일 수 있다. (A) ❻ 그러나 사람들은 두 다리로 달려서 공중에서 균형을 잃기 쉽기 때문에 이것을 할 수 없다. ❼ 그래서 두 번째 방법이 인간이 더 빨리 달리기 위한 유일한 선택이다. (C) ❽ 그 방법에서는 땅을 더 세게 차는 게 중요하다. ❾ 세계에서 가장 빠른 달리기 선수는 그의 몸무게보다 2.5배 더 강하게 땅을 친다. ❿ 만약 우리가 그 힘을 더 강하게 한다면, 세계 기록을 깰 수 있을 것이다.

정답인 이유

1 내용 일치

정답 ③

해설 ❻에서 인간이 두 발로 달려 공중에서 균형을 잃기 쉽다는 내용을 알 수 있다. 따라서 ③은 글의 내용과 일치하지 않는다.

2 순서 파악

정답 ②

해설 빨리 달리기 위한 두 가지 방법 소개 → (B) 첫 번째 방법을 사용하는 동물 소개 → (A) 그렇지 않은 인간의 달리기 방법 → (C) 마지막으로 인간이 더 빨리 달릴 수 있는 방법을 소개하는 것으로 이어지는 것이 적절하다.

해석 이 글의 순서로 가장 적절한 것은?

3 서술형

정답

(1) 네 다리로 달려서 점프해 공중에 더 오래 머무른다.

(2) 땅을 더 힘차게 찬다.

해설

(1) (B)에서 치타가 빨리 뛰기 위해 공중에 더 오래 머무른다는 것을 알 수 있다.

(2) (A)에서 사람은 땅을 힘차게 차는 것(두 번째 방법)으로 빨리 뛴다는 것을 알 수 있다.

제대로 독해법

어휘 Level Up

1 ⓑ 2 ⓜ 3 ⓘ 4 ⓖ 5 ⓕ 6 ⓚ 7 ⓓ 8 ⓒ 9 ⓐ 10 ⓙ 11 ⓛ 12 ⓗ 13 ⓔ

내신 Level Up

정답 stronger

해설 harder는 '더 세게, 더 강하게'의 의미로 바로 다음 문장의 stronger와 같은 의미를 나타낸다.

구문 Level Up

정답 1. would 2. came

해설

1. 가정법 과거 문장으로 if절에 동사의 과거형(had)이 왔으므로 주절에는 「조동사의 과거형+동사원형」 형태가 되도록 would가 알맞다.
2. 가정법 과거 문장으로 주절에 「조동사의 과거형+동사원형(could take)」이 쓰였으므로 if절에는 동사의 과거형인 came이 알맞다.

▸ pp.14~15

요즘 유행하는 방탈출 게임 해봤니?

지문 분석

❶ Do you like playing room escape games? ❷ In these games, you will be locked up in a certain room. ❸ There is no explanation and no exit at all. ❹ You need to look around the room, check everything, and (A) gather / gathering hints and items in the room.

(Do you like -ing?: ~하는 것을 좋아하니? / 방탈출 게임 / 갇히다 / ~이 없다 / (there is) / 전혀 / A, B, and C 병렬구조)

❺ It usually provides some puzzles to find an exit. (ⓐ) ❻ ㉠They are really fun and (B) interested / interesting to solve. (ⓑ) ❼ For example, you may need to find an invisible password on a wall with special goggles, then (C) put it in / put in it the keypad to go to the next stage. (ⓒ) ❽ Escaping room games usually take you about one hour. (ⓓ) ❾ Generally, you need to escape in a given time. (ⓔ If you can't, you have to pay extra money for more hints or give up the game.)

(보통 / to부정사(some puzzles 수식) / to부정사(~하기에) / 예를 들어 / 전 ~을 쓰고 / 그러고 나서 / to부정사(~하기 위해서) / 주어 / 동사 / 부 약, 대략 / 일반적으로)

지문 해석

❶ 방탈출 게임하는 것을 좋아하는가? ❷ 이 게임에서, 당신은 어떤 방에 갇힐 것이다. ❸ 설명이나 출구가 전혀 없다. ❹ 당신은 방을 둘러보고, 모든 것을 확인하고 방에 있는 힌트와 소품들을 모아야 한다. ❺ 그것은 보통 출구를 찾기 위한 퍼즐들을 제공한다. ❻ 그것들은 풀기에 정말 재밌고 흥미 있다. ❼ 예를 들어, 당신은 특수 고글을 쓰고 벽에 있는 눈에 보이지 않는 암호를 찾고 나서 다음 단계로 가기 위해 키패드에 그걸 입력해야 한다. ❽ 방탈출 게임은 보통 한 시간이 걸린다. ❾ 일반적으로, 당신은 주어진 시간 내에 탈출해야 한다. ❿ 그렇게 하지 못하면, 더 많은 힌트를 위해 추가로 돈을 더 내거나 게임을 포기해야 한다.

정답인 이유

1 어법성 판단

정답 ⑤

해설

(A) 앞에 나온 동사 look, check와 병렬구조이므로 동사원형인 gather가 적절하다.

(B) '흥미로운'이라는 뜻이므로 interesting이 적절하다.

(C) 「동사+부사」 형태의 put in(입력하다)의 목적어가 대명사이므로 put과 in 사이에 써야 한다. 따라서 put it in이 적절하다.

2 문장 삽입

정답 ⑤

해설 ⓔ 앞에서 한 시간 안에 탈출해야 한다는 내용이 나오고 주어진 문장에서 'If you can't ~'라고 서술하며 그러지 못했을 경우 해야 하는 일이 나오고 있으므로 ⓔ에 들어가는 것이 적절하다.

해석 주어진 문장이 들어가기에 가장 적절한 곳은?
그렇게 하지 못하면, 더 많은 힌트를 위해 추가로 돈을 더 내거나 게임을 포기해야 한다.

3 서술형

정답 특수 고글을 쓰고 벽에 있는 숨겨진 암호를 찾아서 키패드에 입력한다.

해설 ❼~❾에서 방탈출 게임의 예시를 들고 있다.

제대로 독해법

어휘 Level Up

1 ⓞ 2 ⓑ 3 ⓙ 4 ⓗ 5 ⓝ 6 ⓜ 7 ⓔ 8 ⓕ 9 ⓐ 10 ⓚ 11 ⓒ 12 ⓘ 13 ⓖ 14 ⓓ 15 ⓛ

내신 Level Up

정답 some puzzles

해설 They는 앞 문장의 some puzzles를 가리킨다. 출구를 찾기 위해 제공되는 퍼즐들이 재밌고 흥미 있다는 내용이다.

구문 Level Up

정답 1. jog 2. camels

해설

1. read ~, listen ~, and jog가 병렬구조를 이루어야 하므로 동사 jog가 알맞다.

2. monkeys, elephants, and camels가 병렬구조를 이루어야 하므로 명사 camels가 알맞다.

▸ pp.16~17

볼링과 터키의 관계는?

지문 분석

❶ "Turkey" has several meanings. ❷ It (= Turkey) may be a kind of bird or a country in Europe. ❸ But few (거의 없는) people come up with ㉠another meaning. (come up with: (해답, 아이디어 등을) 내놓다) ❹ This word may mean triple strikes in a bowling game. ❺ Bowling is a sport with a heavy ball and 10 pins. ❻ You have to (~해야 한다) roll the ball to knock down (to부정사(~하기 위해서)) as many pins as possible (as ~ as possible: 가능한 한 ~한[하게]). ❼ If you knock over all of them (전부) at once (한 번에), you call it a strike (call+목적어+목적격보어: ~를 …라고 부르다). ❽ And if you do this (= strike) three times in a row (연속으로), you call it a turkey. ❾ Then, why is it called (수동태(be동사+p.p.)) a turkey? ❿ In America, turkey meat was a common prize in the past (과거에). ⓫ One owner of the bowling game center (주어) decided (동사) to give (to부정사(목적어)) a turkey to (전 ~에게) people if (접 ~라면(조건)) they made three strikes in a row (연속으로). ⓬ From that time on (그때부터), bowling players named it a turkey (name+목적어+목적격보어: ~를 …라고 이름 짓다) and still use the word (= turkey).

지문 해석

❶ '터키'에는 여러 가지 의미가 있다. ❷ 이것은 새의 한 종류일 수도 있고, 유럽에 있는 나라일 수도 있다. ❸ 그러나 또 다른 의미를 내놓는 사람은 거의 없다. ❹ 이 단어는 볼링 경기에서 3연속 스트라이크를 의미할 수 있다. ❺ 볼링은 무거운 공과 열 개의 핀을 가지고 하는 운동이다. ❻ 당신은 가능한 한 많은 핀을 넘어뜨리기 위해 공을 굴려야 한다. ❼ 만약 당신이 한 번에 전부 넘어뜨린다면, 당신은 그것을 스트라이크라고 부른다. ❽ 그리고 연속으로 그것을 세 번하면, 당신은 그것을 터키라고 부른다. ❾ 그렇다면, 왜 그것이 터키라고 불릴까? ❿ 미국에서는, 과거에 칠면조(터키) 고기가 흔한 상품이었다. ⓫ 한 볼링 경기장 소유자가 사람들이 연속으로 세 번 스트라이크를 하면 그들에게 칠면조를 주기로 결정했다. ⓬ 그때부터 볼링 선수들은 이것을 터키라고 이름 붙였고, 여전히 그 단어를 사용한다.

정답인 이유

1 요약문 완성

정답 ③

해설 볼링 경기에서 3연속 스트라이크를 하는 것은 터키라고 불리고, 이 단어는 과거에 우승 상품에서 유래했다.

① 치킨 ---- 볼링 선수 ② 터키 ---- 나라 이름
③ 터키 ---- 우승 상품 ④ 치킨 ---- 칠면조 고기
⑤ 터키 ---- 아메리칸 드림

2 주제 추론

정답 ①

해설 이 글은 볼링 경기에서 '터키'라는 용어의 유래에 대한 것이므로 ①이 주제로 가장 적절하다.

해석 이 글의 주제로 가장 적절한 것은?
① 볼링 경기에서 터키의 유래
② 야생에서 칠면조를 사냥하는 방법
③ 가장 재미있는 방법으로 볼링 경기 하기
④ 볼링 경기에서 높은 점수를 받는 방법
⑤ 유럽 국가인 터키의 역사

3 서술형

정답
(1) 새 이름
(2) 나라 이름
(3) 볼링에서 세 번 연속 스트라이크가 나온 경우

해설 '터키'에는 여러 가지 의미가 있는데, 새의 한 종류, 유럽에 있는 나라, 그리고 볼링 경기에서 3연속 스트라이크를 의미할 수도 있다고 하였다.

제대로 독해법

어휘 Level Up

1 ⓖ 2 ⓘ 3 ⓚ 4 ⓔ 5 ⓙ 6 ⓐ 7 ⓓ 8 ⓕ 9 ⓜ 10 ⓗ 11 ⓒ 12 ⓝ 13 ⓛ 14 ⓑ

내신 Level Up

정답 triple strikes in a bowling game

해설 바로 다음에 이어지는 문장 ❹에서 another meaning이 가리키는 것이 볼링 경기에서의 3연속 스트라이크임을 알 수 있다.

구문 Level Up

정답 was made angry

해설 5형식 문장에서 수동태를 만들 때 목적격보어는 「be동사+p.p.」 뒤에 써 준다.

어휘 테스트

▸ p.18

A 1 table tennis 2 faster 3 balance 4 exit 5 roll 6 meat

B 1 ⓒ 2 ⓐ 3 ⓑ

해석 1 신체적인 2 앞으로 3 눈에 보이지 않는
ⓐ 당신 앞에 있는 방향으로
ⓑ 보이지 않는
ⓒ 신체와 관련된

Chapter 2 Environment

Day 03 Reading 01

▸ pp.22~23

기후 변화의 원인에 대한 논쟁

지문 분석

❶ Scientists are arguing why climate change is happening. (현재진행시제(be동사+-ing)) ❷ Most of them believe [that the recent climate change is due to human activity]. (대부분의 / = scientists / 명사절(believe의 목적어) / ~ 때문에) ❸ Many data from satellite support the fact [that the development of cities and factories actually is causing climate change]. (주어 / 동사 / the fact를 설명해 주는 동격절(접속사 that) / 사실상 / 현재진행시제(be동사+-ing)) ❹ Researchers also agree [that fossil fuel gas from cars is raising the temperature of the Earth]. (명사절(agree의 목적어) / 현재진행시제(be동사+-ing)) ❺ However, some people question the truth of ㉠this argument. (통 ~을 의심하다) ❻ ⓐ They are saying [that climate change is a part of the natural change in Earth's climate and temperature]. (명사절(saying의 목적어) / 명 변화 / 전치사구) ❼ ⓑ The Earth gets most energy from the Sun. ❽ ⓒ They think [it is difficult to connect climate change and certain weather events]. (가주어 / (think의 목적어절을 이끄는 접속사 that 생략) / 진주어(to부정사구)) ❾ ⓓ For example, the summer is getting hotter and hotter around the world, but nobody knows the reason exactly. (예를 들어 / get+비교급 and 비교급: 점점 더 ~해지다 / 전 세계적으로 / 아무도 ~않다) ❿ ⓔ Some people say [it might be a natural change as the Earth ages]. ((say의 목적어절을 이끄는 접속사 that 생략) / 접 ~함에 따라 / 통 나이가 들다)

지문 해석

❶ 과학자들은 기후 변화가 일어나고 있는 원인에 대해 논쟁하고 있다. ❷ 대부분의 과학자들은 최근의 기후 변화가 인간의 활동 때문이라고 믿는다. ❸ 위성에서 오는 많은 자료가 도시와 공장의 발전이 사실상 기후 변화를 일으키고 있다는 사실을 뒷받침하고 있다. ❹ 연구자들은 또한 자동차에서 나오는 화석 연료 가스가 지구의 온도를 올리고 있다는 것에 동의한다. ❺ 그러나 일부 사람들은 이 논쟁의 사실 여부를 의심한다. ❻ 그들은 기후 변화는 지구 기후와 온도의 자연스러운 변화의 한 부분이라고 말하고 있다. ❼ (지구는 대부분의 에너지를 태양으로부터 얻는다.) ❽ 그들은 기후 변화와 특정 날씨 발생을 연관 짓기가 어렵다고 생각한다. ❾ 예를 들어, 여름이 전 세계적으로 점점 더 더워지고 있지만, 아무도 정확히 이유를 알지 못한다. ❿ 일부 사람들은 이것은 지구가 나이 들면서 일어나는 자연적인 변화라고 말한다.

정답인 이유

1 무관한 문장

정답 ②

해설 기후 변화에 대한 내용의 글이므로, 지구가 에너지를 받는 원천에 대한 내용의 ⓑ는 전체 흐름과 어울리지 않는다.

2 제목 추론

정답 ①

해설 이 글은 지구 기후 변화의 원인에 대한 논쟁을 제시한 글이다. 따라서 이 내용을 포괄할 수 있는 ①이 제목으로 적절하다.

해석 이 글의 제목으로 가장 적절한 것은?
① 왜 기후 변화가 일어나는가?
② 인간 활동의 정수: 도시와 공장
③ 인간의 활동으로 변한 기후
④ 지구가 나이 들수록, 기후는 더 나빠진다
⑤ 기후 변화: 지구에게 자연스러운 것

3 서술형

정답 **인간의 활동이 기후 변화를 만든다는 것**

해설 this argument가 의미하는 것은 ❷에서 알 수 있다. '기후 변화가 인간의 활동 때문이라는 것'도 유사 답으로 인정한다.

제대로 독해법

어휘 Level Up

1ⓓ 2ⓒ 3ⓠ 4ⓐ 5ⓞ 6ⓜ 7ⓕ 8ⓖ 9ⓗ
10ⓑ 11ⓙ 12ⓔ 13ⓛ 14ⓚ 15ⓝ 16ⓘ 17ⓡ 18ⓟ

내신 Level Up

정답

(1) 인간의 활동

(2) 지구 기후와 온도의 자연스러운 변화

해설 과학자들은 기후 변화가 일어나고 있는 원인에 대해 논쟁하고 있는데, 대부분의 과학자들은 최근의 기후 변화가 인간의 활동 때문이라고 말하고, 일부 사람들은 지구 기후와 온도의 자연스러운 변화의 한 부분이라고 말한다.

구문 Level Up

정답

1. that we can do it
2. that you were a high school teacher

해설

1, 2. 접속사 that이 이끄는 절은 각각 believe, heard의 목적어 역할을 한다.

▸ pp.24~25

우리는 매일 플라스틱을 먹고 있다

지문 분석

❶ We are eating plastic every day, but few of us realize it. ❷ The biggest reason is [that we don't care whether it returns to us].

(현재진행시제(be동사+-ing) / 거의 없는 / 형 big의 최상급 / 명사절(보어) / 접 ~인지 아닌지)

(C) ❸ Let me give you an example. ❹ If we throw plastic pieces into the ocean, ⓒthey are broken down into smaller and smaller pieces. ❺ ⓓThey sink deep into the ocean and plankton absorbs ⓔthem. ❻ Then, some fish eat the plankton and the plastic pieces stay in the fish.

(예를 들다 / 접 ~라면(조건) / = plastic pieces / 점점 더 작은(비교급 and 비교급: 점점 더 ~한) / = Plastic pieces / = plastic pieces)

(B) ❼ Finally, fishermen catch ⓐthem and then the tiny plastic pieces go into our food. ❽ We don't know much about its effect to the human body. ❾ However, ⓑthey do not seem good for our health.

(결국 / fisherman의 복수형 / = fish / 부 많이 / ~인 것 같지 않다)

(A) ❿ Many fish and sea creatures are dying because of plastic concentration inside their body. ⓫ It could be the same to human. ⓬ Therefore, scientists suggest [that we stop using plastic products and recycle them as much as possible].

(현재진행시제(be동사+-ing) / die의 현재분사(die+-ing → dying) / 전 ~ 안에 / 전 ~에게 / 그래서 / 명사절(suggest의 목적어) / 동사 1 / 동명사(목적어) / 동사 2 / 가능한 한 많이)

지문 해석

❶ 우리는 매일 플라스틱을 먹고 있지만, 그것을 깨닫고 있는 사람은 거의 없다. ❷ 가장 큰 이유는 우리가 이것이 우리에게 돌아오는지 신경을 안 쓴다는 것이다. (C) ❸ 예를 한번 들어보자. ❹ 우리가 플라스틱 조각을 바다에 버린다면, 그것들은 점점 더 작은 조각으로 분해된다. ❺ 그것들은 바다 깊숙한 곳에 가라앉고 플랑크톤이 그것들을 흡수한다. ❻ 그런 다음, 어떤 물고기가 그 플랑크톤을 먹고 플라스틱 조각들은 물고기 안에 남는다. (B) ❼ 결국, 어부들이 그것들을 잡은 다음 작은 플라스틱 조각들은 우리 음식으로 간다. ❽ 우리는 이것이 인체에 미치는 영향에 대해 많이 알지 못한다. ❾ 그러나, 그것들은 우리 건강에 좋아 보이지 않는다. (A) ❿ 많은 물고기와 해양 생물들은 그들의 몸 안의 플라스틱 농축물 때문에 죽어가고 있다. ⓫ 그것은 인간에게도 마찬가지일 수 있다. ⓬ 그래서 과학자들은 우리가 플라스틱 제품을 사용하는 것을 멈추고 가능한 한 많이 재활용해야 한다고 제안한다.

정답인 이유

1 지칭 추론

정답 ①

해설 ⓑ, ⓒ, ⓓ, ⓔ는 플라스틱(조각)을 가리키지만 ⓐ는 어부가 잡은 물고기를 가리킨다.

2 순서 파악

정답 ⑤

해설 플라스틱이 우리에게 돌아온다는 주어진 글 뒤에 플라스틱이 돌아오는 과정을 묘사하는 (C), (B)가 오고 플라스틱이 건강에 좋지 않으니 사용을 줄이자는 내용의 (A)가 오는 것이 적절하다.

해석 이 글의 순서로 가장 적절한 것은?

3 서술형

정답 바다 / 플랑크톤 / 물고기 / 어부

해설 (C), (B)에서 플라스틱이 우리 몸에 들어오는 과정을 묘사하고 있다.

제대로 독해법

어휘 Level Up

1ⓝ 2ⓖ 3ⓔ 4ⓓ 5ⓛ 6ⓚ 7ⓘ 8ⓗ 9ⓜ 10ⓙ 11ⓕ 12ⓐ 13ⓑ 14ⓞ 15ⓟ 16ⓒ

내신 Level Up

정답 recycle

해설 '어떤 것을 다른 목적으로 다시 사용하다'라는 뜻을 갖는 단어는 recycle(재활용하다, 재사용하다)이다.

구문 Level Up

정답 1. chatting 2. drinking

해설

1, 2. 동사 stop의 목적어가 와야 하므로 동명사(-ing)가 알맞다. 「stop+-ing」는 '~하는 것을 멈추다'라는 의미이다.

▸ pp.26~27

아보카도는 과연 좋기만 할까?

지문 분석

❶ Do you like eating avocados? ❷ Avocados are
favored around the world because they taste like
수동태(be동사+p.p.) 전 세계적으로 접 ~ 때문에(이유)
butter, but are much ⓐhealthier than real butter. ❸ So
(they) 훨씬(비교급 강조) 비교급+than: ~보다 더 …한
many restaurants are inventing menu with avocados.
현재진행시제(be동사+-ing)
❹ However, there are problems about this green fruit.
there are+복수명사: ~들이 있다
❺ They usually grow in Mexico and need a lot of water.
주로
명사절(say의 목적어)
❻ Many researchers say [that it makes the land of Mexico
= this green fruit(= avocado)
drier and drier like ⓑthe desert]. ❼ In other words, they
다시 말해서 avocados =
are killing the land. ❽ They also ⓒharm the economy in
현재진행시제(be동사+-ing) = Avocados
Mexico. ❾ Because many local farmers prefer planting
접 ~ 때문에(이유) prefer A to B: B보다 A를 선호하다
avocados to any other crop, they spend a lot of money
spend+돈+on: ~에 (돈)을 쓰다
on the seeds. ❿ However, the supply is ⓓlimitless, and
그러나 (×) → limited(○)
the price keeps going up. ⓫ So the farmers need to pay
그래서 = have to
more and more for avocado farms. ⓬ Some even call
비교급 and 비교급: 점점 더 ~한[하게] 부 ~도[조차]
it a blood avocado because a number of people ⓔlose
call+목적어+목적격보어: ~을 …라고 부르다 주어/a number of(= many) 동사 1
money and leave their farms.
동사 2

지문 해석

❶ 아보카도 먹는 것을 좋아하는가? ❷ 아보카도는 버터와 같은 맛이 나지만, 진짜 버터보다 훨씬 더 건강하기 때문에 전 세계적으로 선호된다. ❸ 그래서 많은 식당들이 아보카도로 메뉴를 개발하고 있다. ❹ 그러나 이 녹색 과일에는 문제가 있다. ❺ 그것들은 주로 멕시코에서 자라고 많은 물을 필요로 한다. ❻ 많은 연구자들이 이것이 멕시코 땅을 사막처럼 점점 더 메마르게 만든다고 말한다. ❼ 다시 말해서, 그것들이 땅을 죽이고 있는 것이다. ❽ 그것들은 또한 멕시코의 경제에 해가 되고 있다. ❾ 많은 지역 농민들이 다른 작물보다 아보카도를 심는 걸 선호하기 때문에, 그들은 종자에 많은 돈을 쓴다. ❿ 그러나 공급이 무제한(→ 제한적)이고 가격은 오르고 있다. ⓫ 그래서 농부들은 아보카도 농장을 위해 점점 더 많이 돈을 써야 한다. ⓬ 어떤 이들은 이것을 피의 아보카도라고도 부르는데, 왜냐하면 많은 사람들이 돈을 잃고 농장을 떠나기 때문이다.

정답인 이유

1 주제 추론

정답 ④

해설 이 글은 인기를 끌고 있는 아보카도를 경작할 때 생기는 문제점에 대한 글이므로 ④가 주제로 가장 적절하다.

2 어휘 파악

정답 ④

해설 ⓓ 공급이 무제한이라는 것은 바로 뒤에 나오는 가격이 올라간다는 내용과 맞지 않다. 따라서 limitless(무제한)가 아니라 limited(제한적)가 오는 것이 적절하다.

해석 ⓐ~ⓔ 중에서 낱말의 쓰임이 적절하지 않은 것은?

3 서술형

정답 **버터맛이 나지만, 진짜 버터보다 훨씬 더 건강에 좋다.**

해설 ❷에서 아보카도가 전 세계에서 선호되는 이유를 설명하고 있다.

제대로 독해법

어휘 Level Up

1 ⓜ 2 ⓓ 3 ⓛ 4 ⓚ 5 ⓘ 6 ⓕ 7 ⓟ 8 ⓜ 9 ⓝ
10 ⓑ 11 ⓞ 12 ⓖ 13 ⓔ 14 ⓐ 15 ⓗ 16 ⓒ 17 ⓙ

내신 Level Up

정답 (1) crop (2) spend (3) leave

해설 많은 지역 농민들이 다른 작물보다 아보카도를 심는 걸 선호하기 때문에 그들은 종자에 많은 돈을 쓰고 그로 인해 많은 사람들이 돈을 잃고 농장을 떠나게 된다고 하였다.

구문 Level Up

정답 much

해설 much는 비교급을 강조하여 '훨씬'의 의미를 나타낸다. very는 원급을 강조한다.

▸ pp.28~29

따뜻한 롱패딩을 위해 죽어 가는 동물들

지문 분석

❶ Long padding coats, or bench coats, are in trend these days, because they can make us warm even if the weather is freezing. ❷ However, you should know [that quite a few animals are killed for this trend]. ❸ Most of these coats contain thick volume of birds' feathers. (ⓐ)
❹ In clothing factories, the workers pull feathers from ducks and geese. ❺ (ⓑ The birds stay still but feel strong pain because they are alive during this process.)
❻ Mammals such as rabbits, racoons, or foxes are also losing their lives for this fashion. (ⓒ) ❼ Because their fur is colorful and smooth, fashion designers want to use it for styling the hoods and collars of these coats. (ⓓ)
❽ Consumers should be aware of ㉠these facts and (should) be more careful when they buy long padding coats. (ⓔ)

(주어: Long padding coats, or bench coats / 동사: are / 요즘: these days / 접 왜냐하면(이유): because / 접 ~하더라도: even if / ~해야 한다: should / 명사절: that quite a few ... trend / 상당히 많은: quite a few / 수동태(be동사+p.p.): are killed / 대부분의: Most of / 동사: contain / 목적어: thick volume of birds' feathers / 주어: the workers / 동사: pull / 목적어: feathers / 전 ~에서: from / goose(거위)의 복수형: geese / ~와 같은: such as / 병렬구조: rabbits, racoons, or foxes / lose one's life: 목숨을 잃다 / 접 ~ 때문에(이유): Because / 전치사+(동)명사: for styling / 주어: fashion designers / 동사: want / 목적어: to use / it = their fur / ~을 알다: be aware of / 접 ~할 때(시간): when)

지문 해석

❶ 롱패딩코트 또는 벤치코트는 요즘 유행인데, 왜냐하면 그것들은 날씨가 엄청 춥더라도 우리를 따뜻하게 해주기 때문이다. ❷ 그러나 당신은 상당히 많은 동물들이 이 유행 때문에 죽고 있다는 것을 알아야 한다. ❸ 대부분의 이러한 코트는 두꺼운 부피의 새 깃털을 포함한다. ❹ 의류 공장에서, 노동자들은 오리와 거위에서 깃털을 뽑는다. ❺ 새들은 이 과정에서 살아 있기 때문에 가만히 있지만 큰 고통을 느낀다. ❻ 토끼, 라쿤(미국너구리), 여우 같은 포유류들도 이 유행 때문에 목숨을 잃고 있다. ❼ 그것들의 모피가 색이 다채롭고 윤이 나기 때문에 패션 디자이너들은 이 코트의 모자나 옷깃을 꾸미는 데 그것을 사용하길 원한다. ❽ 소비자들은 이러한 사실들을 알아야 하고 롱패딩코트를 구입할 때 좀 더 신중해야 한다.

정답인 이유

1 문장 삽입

정답 ②

해설 새들이 의류 공장에서 깃털이 뽑히는 내용 뒤에 그 과정에서 새들이 고통을 느낀다는 내용이 나오는 게 자연스러우므로 ⓑ에 들어가는 것이 적절하다.

해석 새들은 이 과정에서 살아 있기 때문에 가만히 있지만 큰 고통을 느낀다.

2 주제 추론

정답 ③

해설 이 글은 롱패딩코트나 벤치코트를 만드는 데 많은 동물들이 고통 속에 희생당하고 있다는 내용이므로 ③ '많은 동물들이 벤치코트 유행으로 고통 속에 죽임을 당한다.'가 주제로 가장 적절하다.

해석 이 글의 주제로 가장 적절한 것은?
① 벤치코트는 충분히 따뜻하지 않다.
② 우리는 패션을 위해서 동물을 어떤 경우에도 죽여선 안 된다.
③ 많은 동물들이 벤치코트 유행으로 고통 속에 죽임을 당한다.
④ 패션 유행은 항상 변하고 있다.
⑤ 동물들은 그들의 영혼을 가지고 있고 고통을 느낀다.

3 서술형

정답 **그것들의 모피가 색이 다채롭고 윤이 나기 때문에**

해설 ❼에 패션 디자이너들이 모피를 사용하는 이유가 나타나 있다.

제대로 독해법

어휘 Level Up

1ⓔ 2ⓞ 3ⓖ 4ⓓ 5ⓝ 6ⓛ 7ⓒ 8ⓘ 9ⓕ 10ⓐ 11ⓗ 12ⓜ 13ⓙ 14ⓑ 15ⓚ

내신 Level Up

정답 Quite a few animals are killed for this trend.

해설 '많은 동물들이 이 유행 때문에 죽어가고 있다'는 사실들을 알고 롱패딩코트를 구입할 때 신중해야 한다는 내용이다.

구문 Level Up

정답 1. thought the chair old 2. left the door open

해설

1, 2. 5형식 문장은 「주어+동사+목적어+목적격보어」의 어순으로 나타낸다.

어휘 테스트

▸ p.30

A 1 recycle 2 land 3 crop 4 freezing 5 feathers 6 geese

B 1ⓑ 2ⓐ 3ⓒ

해석 1 동의하다 2 선호하다 3 소비자
ⓐ 다른 것보다는 한 가지를 좋아하거나 선택하거나 원하다
ⓑ 같은 의견을 가지다
ⓒ 자신들이 사용하는 물건이나 서비스를 사는 사람

Travel · Places

▸ pp.34~35

몰디브에서 볼 수 있는 동물은?

지문 분석

❶ Maldives have beautiful blue seas and white beaches. ❷ There are more than(~이상) 2,000 kinds(명 종류) of tropical fish around(전 ~ 주위에) the islands. ❸ Sea creatures(주어) like(전 ~와 같은) jellyfish, octopus, squid, and clams are(동사) also common(↔ uncommon(드문, 흔하지 않은)). ❹ Coral reefs are very popular with the seasonal movement of fish(단수형과 복수형이 같은 명사) and whales. ❺ Maldives'(-s로 끝나는 명사의 소유격) oceans and beaches are becoming one of the most popular tourist attractions(one of the 최상급+복수명사: 가장 ~한 것들 중 하나) in the world to see(to부정사(tourist attractions 수식)) these colorful sea creatures, including(~을 포함하여) aquariums. ❻ However, if(접 ~라면(조건)) you are looking for(look for: ~을 찾다) zoos, you may be(~일지도 모른다) disappointed(형 실망한). ❼ There are very few(거의 없는) land animals, and even(심지어 ~도) no house dogs live in Maldives. ❽ In fact(사실), Maldives(주어1) are(동사1) a group of very small islands and most animals(주어2) live(동사2) in the water. ❾ They simply don't have enough space to raise land animals.

지문 해석

❶ 몰디브에는 아름다운 푸른 바다와 하얀 해변이 있다. ❷ 이 섬들 주위에는 2천 종이 넘는 열대어들이 있다. ❸ 해파리, 문어, 오징어 그리고 조개와 같은 해양 생물들 또한 흔하다. ❹ 산호초는 물고기들과 고래들의 계절 이동과 함께 매우 인기가 있다. ❺ 몰디브의 바다와 해변은 아쿠아리움(수족관)을 포함하여 이러한 다채로운 색깔의 해양 생물을 볼 수 있는 세계에서 가장 인기 있는 관광지 중 하나가 되고 있다. ❻ 하지만 만약 동물원을 찾는다면, 당신은 실망할지도 모른다. ❼ 몰디브에는 육지 동물이 거의 없고 심지어 집 지키는 개도 살지 않는다. ❽ 사실 몰디브는 매우 작은 섬들의 집합이고 대부분의 동물들은 물속에서 산다. ❾ 그들은 단지 육지 동물을 기를 만한 충분한 공간을 가지고 있지 않다.

정답인 이유

1 요약문 완성

정답 ③

해설 이 글은 세계에서 가장 유명한 관광지 중 하나인 몰디브에는 육지 동물이 거의 없고 대부분의 동물들은 물속에서 산다는 내용으로 정답은 ③이다.

해석
세계에서 가장 유명한 관광지 중 하나인 몰디브에서는 대부분의 동물들이 육지가 아니라 물속에 산다.
① 도시 지역 ---- 물 ② 무역 국가 ---- 수족관
③ 관광지 ---- 물 ④ 화산섬 ---- 동굴 ⑤ 유적 ---- 동굴

2 빈칸 추론

정답 ②

해설 빈칸에는 육지 동물이 많이 없는 이유가 들어가야 한다. 바로 앞 문장에서 몰디브가 매우 작은 섬이라고 말한 것을 고려했을 때 육지 동물을 기를 만한 공간이 없다는 ②가 적절하다.

해석 빈칸에 들어갈 말로 가장 적절한 것은?
① 동물원을 운영할 충분한 예산
② 육지 동물을 기를 만한 충분한 공간
③ 육지 동물을 위한 좋은 기후
④ 육지 동물에게 먹이를 줄 사육사
⑤ 육지 동물을 수입할 시장

3 서술형

정답 **몰디브의 파란 바다와 하얀 해변에서 다채로운 색깔의 해양 생물을 볼 수 있어서**

해설 '다채로운 색깔의 해양 생물을 볼 수 있다'는 내용을 포함하면 정답으로 인정한다.

제대로 독해법

어휘 Level Up

1 ⓛ 2 ⓗ 3 ⓜ 4 ⓔ 5 ⓘ 6 ⓝ 7 ⓐ 8 ⓚ 9 ⓑ
10 ⓒ 11 ⓕ 12 ⓖ 13 ⓙ 14 ⓓ

내신 Level Up

정답 **열대어, 해파리, 문어, 오징어, 조개, 산호초, 물고기, 고래**

해설 글의 앞부분에 몰디브 주변에는 2천 종이 넘는 열대어들이 있고, 해파리, 문어, 오징어, 조개 같은 해양 생물들 또한 흔하고, 산호초는 물고기와 고래들의 계절 이동과 함께 매우 인기가 있다는 내용이 언급되어 있다.

구문 Level Up

정답 **1. is 2. aren't**

해설
1. 주어가 단수명사(a cow)이므로 is가 알맞다.
2. 주어가 복수명사(many trees)이므로 aren't가 알맞다.

▸ pp.36~37

당신은 어떤 유형의 여행자인가요?

지문 분석

❶ Here are three types of travelers. (Here are + 복수명사: 여기 ~들이 있다) ❷ [Read and check what type of traveler you are]. (명령문(동사원형으로 시작) / 간접의문문(의문사 + 주어 + 동사))

❸ 1. The Lifetime Traveler

❹ They live to travel. (to부정사(~하기 위해서)) ❺ When they aren't traveling, they are thinking about the next place to go. (to부정사(place 수식)) ❻ They just enjoy traveling (동명사(목적어)) and (they) are not concerned about (= worried about) whether their situation (주어) during (전 ~동안) the journey is (동사) good (A) or bad (B). (whether ~ A or B: A이든 B이든)

❼ 2. The Athlete Traveler

❽ They like to plan (= planning) vacations around (전 ~을 중심으로) sports. ❾ They go on golfing, mountain-climbing, or scuba-diving vacations. ❿ They may love to sit (= sitting) on a beach but only after sailing or kayaking.

⓫ 3. The Comfort Traveler

⓬ They are almost the opposite of the athlete travelers. ⓭ They love traveling (= to travel) only when it is easy and comfortable. ⓮ One thing (주어/선행사) [that's important to them] (관계대명사절(주격)) is (동사) the view from their room or from warm and sunny beaches. (병렬구조(전치사구 대등 연결))

지문 해석

❶ 여기 세 가지 여행자 유형이 있다. ❷ 당신은 어떤 유형의 여행자인지 읽고 확인해라.
❸ 1. 생애형 여행자 ❹ 그들은 여행하기 위해 산다. ❺ 그들은 여행을 하지 않을 때는 다음에 갈 장소를 생각 중이다. ❻ 그들은 그저 여행을 즐기고 여행 동안에 그들의 상황이 좋든 나쁘든 걱정하지 않는다.
❼ 2. 운동선수형 여행자 ❽ 그들은 운동 중심으로 휴가를 계획하는 것을 좋아한다. ❾ 그들은 골프, 등산 또는 스쿠버 다이빙 휴가를 간다. ❿ 그들은 해변에 앉아 있는 것을 즐길 수도 있지만 그것은 오직 보트 타기나 카약 타기를 한 후이다.
⓫ 3. 안락형 여행자 ⓬ 그들은 운동선수형 여행자와 거의 반대이다. ⓭ 그들은 오직 쉽고 편안한 여행만을 좋아한다. ⓮ 그들에게 중요한 한 가지는 그들의 방에서 혹은 따뜻하고 화창한 해변에서의 풍경이다.

정답인 이유

1 목적 추론

정답 ⑤

해설 이 글은 세 가지 여행자 유형에 대한 정보를 주는 글이므로 ⑤가 글의 목적으로 가장 적절하다.

해석
① 예약을 확인하려고 ② 여행에 대해 불평하려고
③ 관광지를 광고하려고 ④ 위험한 장소에 대해 경고하려고
⑤ 각기 다른 여행자 유형을 소개하려고

2 내용 일치

정답 ⑤

해설 세 가지 유형의 여행자 모두가 여행을 위한 돈과 시간을 걱정한다는 내용은 언급되지 않았으므로 ⑤는 내용과 일치하지 않는다.

해석 이 글의 내용과 일치하지 않는 것은?
① 세 가지 유형의 여행자가 있다.
② 생애형 여행자는 새로운 여행을 계획하는 것을 좋아한다.
③ 운동선수형 여행자는 여행하는 동안 운동하려는 경향이 있다.
④ 안락형 여행자는 운동선수형 여행자와 완전히 다르다.
⑤ 모든 유형의 여행자들은 여행을 위한 돈과 시간을 걱정한다.

3 서술형

정답
(1) The comfort traveler (안락형 여행자)
(2) ① 쉽고 편안한 여행을 좋아한다.
② 풍경을 중요하게 생각한다.

해석 당신은 훌륭한 서비스를 제공하는 호텔에 머물 수 있다. 전용 해변에서 당신은 멋진 풍경과 함께 일광욕과 휴식을 할 수 있다. 심지어 당신은 언제든지 마사지를 받을 수 있다.

제대로 독해법

어휘 Level Up

1 ⓜ 2 ⓙ 3 ⓚ 4 ⓐ 5 ⓖ 6 ⓘ 7 ⓑ 8 ⓠ 9 ⓒ
10 ⓓ 11 ⓗ 12 ⓕ 13 ⓞ 14 ⓔ 15 ⓛ 16 ⓟ 17 ⓝ

내신 Level Up

정답 (1) Athlete (2) Comfort (3) Lifetime

해석
(1) 운동선수형 여행자
"나는 이번 여름휴가에 번지 점프를 하러 갈 계획이야."
(2) 안락형 여행자
"나는 그냥 해변 의자에 누워서 소설을 읽고 싶어."
(3) 생애형 여행자
여행하는 것은 정말 내 삶의 모든 것이야."

구문 Level Up

정답 makes

해설 현재시제이고, 선행사(someone)가 3인칭 단수이므로 makes가 알맞다.

▸ pp.38~39

미국의 가장 특이한 주, 알래스카

지문 분석

❶ Alaska, a state of the United States, is a really interesting place in the world. ❷ People usually think [ⓐit is cold all year long], but it actually has four seasons, too. ❸ The temperature even rose up to about 38 degree Celsius in the summer of 1915. ❹ However, ⓑit is true that Alaska freezes all over during wintertime. ❺ The sea between Alaska and Russia also freezes in winter, so some travelers successfully crossed the sea border on foot. ❻ ㉠The land has another interesting point. ❼ ⓒIt has the highest mountain in North America, Denali, and the longest coastline among the States. ❽ Although ⓓits size is quite big and wide, Alaska has the smallest population in the country. ❾ For your information, one of ⓔits towns, Barrow, has the longest and the shortest daytime records in the U.S. at the same time.

(a state of the United States: 동격 / think의 목적어절을 이끄는 접속사 that 생략 / usually: 보통 / all year long: 일 년 내내 / too: 부 역시, 또한 / it: 가주어 / that Alaska freezes all over during wintertime: 진주어(that절) / between A and B: A와 B 사이에 / so: 접 ~해서(결과) / on foot: 걸어서 / The land = Alaska / interesting: 현재분사가 명사 앞에서 수식 / Denali: 동격 / longest: long의 최상급 / the States: 미국(미합중국) / Although: 접 비록 ~이지만(양보) / quite: 부 꽤, 상당히 / smallest: small의 최상급 / For your information: 참고로 / Barrow: 동격 / longest: long의 최상급 / shortest: short의 최상급 / at the same time: 동시에)

지문 해석

❶ 미국의 한 주인 알래스카는 세계에서 정말 흥미로운 장소이다. ❷ 사람들은 보통 그곳이 일 년 내내 추울 것이라고 생각하지만, 사실은 그곳에도 사계절이 있다. ❸ 1915년 여름에는 기온이 약 섭씨 38도까지 올라가기도 했다. ❹ 그러나 알래스카 전체가 겨울 동안 얼어붙는 것은 사실이다. ❺ 알래스카와 러시아 사이의 바다 역시 겨울에 얼어붙어서, 몇몇 여행자들은 걸어서 해상 국경을 성공적으로 건너기도 했다. ❻ 그 땅은 또 다른 흥미로운 점이 있다. ❼ 그곳은 북미에서 가장 높은 디날리산과 미국에서 가장 긴 해안선을 가지고 있다. ❽ 비록 그곳의 크기는 상당히 크고 넓지만, 알래스카는 그 나라에서 가장 적은 인구를 가지고 있다. ❾ 참고로, 그곳의 마을 중 하나인 배로는 미국에서 가장 길고 가장 짧은 낮 시간 기록을 동시에 가지고 있다.

정답인 이유

1 지칭 추론

정답 ②

해설 ⓐ, ⓒ, ⓓ, ⓔ는 모두 알래스카를 의미하지만 ⓑ는 문법적으로 가주어 it으로 아무것도 지칭하지 않는다.

2 내용 일치

정답 ③

해설 ❼에서 알래스카에는 북미에서 가장 높은 산(Denali)이 있다는 내용이 언급되어 있으므로 ③이 글의 내용과 일치한다.

해석 이 글의 내용과 일치하는 것은?

① 알래스카는 일 년 내내 춥다.
② 아무도 알래스카와 러시아 사이의 바다를 걸어서 건너지 않았다.
③ 알래스카에는 북미에서 가장 높은 산이 있다.
④ 알래스카에는 해안선이 없다.
⑤ 알래스카는 미국에서 인구가 가장 많다.

3 서술형

정답

(1) 북미에서 가장 높은 산을 가지고 있다.
(2) 미국에서 가장 긴 해안선을 가지고 있다.
(3) 미국에서 가장 인구가 적다.
(4) 미국에서 가장 길고 가장 짧은 낮시간 기록을 동시에 가진 배로라는 마을이 있다.

해설 ❼~❾에 알래스카가 가진 최고 기록들이 언급되어 있다.

제대로 독해법

어휘 Level Up

1 ⓙ 2 ⓜ 3 ⓞ 4 ⓝ 5 ⓑ 6 ⓐ 7 ⓛ 8 ⓚ 9 ⓕ
10 ⓔ 11 ⓓ 12 ⓒ 13 ⓗ 14 ⓟ 15 ⓖ 16 ⓘ

내신 Level Up

정답 Alaska

해설 Alaska(알래스카)의 다양한 특징을 설명하는 글이다.

구문 Level Up

정답 that he studies well

해설 that절이 주어로 쓰이면 가주어 It을 주어 자리에 두고 that절은 문장 끝에 온다.

▸ pp.40~41

세계에서 가장 깊은 곳, 마리아나 해구

지문 분석

❶ Mariana Trench, located near the Philippines, is the deepest place in the Earth's oceans. ❷ In 2010, American researchers measured ㉠이곳이 얼마나 깊은지.

(마리아나 해구 / deep의 최상급(deep-deeper-deepest))

(C) ❸ They found [that it is 1.6 km deeper than Mount Everest, the highest mountain on Earth]. ❹ This place is also famous for its pressure by the weight of water above.

(명사절(found의 목적어) / 비교급+than: ~보다 더 …한 / 동격 / be famous for: ~으로 유명하다 / 부 위에서)

(A) ❺ For example, if you put a can into Mariana Trench, it will be flat right away by the amazing pressure of water. ❻ Adventurers around the world tried to dive into the ground of this point, but many of them were killed or hurt by the water's pressure.

(접 ~라면(조건) / 예를 들면 / 조건의 부사절에서 현재시제가 미래를 나타냄 / 전 ~에 의해 / 전 세계의 / try+to부정사: ~하려고 노력하다 / 그들 중 많은 사람들이)

(B) ❼ Thanks to recent technology, however, a famous movie director, James Cameron, successfully reached the bottom of this place and recorded the unbelievable view of Mariana Trench.

(~ 덕분에 / 그러나 / 동격 / 동사 1 / 동사 2)

지문 해석

❶ 필리핀 근처에 위치한 마리아나 해구는 지구의 바다에서 가장 깊은 장소이다. ❷ 2010년에 미국 연구자들은 이곳이 얼마나 깊은지 측정했다. ❸ (C) 그들은 이곳이 지구에서 가장 높은 산인 에베레스트 산보다 1.6km 더 깊다는 것을 발견했다. ❹ 이 장소는 또한 위에서 누르는 물의 무게에 의한 압력으로 유명하다. ❺ (A) 예를 들면, 마리아나 해구에 캔을 놓으면, 엄청난 물의 압력(수압)으로 바로 납작해질 것이다. ❻ 전 세계의 모험가들이 이곳 지면으로 뛰어들려고 노력했지만, 그들 중 많은 사람들이 물의 압력(수압)에 의해 죽거나 다쳤다. ❼ (B) 그러나, 최근 기술 덕분에, 유명한 영화감독인 제임스 캐머런이 이 장소의 바닥에 성공적으로 도달해서 마리아나 해구의 믿기 어려울 정도의 장면을 녹화했다.

정답인 이유 

1 내용 일치

정답 ⑤

해설 영화감독 제임스 카메론이 성공적으로 해저면에 도달했다고 했으므로 ⑤는 내용과 일치하지 않는다.

2 순서 파악

정답 ④

해설 얼마나 깊은지 깊이를 측정했다는 주어진 문장 다음에 얼마나 깊은지에 대한 설명이 나오는 (C)가 오고 수압이 강하다는 (C)의 마지막 문장 뒤에 수압이 얼마나 강한지 예시가 나오는 (A), 그리고 많은 모험가들이 목숨을 잃었지만 결국 제임스 카메론이 성공했다는 (B)가 오는 것이 가장 적절하다.

해석 이 글의 순서로 가장 적절한 것은?

3 서술형

정답 **캔을 놓으면 높은 수압 때문에 즉시 납작해질 것이다.**

해설 ❺에서 마리아나 해구에 캔을 놓으면 엄청난 수압으로 바로 납작해질 것이라고 말하고 있다.

제대로 독해법

어휘 Level Up

1 ⓙ 2 ⓜ 3 ⓓ 4 ⓒ 5 ⓛ 6 ⓑ 7 ⓖ 8 ⓕ 9 ⓔ
10 ⓞ 11 ⓐ 12 ⓝ 13 ⓚ 14 ⓘ 15 ⓗ

내신 Level Up

정답 how deep it is

해설 '얼마나 깊은'이라는 뜻의 의문사 how deep을 사용하여 간접의문문을 만든다. 간접의문문은 「의문사+주어+동사」의 어순으로 나타낸다.

구문 Level Up

정답 1. rains 2. practices

해설

1, 2. 조건을 나타내는 부사절에서는 현재시제로 미래를 나타내므로 각각 rains, practices로 고쳐 써야 한다.

어휘 테스트

▸ p.42

A 1 travelers 2 scuba-diving 3 kayaking
4 tropical fish 5 squid 6 measured

B 1 ⓑ 2 ⓐ 3 ⓒ

해석 1 국경 2 해변 3 최근의

ⓐ 바다 근처에 모래나 작은 돌멩이가 있는 지역

ⓑ 한 나라와 다른 나라를 나누는 선

ⓒ 얼마 전에 일어나거나 시작한

Information

Day 07 Reading 01

▸ pp.46~47

슈퍼마켓에 이런 전략이!

지문 분석

❶ Can you easily find milk in supermarkets? ❷ Probably not. ❸ Here lies a marketing strategy. ❹ It is usually placed on the opposite ends from the entrances. ❺ It means [that if you want to buy it, you have to walk passed all of the aisles]. ❻ Then, you may buy items [which you didn't plan to]. ❼ Some big-box retailers change the display of goods so that customers must wander around the store. ❽ Why do you think they do that? ❾ It is the same reason. ❿ They want you to look around the store and pick up some more items [which you didn't plan to buy]. ⓫ The more we wander, the more likely we are to buy items. ⓬ Also, chewing gum and other snacks are set near the counters to encourage customers to pick them up while they are waiting in line to pay.

- Probably: 아마도
- Here lies a marketing strategy: here + 동사 + 주어 → 도치
- It: = Milk
- [that if you want to buy it, you have to walk passed all of the aisles]: 명사절(means의 목적어)
- if: 접 ~라면(조건)
- to buy: to부정사(목적어)
- have to: ~해야 한다
- Then: 그러면
- may buy: ~일지도 모른다
- to: (buy)
- items [which you didn't plan to]: 관계대명사절(목적격)
- big-box retailers: 대형 할인점
- goods: 명 상품
- so that: ~하기 위해서
- Why do you think they do that?: 주절에 think 동사가 쓰인 간접의문문(의문사 + think + 주어 + 동사)
- to look around the store and (to) pick up: 병렬구조
- items: 선행사 / [which you didn't plan to buy]: 관계대명사절(목적격)
- plan to buy: plan + to부정사(목적어)
- The more ~, the more likely: the 비교급 ~, the 비교급 … : ~할수록 더 …한
- be likely to부정사: ~하기 쉽다
- are set: 수동태(be동사 + p.p.) / set-set-set
- to encourage: to부정사(~하기 위해서)
- pick them up: 동사 + 대명사 + 부사 → 어순 주의!
- wait in line: 줄을 서서 기다리다
- to pay: to부정사(~하기 위해서)

지문 해석

❶ 당신은 슈퍼마켓에서 우유를 쉽게 찾을 수 있는가? ❷ 아마 아닐 것이다. ❸ 여기에 마케팅 전략이 있다. ❹ 그것은 보통 출입구에서 정반대 끝에 놓여 있다. ❺ 그것은 당신이 그것을 사길 원하면 모든 통로들을 지나가야 한다는 것을 의미한다. ❻ 그러면 당신은 아마 사려고 계획하지 않았던 것들을 살지 모른다. ❼ 몇몇 대형 할인점들은 고객들이 상점 안을 돌아다니게 하기 위해서 상품 진열을 바꾼다. ❽ 당신은 왜 그들이 그렇게 한다고 생각하는가? ❾ 같은 이유이다. ❿ 그들은 당신이 가게 안을 둘러보고 당신이 사려고 계획하지 않았던 좀 더 많은 상품들을 집어 들기를 바란다. ⓫ 우리는 더 많이 돌아다닐수록 더 많이 물건을 사기 쉽다. ⓬ 또한 껌이나 다른 간식거리들은 고객들이 돈을 지불하려고 줄을 서서 기다리는 동안 그것들을 집어 들도록 권하기 위해서 계산대 근처에 놓인다.

정답인 이유

1 빈칸 추론

정답 ③

해설 문맥상 더 많이 걸을수록 물건을 많이 집게 되어 더 많이 사게 될 것이라는 내용이 오는 것이 자연스러우므로 ③ '물건을 사다'가 적절하다.

해석

① 우유를 찾다 ② 배고파지다 ③ 물건을 사다
④ 사람들을 만나다 ⑤ 적게 돈을 쓰다

2 목적 추론

정답 ⑤

해설 이 글은 우유의 위치 속에 숨겨진 슈퍼마켓의 마케팅 전략을 우리에게 알려주고 있으므로 ⑤ '우리에게 마케팅 전략을 알려주려고'가 목적으로 적절하다.

해석 이 글의 목적으로 가장 적절한 것은?

① 왜 걷는 것이 우리에게 좋은지 설명하려고
② 건강에 좋은 우유 제품을 홍보하려고
③ 농장주들을 위해 우리에게 더 많은 우유를 구매하라고 설득하려고
④ 쓰레기를 줄이기 위해 우리에게 쇼핑을 적게 하라고 장려하려고
⑤ 우리에게 마케팅 전략을 알려주려고

3 서술형

정답 고객들이 물건을 사기 위해 가게 안을 돌아다니면서 계획하지 않았던 물건들을 더 사게 하려고

해석 ❼~❿에서 대형 할인점은 상품 진열을 바꿔 고객들이 가게 안을 돌아다니게 만들어 그들이 사려고 계획하지 않았던 것들까지 사기를 바란다고 설명하고 있다.

제대로 독해법

어휘 Level Up

1 ⓗ 2 ⓘ 3 ⓙ 4 ⓚ 5 ⓜ 6 ⓑ 7 ⓛ 8 ⓖ 9 ⓓ
10 ⓕ 11 ⓒ 12 ⓝ 13 ⓔ 14 ⓐ

내신 Level Up

정답 (1) F (2) T (3) F

해설

(1) 우유는 고객들이 통로를 따라 걷게 하기 위해 출입구의 정반대 끝에 놓인다고 했다.

(3) 껌이나 다른 간식거리들은 고객들이 계산하려고 기다리는 동안 집어 들게 하기 위해 계산대와 가까운 곳에 놓인다고 했다.

구문 Level Up

정답 What do you think he did there?

해설 간접의문문(what he did there)이 동사 think의 목적어이므로 의문사(what)가 문장의 맨 앞에 온다.

▸ pp.48~49

혈액형 이야기

지문 분석

❶ What's your blood type? ❷ Here is the ratio of blood types. ❸ There are four basic blood types: A, B, O, and AB. ❹ The most common is type O. ❺ About 40 to 60% of the world's population has this blood type. ❻ The rarest is type AB. (ⓐ) ❼ However, blood type percentages vary among different countries. (ⓑ) ❽ For example, although type O is the most common in most countries, type A is the most common among Scandinavians and Australians. ❾ (ⓒ Type O is not only the most common, but it is the most generous blood type.) ❿ Do you know why? (ⓓ) ⓫ In an emergency, type O blood can be given to people of any blood type. (ⓔ) ⓬ On the other hand, type AB can receive blood from any blood type.

- blood type: 혈액형
- Here is + 단수명사: 여기에 ~이 있다
- There are + 복수명사: ~들이 있다
- most common: common의 최상급
- About: 약, 대략
- 40 to 60%: 40~60%
- rarest: rare의 최상급
- among: 전 ~ 사이에
- For example: 예를 들어
- although: 접 ~이지만(양보)
- most common: common의 최상급
- Scandinavians: 명 스칸디나비아인들
- Australians: 명 오스트레일리아(호주)인들
- can be given: 조동사가 있는 수동태(조동사+be+p.p.)
- On the other hand: 반면에

지문 해석

❶ 당신의 혈액형은 무엇인가? ❷ 여기 혈액형의 비율이 있다. ❸ 4가지의 기본적인 혈액형이 있다. 즉 A, B, O, 그리고 AB형이다. ❹ 가장 흔한 것은 O형이다. ❺ 대략 세계 인구의 40~60%가 이 혈액형이다. ❻ 가장 드문 것은 AB형이다. ❼ 그러나 혈액형 비율은 각각 다른 나라들 사이에서 서로 다르다. ❽ 예를 들어, O형이 대부분의 나라들에서 가장 흔하지만, 스칸디나비아인들과 오스트레일리아(호주)인들 사이에서는 A형이 가장 흔하다. ❾ O형은 가장 흔할 뿐만 아니라, 가장 관대한 혈액형이다. ❿ 왜 그런지 아는가? ⓫ 응급 상황에서, O형 혈액은 어떤 혈액형의 사람들에게도 수혈될 수 있다. ⓬ 반면에 AB형은 어떤 혈액형으로부터라도 수혈받을 수 있다.

정답인 이유

1 문장 삽입

정답 ③

해설 주어진 문장에서 O형이 가장 흔할 뿐만 아니라, 가장 관대한 혈액형이라고 소개하고 있으므로 그 이유(O형이 가장 관대한 이유)를 설명하는 내용이 시작되는 앞인 ⓒ에 들어가는 것이 문맥상 가장 적절하다.

해석 O형은 가장 흔할 뿐만 아니라, 가장 관대한 혈액형이다.

2 내용 일치

정답 ⑤

해설 AB형은 다른 혈액형의 피에서 수혈을 받을 수 있다는 내용만 언급되었고, ⑤ 'AB형은 병원에서 가장 유용한 혈액형이다.'라는 내용은 언급되지 않았다.

해석 이 글의 내용과 일치하지 않는 것은?

① 혈액형은 4개의 분류로 나뉠 수 있다.
② 가장 덜 흔한 혈액형은 AB형이다.
③ 각각의 나라는 다른 혈액형 비율을 가지고 있다.
④ O형은 어떤 혈액형에게도 수혈될 수 있다.
⑤ AB형은 병원에서 가장 유용한 혈액형이다.

3 서술형

정답 (1) 가장 흔하다. (2) 모든 혈액형에게 수혈될 수 있다.

해설

(1) ❹에 O형이 가장 흔하다는 내용이 나와 있다.
(2) ⓫에 O형이 모든 혈액형에게 수혈될 수 있다는 내용이 나와 있다.

제대로 독해법

어휘 Level Up

1 ⓗ 2 ⓒ 3 ⓑ 4 ⓙ 5 ⓔ 6 ⓚ 7 ⓓ 8 ⓐ 9 ⓘ 10 ⓕ 11 ⓖ

내신 Level Up

정답

(1) 세계에서 가장 드물다.
(2) 모든 혈액형에게 수혈받을 수 있다.

해설 ❻과 ⓬에서 AB형의 특징을 알 수 있다.

구문 Level Up

정답 was a new computer

해설 장소를 나타내는 부사구 in the room을 강조하여 문장의 맨 앞에 쓰면 주어와 동사가 도치된다.

▸ pp.50~51

기억을 잡아 두고 싶나요?

지문 분석

❶ According to (~에 따르면) a new study (명 연구), making a fist can improve your memory. ❷ Here's how: Are you a right-handed person (= you are a right-handed person)? ❸ If so, tighten (명령문(동사원형으로 시작)) your right fist before taking in (전치사+동명사) new information. ❹ Then (그 다음에) tighten (명령문(동사원형으로 시작)) your left fist when (접 ~할 때(시간)) you want to remember (want+to부정사(목적어)) it later. ❺ This strange trick would work (동 효과가 있다) because making a fist (동명사(주어) → 단수 취급) activates the side of the brain (선행사) [that handles memory] (관계대명사절(주격)). ❻ For example (예를 들어), if (접 ~라면(조건)) you are a right-handed person, the left side of the brain is mainly responsible for storing (전치사+동명사) information. ❼ On the other hand (반면에), the right side of the brain is responsible for (~을 맡다, 담당하다) remembering it. ❽ However (하지만), if (접 ~라면(조건)) you are left-handed, ㉠the opposite applies. ❾ Are you willing to make (be willing to부정사: 기꺼이 ~하다) fists while (접 ~ 동안(시간)) (you are) studying for a test or an important speech? ❿ Just remember which (의문사) hand you need to use.

지문 해석

❶ 새로운 연구에 따르면, 주먹을 쥐는 것이 당신의 기억력을 향상시킬 수 있다. ❷ 여기에 그 방법이 있다. 당신은 오른손잡이인가? ❸ 만약 그렇다면 새로운 정보를 받아들이기 전에 당신의 오른쪽 주먹을 꽉 쥐어라. ❹ 그 다음 나중에 그것을 기억하고자 할 때 왼쪽 주먹을 꽉 쥐어라. ❺ 이 이상한 요령은 주먹을 쥐는 것이 기억을 다루는 쪽의 뇌를 활성화시키기 때문에 효과가 있을 것이다. ❻ 예를 들어, 당신이 오른손잡이라면, 좌뇌가 주로 정보 저장을 담당한다. ❼ 반면에 우뇌는 기억하는 것을 담당한다. ❽ 하지만 당신이 왼손잡이라면, 그 반대로 적용된다. ❾ 시험 또는 중요한 발표를 위해 공부하는 동안 주먹을 쥐겠는가? ❿ 어떤 손을 사용해야 할지만 기억해라.

정답인 이유

1 빈칸 추론

정답 ①

해설 주로 쓰는 손의 방향에 유의하여 주먹을 쥐면 정보를 쉽게 기억하고 떠올릴 수 있다는 내용의 글이므로 빈칸에는 ① '주먹을 쥐는 것이 당신의 기억력을 향상시킬 수 있다'가 적절하다.

해석
① 주먹을 쥐는 것이 당신의 기억력을 향상시킬 수 있다
② 당신의 뇌는 감정에 의해 쉽게 속는다
③ 사람들은 항상 양쪽 뇌를 균등하게 사용하기 위해 노력한다
④ 양손을 쓰는 것이 당신이 더 좋은 성적을 받도록 도와준다
⑤ 오른손잡이 사람들이 정보를 더 잘 기억할 수 있다

2 내용 일치

정답 ③

해설 ③ 오른손잡이가 왼손잡이보다 기억을 더 잘한다는 내용은 언급되지 않았다.

해석 이 글의 내용과 일치하지 않는 것은?
① 우리는 기억력을 향상시키기 위해 양손을 사용해야 한다.
② 우리의 뇌는 우리의 손과 연결되어 있다.
③ 오른손잡이 사람들은 왼손잡이 사람들보다 기억을 더 잘한다.
④ 주된 손의 반대 방향의 뇌는 정보를 저장한다.
⑤ 주먹을 쥐는 것이 뇌를 활성화시킬 수 있다.

3 서술형

정답 **우뇌가 정보 저장을 하고, 좌뇌가 그것을 기억하는 것을 담당한다.**

해설 오른손잡이일 경우 좌뇌가 주로 정보 저장을 담당하고, 우뇌는 기억하는 것을 담당하며, 왼손잡이일 경우에 그 반대로 적용된다고 했으므로 우뇌가 정보 저장을 하고, 좌뇌가 기억하는 것을 담당한다는 내용을 의미한다.

제대로 독해법

어휘 Level Up

1 ⓔ 2 ⓝ 3 ⓜ 4 ⓐ 5 ⓑ 6 ⓗ 7 ⓖ 8 ⓞ 9 ⓓ
10 ⓒ 11 ⓛ 12 ⓘ 13 ⓚ 14 ⓕ 15 ⓙ

내신 Level Up

정답 1. (1) right (2) left 2. (1) left (2) right

해석
1. 당신이 오른손잡이라면, 기억을 저장하기 위해 오른쪽 주먹을 쥐고, 기억을 불러오기 위해 왼쪽 주먹을 쥐어라.
2. 당신이 왼손잡이라면, 기억을 저장하기 위해 왼쪽 주먹을 쥐고, 기억을 불러오기 위해 오른쪽 주먹을 쥐어라.

구문 Level Up

정답 while

해설 괄호 뒤에 「주어+동사(you were)」가 이어지므로 접속사 while이 알맞다.

▸ pp.52~53

눈썹이 있는 이유

지문 분석

❶ Look at yourself in the mirror. ❷ Short hairs are lined up on your forehead above your eyes. ❸ ⓐThey are eyebrows. ❹ Everybody has eyebrows above their eyes. ❺ Are you able to move ⓑthem up and down? ❻ Sure you can. ❼ But people don't have eyebrows just to move ⓒthem for fun. ❽ Eyebrows play an important role for people to express ⓓtheir emotions. ❾ Take a good look at your mom's eyebrows. ❿ You can easily know whether she is happy or not. ⓫ But there is a more important reason [why people have eyebrows]. ⓬ ⓔThey keep the eyes dry when sweating or walking around in the rain. ⓭ The arch-shaped eyebrows send the raindrops or sweat on your forehead around to the side of your face.

(yourself: 재귀대명사(재귀 용법) / are lined: 수동태(be동사+p.p.) / Everybody: 항상 단수 취급 → has: 단수동사 / be able to: ~할 수 있다(= can) / up and down: 위아래로 / you can: = can move them up and down / to move: to부정사(~하기 위해서) / play a role: 역할을 하다 / for people: 의미상 주어 / Take a good look at: ~을 잘 살펴보다 / whether ~ or not: ~인지 아닌지 / reason: 선행사, why ~: 관계부사절(이유) / They: = Eyebrows / keep+목적어+목적격보어(형용사) / sweating or walking: 병렬구조 / to: 전 ~로)

지문 해석

❶ 거울 속의 당신을 들여다보라. ❷ 눈 위 이마에 짧은 모발이 선을 이루고 있다. ❸ 그것들은 눈썹이다. ❹ 누구나 눈 위에 눈썹이 있다. ❺ 당신은 그것들을 위아래로 움직일 수 있는가? ❻ 물론 그럴 수 있다. ❼ 그러나 사람들은 눈썹을 재미 삼아 움직이려고 갖고 있는 것이 아니다. ❽ 눈썹은 사람들이 그들의 감정을 표현하는 데 중요한 역할을 한다. ❾ 당신의 어머니의 눈썹을 잘 살펴보라. ❿ 당신은 그녀가 행복한지 아닌지 쉽게 알 수 있다. ⓫ 그러나 사람들에게 눈썹이 있는 더 중요한 이유가 있다. ⓬ 그것들은 땀을 흘리거나 빗속에서 걸을 때 눈이 젖지 않게 해 준다. ⓭ 아치 모양의 눈썹이 이마 위의 빗방울이나 땀을 얼굴의 측면으로 보낸다.

정답인 이유

1 지칭 추론

정답 ④

해설 ⓐ, ⓑ, ⓒ, ⓔ는 '눈썹'을 가리키고, ⓓ는 '사람들'을 가리킨다.

2 제목 추론

정답 ①

해설 눈썹의 역할(눈썹이 있는 이유)에 대해 설명하고 있으므로 ① '눈썹이 우리를 위해 하는 일'이 제목으로 적절하다. ③, ⑤는 글의 내용 중 일부만 다루고 있어서 전체 내용을 포괄하는 제목이 될 수 없다.

해석 이 글의 제목으로 가장 적절한 것은?
① 눈썹이 우리를 위해 하는 일
② 눈썹은 당신을 위험으로부터 보호한다
③ 눈썹은 표정을 짓는다
④ 눈은 어떻게 눈썹과 연결되어 있는가?
⑤ 눈썹은 사람의 감정을 표현한다

3 서술형

정답
(1) 감정을 표현한다.
(2) 땀이나 빗물에 눈이 젖지 않게 해 준다.

해설
(1) ❽에 눈썹이 감정을 표현하는 역할을 한다는 내용이 나와 있다.
(2) ⓬에 눈썹이 땀이나 빗물에 눈이 젖지 않게 해준다는 내용이 나와 있다.

제대로 독해법

어휘 Level Up

1ⓑ 2ⓓ 3ⓛ 4ⓐ 5ⓘ 6ⓚ 7ⓗ 8ⓜ 9ⓒ 10ⓙ 11ⓔ 12ⓖ 13ⓕ

내신 Level Up

정답 ⑤

해설 마지막 문장에서 눈썹이 빗방울이나 땀을 얼굴의 측면으로 흘려보낸다고 했으므로 ⑤는 내용과 일치하지 않는다.

구문 Level Up

정답 **강조 용법**

해설 생략된 주어(You)를 강조하는 강조 용법으로, yourselves는 생략이 가능하다.

어휘 테스트

▸ p.54

A 1 entrances 2 aisles 3 percentages 4 fist 5 mirror 6 lined up

B 1ⓑ 2ⓐ 3ⓒ

해석 1 돌아다니다 2 활성화시키다 3 표현하다
ⓐ 무언가를 시작하게 하다
ⓑ 어떤 명확한 목적이나 방향 없이 천천히 주위를 걸어 다니다
ⓒ 감정이나 의견, 사실을 보여 주다

Food · Health

▸ pp.58~59

다이어트를 돕는 메뉴판

지문 분석

❶ New research shows [that if restaurant menus show how much exercise is needed to burn off calories, it would be good for helping customers lose weight].
(명사절(shows의 목적어) / 간접의문문(의문사+주어+동사) / to부정사(~하기 위해서) / ~에 좋다 / help+목적어+(to) 동사원형: (목적어)가 ~하는 것을 돕다)

(B) ❷ For example, telling customers [how many minutes they must walk to burn off the calories] is helpful.
(간접의문문(의문사+주어+동사~) / 예를 들어 / 동명사(주어) → 단수 취급 / to부정사(~하기 위해서) / 단수동사)

(C) ❸ When someone orders a hamburger, ㉠the information is more effective than only showing [how many calories the hamburger has].
(접 ~할 때(시간) / 비교급+than: ~보다 더 …한 / 간접의문문(의문사+주어+동사))

(A) ❹ Researchers say [people do not really understand calories].
((say의 목적어절을 이끄는 접속사 that 생략))

❺ Instead, they understand [that they have to walk for 30 minutes]. ❻ This new style of menu really helps people make healthier choices. ❼ One researcher said: "We are sure that it is possible [to encourage people to order food with fewer calories by Ⓐthe new style of menu]." ❽ Indeed, the people [who had the menus with the exercise information] tended to order food with the fewest calories.
(부 대신에 / = people / 명사절(understand의 목적어) / help+목적어+(to) 동사원형: (목적어)가 ~하는 것을 돕다 / healthy의 비교급 / 진주어(to부정사구) / ~을 확신하다 / 가주어 / encourage+목적어+to부정사: ~가 …하도록 권장하다 / few의 비교급 / 부 실제로 / 주어 / 관계대명사절(주격) / 동사 / few의 최상급)

지문 해석

❶ 새로운 연구는 레스토랑 메뉴가 칼로리를 태우기 위해 얼마나 많은 운동이 필요한지를 보여 준다면, 고객들이 살을 빼는 것을 도와주는 데 좋을 것이라고 설명한다. (B) ❷ 예를 들어, 고객들에게 칼로리를 태우기 위해 몇 분이나 걸어야 하는지를 알려주는 것은 도움이 된다. (C) ❸ 누군가가 햄버거 한 개를 주문할 때, 그 정보는 단지 그 햄버거가 가진 칼로리만을 보여 주는 것보다 더 효과적이다. (A) ❹ 연구원들은 사람들이 실제로 칼로리를 이해하지 못한다고 말한다. ❺ 대신에 그들은 30분간 걸어야 한다는 것은 이해한다. ❻ 이런 새로운 스타일의 메뉴는 정말 사람들로 하여금 더 건강한 선택을 하도록 돕는다. ❼ 한 연구원은 "우리는 그 새로운 스타일의 메뉴를 통해서 사람들이 더 낮은 칼로리의 음식을 주문하도록 권장하는 것이 가능하다고 확신합니다."라고 말했다. ❽ 실제로, 운동 정보가 있는 메뉴를 받은 사람들은 가장 낮은 칼로리의 음식을 주문하는 경향을 보였다.

정답인 이유

1 밑줄 추론

정답 ⑤

해설 이 글은 섭취한 칼로리를 소비하는 데 필요한 운동 시간을 보여 주는 메뉴의 효과에 대해 말하고 있다.

2 순서 파악

정답 ③

해설 (B) 섭취한 칼로리를 소비하기 위한 운동량을 알려주는 것이 도움이 됨 → (C) 햄버거의 칼로리보다 칼로리를 소비하는 데 필요한 운동량에 대한 정보가 더 유용함 → (A) 사람들은 칼로리를 이해하지 못함 → 대신에 사람들은 얼마나 운동해야 하는지를 더 잘 이해함

해석 이 글의 순서로 가장 적절한 것은?

3 서술형

정답 (1) menu (2) exercise (3) order (4) fewer

해석 새로운 연구는 레스토랑의 메뉴가 열량을 태우기 위해 얼마만큼의 운동이 필요한지를 보여 주면 사람들이 더 낮은 칼로리의 음식을 주문하는 경향이 있다고 말한다.

제대로 독해법

어휘 Level Up

1ⓗ 2ⓛ 3ⓐ 4ⓚ 5ⓖ 6ⓘ 7ⓕ 8ⓔ 9ⓑ 10ⓓ 11ⓙ 12ⓜ 13ⓒ

내신 Level Up

정답 How many minutes must they walk to burn off the calories?

해설 the information은 칼로리를 태우기 위해 몇 분이나 걸어야 하는지를 알려주는 것을 가리킨다.

구문 Level Up

정답

1. Blaming others is
2. Getting along with classmates is

해설

1, 2. 동명사 주어는 단수 취급하므로 단수동사 is를 쓴다.

▸ pp.60~61

팝콘이 펑펑!

지문 분석

❶ Popcorn is one of the most popular snacks in a movie theater. (one of the 최상급+복수명사: 가장 ~한 것들 중의 하나) ❷ Many people enjoy eating popcorn during a movie. (enjoy+동명사(목적어) / 전 ~ 동안) ❸ By the way, when we eat popcorn, we find some kernels of corn [that don't pop]. (그런데 / 접 ~할 때(시간) / 선행사 / 관계대명사절(주격)) ❹ Why do you think this happens? (think가 쓰인 간접의문문(의문사+think+주어+동사)) ❺ (ⓐ) Popcorn is a small kernel before it pops. (접 ~ 전에(시간)) ❻ The kernel has a thin but very tight coat. ❼ (ⓑ) Inside of the coat, there is a little water. (부 내부에 / there is+단수명사: ~이 있다) ❽ (ⓒ When the kernel is heated up, the water inside the kernel turns to steam.) ❾ The steam breaks through the kernel's coat. (~을 뚫고 나오다) ❿ Pop! ⓫ (ⓓ) The steam is released and popcorn is made. (수동태(be동사+p.p.)) ⓬ (ⓔ) But some kernels don't have enough water inside and that's why they don't pop. (그것이 ~한 이유다 / = kernels)

지문 해석

❶ 팝콘은 영화관에서 가장 인기 있는 간식들 중 하나이다. ❷ 많은 사람들이 영화를 보는 동안 팝콘 먹는 것을 즐긴다. ❸ 그런데 우리는 팝콘을 먹을 때 터지지 않은 옥수수 알갱이들을 보게 된다. ❹ 이런 일이 왜 생긴다고 생각하는가? ❺ 팝콘은 (볶아서) 터지기 전에는 작은 알갱이다. ❻ 그 알갱이는 얇지만 아주 단단한 껍질을 가지고 있다. ❼ 그 껍질의 안쪽에는 수분이 조금 있다. ❽ 알갱이가 뜨거워지게 되면 알갱이 속 수분이 증기로 바뀐다. ❾ 증기가 알갱이의 껍질을 뚫고 나온다. ❿ 펑! ⓫ 증기가 뿜어져 나오고 팝콘이 만들어진다. ⓬ 그러나 어떤 알갱이들은 내부에 수분이 충분하지 않은데 그것이 그것들이 터지지 않는 이유다.

정답인 이유

1 내용 일치

정답 ⑤

해설 ⓬에서 내부에 수분이 충분하지 않은 알갱이들이 터지지 않는다고 했으므로 ⑤는 내용과 일치하지 않는다.

2 문장 삽입

정답 ③

해설 주어진 문장은 (옥수수) 알갱이가 뜨거워지게 되면, 알갱이 속 수분이 증기로 바뀐다는 내용으로, 이 증기가 하는 역할이 ⓒ 이후에 나오므로 주어진 문장은 ⓒ에 들어가는 것이 적절하다.

해석 주어진 문장이 들어가기에 가장 적절한 곳은?
알갱이가 뜨거워지게 되면 알갱이 속 수분이 증기로 바뀐다.

3 서술형

정답 don't pop

해설 이 글은 옥수수 알갱이들이 터지지 않은 채 남아 있는 이유에 대해 설명한 글이다.

해석 옥수수 알갱이들이 터지지 않은 이유

제대로 독해법

어휘 Level Up

1 ⓕ 2 ⓛ 3 ⓑ 4 ⓙ 5 ⓜ 6 ⓚ 7 ⓞ 8 ⓗ 9 ⓘ
10 ⓔ 11 ⓒ 12 ⓓ 13 ⓝ 14 ⓐ 15 ⓖ

내신 Level Up

정답 water

해설 ⓬에서 옥수수 알갱이의 내부에 수분이 충분하지 않아서 터지지 않는다고 설명하고 있다.

해석 왜 어떤 옥수수 알갱이들은 터지지 않는가? → 그것들은 내부에 수분을 충분히 가지고 있지 않기 때문이다.

구문 Level Up

정답 1. holidays 2. most

해설

1. 「one of the 최상급+복수명사」 형태로 복수명사 holidays가 알맞다.
2. famous의 최상급 most famous가 와야 한다.

▸ pp.62~63

건강한 그린 몬스터, 스무디

지문 분석

❶ There is nothing in this smoothie except super-healthy fruits and vegetables! (전 제외하고는 / 정말 건강한) ❷ Don't let the green color scare you — it tastes fruity and delicious. (let+목적어+동사원형(scare): (목적어)가 ~하게 하다 / it = this smoothie)

❸ Ingredients: 1/2 cup of mango, 1/2 cup of pineapple, 1 banana, spinach, 1 kale leaf, 2/3 cup of water

❹ Directions: Add mango, pineapple, and banana to the blender. (add A to B: A에 B를 더하다)

(C) ❺ Add in one kale leaf and spinach. ❻ Spinach adds protein and it will keep you full! ❼ It changes the color, but not the taste, I promise! (it = spinach / keep+목적어+목적격보어(형용사): ~을 …하게 유지시키다)

(B) ❽ Add in 2/3 cup of water, but you may need to add more or less, depending on [how strong your blender is]. ❾ Are you ready to blend them all? (depending on: ~에 따라 / 간접의문문(의문사+주어+동사) / be ready to: ~할 준비가 되다)

(A) ❿ Blend and enjoy! ⓫ You'll have enough for two smoothies, and this one will last for up to two days in the fridge. (one = smoothie / up to: ~까지)

지문 해석

❶ 이 스무디에는 정말 건강한 과일과 채소를 제외하고는 아무것도 들어 있지 않다! ❷ 초록색에 겁먹지 마라. 그것은 과일 맛이 나고 맛있다.
❸ 재료: 망고 1/2컵, 파인애플 1/2컵, 바나나 한 개, 시금치, 케일 잎 한 장, 물 2/3컵
❹ 방법: 믹서기에 망고와 파인애플, 그리고 바나나를 넣어라. (C) ❺ 케일 잎 한 장과 시금치를 넣어라. ❻ 시금치가 단백질을 첨가하고 당신을 배부르게 유지시켜줄 것이다! ❼ 그것(시금치)은 (음료의) 색깔을 바꾸지만 맛은 바꾸지 않는다. 약속한다! (B) ❽ 물 2/3컵을 넣어라. 하지만 여러분의 믹서기가 얼마나 튼튼한지에 따라 더 또는 덜 넣어야 할 것이다. ❾ 그것들 모두를 갈 준비가 되었는가? (A) ❿ 갈아서 즐겨라! ⓫ 당신은 두 잔의 스무디를 충분히 만들 것이고 이것은 냉장고에서 이틀까지는 유지될 것이다.

정답인 이유

1 순서 파악

정답 ⑤

해설 믹서기에 망고, 파인애플, 바나나를 넣음 → (C) 케일과 시금치를 넣음 → (B) 믹서기에 맞게 물을 부음 → (A) 넣은 재료를 모두 갈아 마심

2 목적 추론

정답 ②

해설 처음에 그린 스무디(green smoothie)가 건강에 좋다는 소개를 하고 중반부터 재료(ingredients)와 방법(directions)에 관해 설명하며 그린 스무디를 만드는 방법을 소개하고 있다. 따라서 ② '그린 스무디 만드는 방법을 알려주려고'가 글의 목적으로 적절하다.

해석 이 글의 목적으로 가장 적절한 것은?
① 유기농 음식을 먹으라고 추천하려고
② 그린 스무디 만드는 방법을 알려주려고
③ 왜 그린 스무디가 건강에 좋은지 설명하려고
④ 녹색 채소가 먹기 쉽다는 것을 보여주려고
⑤ 정크 푸드(몸에 안 좋은 음식)를 먹지 못하게 하려고

3 서술형

정답
(1) 단백질을 첨가한다(더해 준다).
(2) 색을 (녹색으로) 변화시킨다.

해설 ❻~❼에서 시금치가 단백질을 첨가하고 스무디의 색을 (녹색으로) 바꾼다는 것을 알 수 있다.

제대로 독해법

어휘 Level Up

1 ⓜ 2 ⓝ 3 ⓑ 4 ⓔ 5 ⓒ 6 ⓛ 7 ⓕ 8 ⓟ 9 ⓘ
10 ⓞ 11 ⓗ 12 ⓓ 13 ⓖ 14 ⓚ 15 ⓐ 16 ⓙ

내신 Level Up

정답 ③
해설 스무디를 만드는 재료와 방법에 대한 글이다.
해석 ① 비평 ② 일기 ③ 요리법 ④ 사용 설명서 ⑤ 처방전

구문 Level Up

정답 1. wash 2. play
해설
1. 「사역동사(had)+목적어(me)+동사원형(wash)」의 형태로 쓴다.
2. 「사역동사(let)+목적어(me)+동사원형(play)」의 형태로 쓴다.

▸ pp.64~65

잠의 중요성

지문 분석

❶ Why is sleep important for children? ❷ ㉠A new study answers the question. ❸ In the study, the research team either added or subtracted one hour of sleep for healthy children. ❹ The goal was to see [if small changes in the amount of sleep could affect a child's behavior].

(either A or B: A이거나 B / 명사절(see의 목적어) / to부정사(보어) / 접 ~인지 아닌지)

❺ Before the survey began, students were asked to sleep the same amount of hours as they usually ㉡would. ❻ Their teachers were asked to score the children on emotional reactions. ❼ After five nights of the changed sleep pattern of the children, the teachers were asked to take the survey again. ❽ The result? ❾ Compared with their original scores, those [who slept one hour less] had worse behavior scores and those [who were allowed to sleep an hour more] had better behavior scores.

(접 ~ 전에(시간) / 5형식 문장의 수동태(→ 2형식이 됨) / the same ~ as...: …와 똑같은 ~ / = would sleep / 5형식 문장의 수동태(→ 2형식이 됨) / 전 ~ 후에(시간) / 과거분사가 명사 앞에서 수식 / 5형식 문장의 수동태(→ 2형식이 됨) / ~와 비교하여 / 주어1 / 관계대명사절(주격) / 동사1 / bad의 비교급(bad-worse-worst) / 주어2 / 관계대명사절(주격) / 동사2 / good의 비교급(good-better-best))

지문 해석

❶ 아이들에게 잠이 왜 중요할까? ❷ 새로운 연구가 그 질문에 대한 답을 준다. ❸ 그 연구에서, 연구팀은 건강한 아이들의 수면 시간을 1시간 더하거나 줄였다. ❹ 목적은 수면 양의 작은 변화가 아이의 행동에 영향을 미칠 수 있는지를 보는 것이었다. ❺ 설문 조사가 시작되기 전에, 학생들이 보통 자던 것과 같은 시간만큼 자게 했다. ❻ 그들의 선생님들에게는 아이들 감정 반응을 평가하라고 했다. ❼ 아이들의 수면 패턴을 바꾸고 난 5일 후에, 선생님들에게 그 설문 조사를 다시 하도록 했다. ❽ 그 결과는 (어땠을까)? ❾ 그들의 원래 점수와 비교하여 1시간을 덜 잔 아이들은 더 나쁜 행동 점수를 받았고 1시간을 더 자도록 허락 받은 아이들은 더 좋은 행동 점수를 받았다.

정답인 이유

1 주제 추론

정답 ⑤

해설 수면 양의 변화에 따른 아이들의 행동 변화에 대한 설문 조사에서, 잠을 덜 잔 아이들은 나쁜 행동 점수를 받고 잠을 더 잔 아이들은 좋은 행동 점수를 받았다는 내용이므로 ⑤가 글의 주제로 가장 적절하다.

2 요약문 완성

정답 ③

해설 수면 양의 변화에 따른 아이들의 행동 변화를 관찰하는 연구를 실행하고 그 결과 잠이 부족할 때 아이들의 행동이 나빠진다는 것을 증명하고 있으므로 ③이 가장 적절하다.

해석 이 글의 내용에 따라 빈칸 (A), (B)에 들어갈 말로 가장 적절한 것은?

며칠 동안의 잠의 부족은 아이들의 행동을 결국 더 나쁘게 할 수 있다.

① 잠 - 자세 ② 학업 - 이해력 ③ 잠 - 행동
④ 학업 - 감정 ⑤ 운동 - 성장

3 서술형

정답

(1) 수면 양의 작은 변화가 아이들의 행동에 미치는 영향을 관찰하기 위해

(2) (실험 전) 아이들 감정 반응을 평가함
(실험 중) 5일 동안 아이들의 수면 패턴을 바꿈
(실험 후) 아이들의 달라진 행동을 설문 조사함

해설

(1) ❹에서 연구의 목적을 알 수 있다.

(2) ❺~❾에 실험 과정이 자세히 묘사되고 있다.

제대로 독해법

어휘 Level Up

1 ⓓ 2 ⓜ 3 ⓗ 4 ⓔ 5 ⓐ 6 ⓚ 7 ⓝ 8 ⓘ 9 ⓙ 10 ⓛ 11 ⓑ 12 ⓕ 13 ⓒ 14 ⓖ

내신 Level Up

정답 sleep

해설 반복되는 어구는 생략할 수 있다. '설문 조사가 시작되기 전에, 학생들은 보통 자던 만큼 자도록 했다.'라는 내용으로 앞에 나온 sleep이 생략되었다는 것을 알 수 있다.

구문 Level Up

정답 was allowed to play

해설 5형식 문장의 수동태로, 동사 allowed를 수동태(be동사+p.p.) 형태로 바꾸고, 목적격보어 to play를 주격보어로 그대로 쓴다.

어휘 테스트

▸ p.66

A 1 calories 2 popcorn 3 corn 4 spinach 5 blender 6 survey

B 1 ⓑ 2 ⓒ 3 ⓐ

해석 1 운동 2 증기 3 약속하다

ⓐ 무언가를 틀림없이 할 거라고 누군가에게 말하다
ⓑ 몸을 강하고 건강하게 만들기 위해 하는 신체적 행동
ⓒ 물이 끓을 때 배출되는 뜨거운 기체

Animals · Nature

▸ pp.70~71

갑자기 땅이 꺼지네!

지문 분석

❶ You would think [that a man could be safe in his house]. (명사절(think의 목적어)) ❷ Unfortunately for Jeffrey Bush, [(A) who / which lived in Florida], that was not true. (선행사 / 관계대명사절(주격)) ❸ On a night [when Mr. Bush was in bed], his bedroom just disappeared. (선행사 / 관계부사절(시간)) ❹ How? ❺ It (= Bedroom) fell into a huge sinkhole under his home. ❻ Sinkholes are common in Florida. ❼ Why are these things called (수동태(be동사+p.p.)) "sinkholes" or "snake holes?" ❽ Sometimes (때때로), if (접 ~라면) the rocks (주어) under the Earth's surface (전치사구) (B) is / are made up of (동사 / ~로 구성되다) some kinds of stone and the underground water keeps rising (keep+-ing: 계속 ~하다), it completely damages the rocks. ❾ This causes a sinkhole (which is) also known as a snake hole. (과거분사구의 수식 / known as: ~로 알려진) ❿ Sinkholes can be (동사 1) small or really huge in size and can be formed (동사 2 / 조동사가 있는 수동태(조동사+be+p.p.)) gradually or suddenly. ⓫ They (= Sinkholes) are (C) finding / found (수동태(be동사+p.p.)) throughout the world (전 세계에서) and even (~도[조차]) in Korea.

지문 해석

❶ 여러분은 사람은 집에서 안전할 것이라고 생각할 것이다. ❷ 플로리다 주에 살고 있던 제프리 부시에게는 불행하게도 그렇지 않았다. ❸ 부시 씨가 잠자리에 들었던 어느 날 밤에 그의 침실이 그냥 사라져버렸다. ❹ 어떻게 된 걸까? ❺ 그것이 그의 집 아래에 있던 거대한 싱크홀로 빠졌다. ❻ 플로리다 주에서 싱크홀은 흔하다. ❼ 왜 이런 것들이 '싱크홀'이나 '스네이크홀'이라고 불릴까? ❽ 때때로 지표면 아래 바위들이 어떤 종류의 암석들로 이루어지고 땅속 물이 계속 올라오면 그것은 그 바위들을 완전히 손상시킨다. ❾ 이것이 스네이크홀이라고도 알려진 싱크홀을 야기한다. ❿ 싱크홀은 크기가 작을 수도 있고 아주 클 수도 있으며 서서히 형성될 수도 있고 갑자기 형성될 수도 있다. ⓫ 그것들은 전 세계에서 발견되고 심지어 한국에서도 발견된다.

정답인 이유

1 어법성 판단

정답 ③

해설

(A) 관계대명사가 꾸며주는 선행사가 Jeffrey Bush라는 사람이므로 who가 적절하다.

(B) 주어가 (명사의) 복수형(the rocks)이므로 복수동사 are가 적절하다.

(C) They가 싱크홀이고 전 세계에서 발견되는 것이(수동의 의미) 문맥상 적절하므로 found가 와서 수동태가 되어야 한다.

2 내용 일치

정답 ③

해설 ③ 홍수가 싱크홀을 야기한다는 내용은 언급되지 않았다.

해석 싱크홀에 관한 글의 내용과 일치하지 않는 것은?

① 그것들은 플로리다에서 자주 발견된다.
② 그것들은 '스네이크홀'이라고도 불린다.
③ 그것들은 때때로 홍수로 인해 일어난다.
④ 그것들은 갑자기 생길 수 있다.
⑤ 그것들은 전 세계에서 발견된다.

3 서술형

정답 물이 계속 올라오면서 지표면 아래 바위들이 완전히 손상되어 싱크홀을 야기시킨다.

해설 ❽, ❾에서 물이 계속 올라오면서 지표면 아래 바위들이 손상되어 싱크홀이 만들어진다고 설명하고 있다.

제대로 독해법

어휘 Level Up

1ⓗ 2ⓙ 3ⓕ 4ⓖ 5ⓐ 6ⓓ 7ⓔ 8ⓜ 9ⓚ 10ⓛ 11ⓑ 12ⓝ 13ⓘ 14ⓒ

내신 Level Up

정답 ③

해설 ❸~❺에서 Bush 씨 집의 침실이 싱크홀로 빠진 것을 알 수 있다.

구문 Level Up

정답 when

해설 선행사(The day)가 시간을 나타내고 관계사 뒤에 완전한 문장(I first met him)이 오므로 관계부사 when으로 고쳐 써야 한다.

▸ pp.72~73

개미가 주는 교훈

지문 분석

❶ Ant colonies generally have at least(적어도) one or more queens and the rest(나머지) are (to) worker ants(일개미들). ❷ The worker ants' job is to get food, and take care of the queen.(병렬구조(to부정사구)) ❸ They collect the food, but they are not able to(= can't) digest it(= the food). ❹ So they give the food to young ants.(3형식 → they give young ants the food (4형식)) ❺ Then the young ants digest the food and give it back(동사+대명사+부사 → 어순 주의!) to worker ants. ❻ Isn't it really interesting? ❼ They are cooperative creatures. ❽ They have a nice support system. ❾ When(접 ~할 때(시간)) a worker ant finds a good food source, he leaves a particular smell trail so that the others can find the source.(so that+주어+can: 주어가 ~할 수 있도록(목적)) ❿ Their unity has made(현재완료시제(has/have+p.p.)) them survive(made의 목적격보어(동사원형)) on our planet for a long time, about 100 million years(동격). ⓫ We can learn a lesson or two from them.

지문 해석

❶ 개미 집단에는 보통 적어도 하나 혹은 그 이상의 여왕개미가 있고 나머지는 일개미들이다. ❷ 일개미들의 일은 식량을 구하고 여왕개미를 돌보는 것이다. ❸ 그들은 식량을 모아 오지만 그것을 소화시키지는 못한다. ❹ 그래서 그들은 그 식량을 어린 개미들에게 준다. ❺ 그러면 어린 개미들이 그 식량을 소화시켜서 일개미들에게 다시 준다. ❻ 정말 흥미롭지 않은가? ❼ 그들은 협동하는 생명체들이다. ❽ 그들에게는 훌륭한 지원 시스템이 있다. ❾ 어떤 일개미가 좋은 식량원을 찾아내면 그는 다른 일개미들이 그것을 찾을 수 있도록 특별한 냄새 흔적을 남긴다. ❿ 그들의 협동이 그들을 약 1억 년 정도의 긴 시간 동안 지구에서 살아남게 했다. ⓫ 우리는 그들에게서 한두 가지의 교훈을 배울 수 있다.

정답인 이유

1 내용 일치

정답 ④

해설 ❺에서 어린 개미들이 음식물을 소화시켜 일개미들에게 다시 준다는 내용은 있지만 ④ '어린 개미는 여왕개미에게 식량을 공급한다.'는 내용은 언급되지 않았다.

2 주제 추론

정답 ③

해설 글 전반적으로 예시를 제시하면서 개미가 협동을 통해 오랫동안 살아남을 수 있었다는 것을 주장하고 있으므로 ③ '협동이 개미를 오랫동안 살아남게 하다'가 글의 주제로 적절하다.

해석 이 글의 주제로 가장 적절한 것은?

① 대부분의 개미가 땅 아래에 사는 이유
② 개미: 세계에서 가장 강한 동물
③ 협동이 개미를 오랫동안 살아남게 하다
④ 개미로부터의 교훈: 근면이 완벽을 만든다
⑤ 개미는 지구상의 어떤 동물보다 더 오래 생존할 수 있다

3 서술형

정답 다른 일개미들에게 식량원의 위치를 알리려고

해설 ❾에서 좋은 식량원을 찾아내면 다른 일개미들이 그것을 찾을 수 있도록 특별한 냄새 흔적을 남긴다고 했다.

제대로 독해법

어휘 Level Up

1 ⓔ 2 ⓘ 3 ⓓ 4 ⓖ 5 ⓝ 6 ⓙ 7 ⓗ 8 ⓒ 9 ⓚ
10 ⓞ 11 ⓜ 12 ⓕ 13 ⓛ 14 ⓐ 15 ⓑ

내신 Level Up

정답 ⑤

해설 이 글은 서로 돕고 지원하는 시스템을 가진 개미에 대한 내용이므로 ⑤ '백지장도 맞들면 낫다.'가 이 글의 내용과 가장 잘 어울린다.

해석

① 벽에도 귀가 있다. ② 돌다리도 두드려보고 건너라.
③ 연습이 완벽을 만든다. ④ 피는 물보다 진하다.
⑤ 백지장도 맞들면 낫다.

구문 Level Up

정답 gave his book to me

해설 간접목적어 me 앞에 전치사 to를 붙여 직접목적어 his book 뒤에 쓴다.

▸ pp.74~75

보디가드 곤충

지문 분석

❶ Plants must stand their ground even when plants are ⓐattacked by bad insects. ❷ There's simply no running away. ❸ But interestingly, some varieties of corn and cotton can call out for help and the helpers frequently come to help in ⓑresponse. ❹ Bodyguard insects eat the bad insects [that attack the plants]. ❺ So if the plants have enemies, then bodyguards are ⓒenemies of the plants' enemies. ❻ Of course, plants don't scream out to those helpers. ❼ Instead, they ⓓdetect chemicals, which easily turn from liquids into gases and travel on the winds. ❽ The smell of the gas makes insects or other helpers called "bodyguards" come to the plants. ❾ Scientists discovered this ⓔsecret signaling in 1988. ❿ This finding has helped farmers increase the amount of crops now.

stand one's ground: 공격에 견디다 / 접 ~할 때(시간) / 수동태(be동사+p.p.) / ~이 없다 / 주어 / 도움을 구하다 / to부정사(~하기 위해서) / 선행사 / 관계대명사절(주격) / 접 ~라면(조건) / 소리 지르다 / 대신에 / (×) → produce(○) / 계속적 용법의 관계대명사 / turn from A into B: A에서 B로 변하다 / 주어 / 동사 / 과거분사구의 명사 수식 / makes의 목적격보어(동사원형) / help+목적어+(to) 동사원형 / 현재완료시제(has/have+p.p.) / has helped의 목적격보어

지문 해석

❶ 식물은 해충에게 공격을 받을 때에도 공격에 견뎌야 한다. ❷ 그야말로 도망이라는 게 없다. ❸ 그런데 흥미롭게도, 몇몇 종의 옥수수와 목화는 도움을 구할 수 있고, 도우미들이 자주 (그에 대한) 응답으로 도와주러 온다. ❹ 보디가드 곤충들은 그 식물을 공격하는 해충들을 잡아먹는다. ❺ 그래서 식물에게 적이 있으면 보디가드들이 그 식물의 적에게 적이 되는 것이다. ❻ 물론, 식물은 그 도우미들에게 소리 지르지 못한다. ❼ 대신, 그들은 화학 물질을 발견하는데(→ 생산하는데) 그것은 쉽게 액체에서 기체로 변하여 바람을 타고 이동한다. ❽ 그 기체의 냄새가 곤충들이나 '보디가드'라고 불리는 다른 도우미들이 그 식물에게 오게 만든다. ❾ 과학자들은 이 비밀스런 신호 교환을 1988년에 발견했다. ❿ 이 발견이 지금은 농부들이 농작물의 양을 증가시키는 데 도움이 되고 있다.

정답인 이유

1 어휘 파악

정답 ④

해설 문맥상 ⓓ는 '식물이 보디가드 곤충을 부르기 위해 화학 물질을 생산한다'라는 내용이 더 자연스러우므로 detect(발견하다)가 아니라 produce(생산하다)가 오는 것이 적절하다.

2 요지 추론

정답 ③

해설 이 글은 식물이 해충으로부터 공격을 받을 때 화학 물질을 이용해 보디가드 곤충을 불러와 스스로를 보호할 수 있다는 내용이므로 ③ '어떤 곤충들은 식물이 공격을 받을 때 그들을 구할 수 있다'가 글의 요지로 적절하다.

해석 이 글의 요지로 가장 적절한 것은?

① 어떤 식물들은 화학 물질로 곤충들을 보호할 수 있다.
② 어떤 곤충들은 그들의 자원을 두고 싸울 수 있다.
③ 어떤 곤충들은 식물이 공격을 받을 때 그들을 구할 수 있다.
④ 각각 다른 곤충들이 생존하기 위해 서로 도울 수 있다.
⑤ 어떤 식물들은 그들의 환경으로부터 독립되어 있다.

3 서술형

정답 식물을 공격하는 해충을 잡아먹는다.

해설 ❹에서 보디가드 곤충이 식물을 공격하는 해충을 잡아먹는다는 것을 알 수 있다.

제대로 독해법

어휘 Level Up

1 ⓐ 2 ⓑ 3 ⓗ 4 ⓞ 5 ⓓ 6 ⓜ 7 ⓛ 8 ⓝ 9 ⓟ 10 ⓘ 11 ⓚ 12 ⓕ 13 ⓖ 14 ⓙ 15 ⓔ 16 ⓒ

내신 Level Up

정답 (1) chemicals (2) gases (3) smell

해설 식물은 화학 물질을 생산하고 그 물질이 기체로 변하여 바람을 타고 이동하면 그 기체의 냄새가 보디가드 곤충들이 식물들에게 오게 만든다고 하였다.

구문 Level Up

정답 which

해설 관계대명사 that은 계속적 용법으로 쓸 수 없고 이 문장은 앞문장 전체가 선행사인 문장이다.

▸ pp.76~77

세계에서 가장 큰 나무, 제너럴셔먼

지문 분석

❶ In a deep forest in California, U.S.A, there is the largest tree in the world, General Sherman. ❷ Other trees may be taller, but not bigger than this. ❸ General Sherman is 31 meters around, and goes up to 84 meters in the sky. ❹ That is, its size is similar to a 25-story apartment building. ❺ In fact, General Sherman is the biggest living creature on the earth. ❻ ⓐIt has been standing in the woods for thousands of years. ❼ To our surprise, ⓑit is still growing. ❽ Many scientists are studying how this tree takes energy from the ground. ❾ Their explanation is [that forest fires helped ⓒit grow]. ❿ ⓓIt burnt other trees down around General Sherman, but ⓔit survived due to its thick skin. ⓫ As a result, the tree could get nutrition from the ashes and ㉠grow bigger and bigger.

(largest: large의 최상급 / largest tree in the world, General Sherman: 동격 / may be: ~일지도 모른다 / bigger than: 비교급+than: ~보다 더 …한 / is: 동사 1 / around: 부 둘레가 ~인 / goes: 동사 2 / up to: ~까지 / That is: 즉 / is similar to: ~와 비슷하다 / 25-story: 25층 / In fact: 사실상 / biggest: big의 최상급 / living: 살아 있는(명사 앞에만 쓰임) / on the earth: 지구상에서 / thousands of: 수천의 / To our surprise: 놀랍게도 / is still growing: 현재진행시제(be동사+-ing) / how this tree takes energy from the ground: 간접의문문(의문사+주어+동사) / that ~ grow: 명사절(보어) / helped ⓒit grow: help+목적어+(to) 동사원형: (목적어)가 ~하는 것을 돕다 / around: 전 ~ 주변에 / due to: ~ 때문에 / its: = General Sherman's / As a result: 결과적으로 / and (the tree could) / grow bigger and bigger: 비교급+and+비교급: 점점 더 ~한[하게])

지문 해석

❶ 미국 캘리포니아 깊숙한 숲속에, 세계에서 가장 큰 나무인 제너럴셔먼이 있다. ❷ 다른 나무들이 키가 더 클 수도 있지만, 이것보다 더 (부피가) 크진 않다. ❸ 제너럴셔먼은 둘레가 31미터이고, 하늘로 84미터까지 뻗어나가 있다. ❹ 즉, 이것의 크기는 25층 아파트 건물 높이와 비슷하다. ❺ 사실상, 제너럴셔먼은 지구상 가장 큰 살아 있는 생명체이다. ❻ 그것은 수천 년 동안 숲속에 서 있다. ❼ 놀랍게도, 이것은 여전히 자라고 있다. ❽ 많은 과학자들은 어떻게 이 나무가 땅으로부터 에너지를 얻는지 연구하고 있다. ❾ 그들의 설명은 산불이 그것(제너럴셔먼)이 자라는 걸 도왔다는 것이다. ❿ 그것(산불)이 제너럴셔먼 주변의 다른 나무들을 태워 넘어뜨렸지만, 그것(제너럴셔먼)은 두꺼운 껍질 때문에 살아남았다. ⓫ 결과적으로, 그 나무는 재로부터 영양분을 얻고 점점 더 크게 자랄 수 있었다.

정답인 이유

1 지칭 추론

정답 ④

해설 ⓐ, ⓑ, ⓒ, ⓔ는 큰 나무 General Sherman을 지칭하지만, ⓓ는 산불을 지칭한다.

2 내용 일치

정답 ②

해설 ❷에서 키가 가장 큰 것이 아니라 부피가 크다는 내용을 확인할 수 있다. 따라서 ② '다른 어떤 나무보다 키가 크다'는 글의 내용과 일치하지 않는다.

해석 General Sherman에 관한 글의 내용과 일치하지 않는 것은?
① 미국 캘리포니아에 위치해 있다.
② 다른 어떤 나무보다 키가 크다.
③ 땅으로부터 에너지를 얻는다.
④ 여전히 살아 있다.
⑤ 두꺼운 껍질을 가지고 있다.

3 서술형

정답 산불로 다른 나무들이 불에 타서 재가 되었을 때 두꺼운 껍질로 살아남아 재에서 영양분을 충분히 얻을 수 있었다.

해설 마지막 부분에서 제너럴셔먼이 영양분을 얻을 수 있었던 이유를 설명하고 있다.

제대로 독해법

어휘 Level Up

1ⓑ 2ⓙ 3ⓓ 4ⓔ 5ⓐ 6ⓚ 7ⓗ 8ⓙ 9ⓜ 10ⓛ 11ⓘ 12ⓕ 13ⓞ 14ⓖ 15ⓒ 16ⓝ

내신 Level Up

정답 the tree could

해석 등위 접속사 and로 연결되어 반복되는 주어와 조동사(the tree could)가 생략되었다.

구문 Level Up

정답 1. are, doing 2. am, taking

해설 1, 2. 현재진행시제는 「be동사+-ing」의 형태로 나타낸다.

어휘 테스트

▸ p.78

A 1 cooperative 2 cotton 3 chemicals 4 secret 5 forest fires 6 burnt

B 1ⓐ 2ⓒ 3ⓑ

해석 1 거대한 2 모으다 3 설명
ⓐ 크기나 양이 매우 큰
ⓑ 무언가를 이해하기 쉽게 또는 명확하게 하기 위해 제공하는 세부사항 또는 이유들
ⓒ (여러 가지 것들을) 함께 가져오거나 모으다

Culture · Psychology

Day 13 Reading 01

▸ pp.82~83

블랙 프라이데이

지문 분석

❶ Most Americans celebrate Thanksgiving. ❷ They share a meal, watch football, and enjoy talking to each other. ❸ (ⓐ) For some people, shopping is a big part of their Thanksgiving tradition as well. ❹ For many years, the day after Thanksgiving has been the busiest shopping day of the year. ❺ Many stores have sales on that day. ❻ (ⓑ) Many people go to the sales ㉠so that they can save money. ❼ (ⓒ) The shoppers are looking for bargains. ❽ This busy shopping day is called "Black Friday." ❾ (ⓓ) Recently, researchers have noticed another busy shopping day. ❿ This day is a little different. ⓫ It is the busiest day of the year for online shopping. ⓬ (ⓔ The Monday after Thanksgiving has become known as "Cyber Monday.") ⓭ On this day, more and more shoppers buy their holiday gifts online.

A, B, and C 병렬구조 / 동명사(목적어) / 역시(= too) / 전 ~동안 / 그다음 날 / 현재완료(have/has+p.p.) / so that 주어+can/could: ~하기 위해서 / look for: ~을 찾다 / 수동태(be동사+p.p.) / 현재완료 / 또 다른 하나의(+단수명사) / 약간 / busy의 최상급 / = Cyber Monday / 비교급 and 비교급: 점점 더 ~한[하게]

지문 해석

❶ 대부분의 미국인들은 추수감사절을 기념한다. ❷ 그들은 음식을 함께 나누고, (미식)축구를 보고, 서로 이야기하는 것을 즐긴다. ❸ 어떤 사람들에게는 쇼핑 역시 추수감사절 전통의 큰 부분이다. ❹ 수년 동안, 추수감사절 그다음 날은 일 년 중 가장 바쁘게 쇼핑하는 날이었다. ❺ 많은 가게들이 그날 세일을 한다. ❻ 많은 사람들이 돈을 절약하기 위해 세일하는 곳에 간다. ❼ 쇼핑객들은 싼 물건을 찾고 있다. ❽ 이 바쁜 쇼핑의 날은 '블랙 프라이데이'라고 불린다. ❾ 최근에 연구원들은 또 다른 바쁜 쇼핑의 날을 주목한다. ❿ 이 날은 약간 다르다. ⓫ 그것은 온라인 쇼핑을 위한 일 년 중 가장 바쁜 날이다. ⓬ 추수감사절 다음의 월요일은 '사이버 먼데이'라고 알려져 있다. ⓭ 이 날 점점 더 많은 쇼핑객들이 온라인에서 명절 선물을 구입한다.

정답인 이유

1 문장 삽입

정답 ⑤

해설 ⓔ의 앞 문장에 '일 년 중 가장 바쁜 온라인 쇼핑의 날'이라는 설명이 있고, ⓔ 바로 뒤에 있는 this day가 무엇인지 언급되어야 하므로 '사이버 먼데이'에 대해 언급한 주어진 문장은 ⓔ에 들어가는 것이 적절하다.

해석 추수감사절 다음의 월요일은 '사이버 먼데이'라고 알려져 있다.

2 내용 일치

정답 ④

해설 사이버 먼데이는 소비자들이 온라인 쇼핑몰을 통해 상품을 구입하는 날이므로 ④ '사이버 먼데이는 백화점의 가장 바쁜 날을 나타낸다.'는 글의 내용과 일치하지 않는다.

해석 이 글의 내용과 일치하지 않는 것은?

① 추수감사절에 미국인들은 다른 사람들과 음식을 나눈다.
② 블랙 프라이데이는 추수감사절과 관련이 있다.
③ 블랙 프라이데이는 한 해 중 쇼핑을 위한 최고의 기회이다.
④ 사이버 먼데이는 백화점의 가장 바쁜 날을 나타낸다.
⑤ 사이버 먼데이에 온라인 구매자들이 증가하고 있다.

3 서술형

정답 to save money

해설 밑줄 친 so that they can save money는 '돈을 절약하기 위해서'라는 의미로 to부정사의 목적을 나타내는 부사적 용법으로 바꿔 쓸 수 있다.

제대로 독해법

어휘 Level Up

1 ⓐ 2 ⓑ 3 ⓜ 4 ⓔ 5 ⓖ 6 ⓚ 7 ⓘ 8 ⓕ 9 ⓓ 10 ⓝ 11 ⓛ 12 ⓗ 13 ⓒ 14 ⓙ

내신 Level Up

정답 (1) day (2) Monday

해설 Black Friday는 추수감사절 다음 날이고, Cyber Monday는 추수감사절 다음의 월요일이다.

구문 Level Up

정답 so that

해설 so that은 '~하기 위해서'의 의미를 가지고 「so that + 주어 + can/could」 형태로 쓴다. so as는 to부정사와 함께 쓰이므로 답이 될 수 없다.

▸ pp.84~85

모자를 벗어주시겠습니까?

지문 분석

❶ I teach science at a university in the United States.

❷ Students call me Professor Singh. (call+목적어+목적격보어(명사) → 5형식) ❸ One day, my wife and I went out for dinner. (저녁 먹으러 나갔다) ❹ When (접 ~할 때(시간)) we got to (= reached) the restaurant, the manager asked me to take off my hat. (ask+목적어+to부정사: (목적어)가 ~하게 (요청)하다) ❺ I told him [(told의 목적어절을 이끄는 접속사 that 생략) mine was not just a hat and I could not ㉠remove it]. ❻ However, the manager didn't listen to me. ❼ He insisted [that I (should) remove my hat or he wouldn't serve us food]. (insist+that+주어+(should)+동사원형 ~) ❽ My wife and I left the restaurant right away. (즉시)

❾ In the United States, men take off (~을 벗다(↔ put on: ~을 입다)) their hats in restaurants. ❿ If (접 ~라면(조건)) they don't, it is considered rude. ⓫ The manager wanted his customers to use good manners (want+목적어+to부정사: (목적어)가 ~하기를 원하다) in his restaurant. ⓬ However, (하지만) Professor Singh is a Sikh from India. ⓭ Sikh men wear a turban at all times. (항상, 언제나) ⓮ For a Sikh, a turban is a symbol of pride.

지문 해석

❶ 나는 미국에 있는 대학에서 과학을 가르친다. ❷ 학생들은 나를 Singh(싱) 교수라고 부른다. ❸ 어느 날 아내와 나는 저녁을 먹으러 나갔다. ❹ 우리가 식당에 도착했을 때 지배인이 나에게 모자를 벗어달라고 청했다. ❺ 나는 그에게 내 것은 그냥 모자가 아니므로 벗을 수 없다고 말했다. ❻ 하지만 그 지배인은 내 말을 듣지 않았다. ❼ 그는 내게 모자를 벗지 않으면 음식을 내주지 않겠다고 주장했다. ❽ 아내와 나는 즉시 식당을 나와 버렸다.

❾ 미국에서 남자들은 식당에서 모자를 벗는다. ❿ 만약 그렇게 하지 않으면 무례하다고 여겨진다. ⓫ 그 지배인은 그의 손님이 식당에서 좋은 예의를 갖춰 주기를 원했다. ⓬ 하지만 싱 교수는 인도 출신의 시크교도이다. ⓭ 남자 시크교도들은 항상 터번을 쓴다. ⓮ 시크교도에게 터번은 자존심의 상징이다.

정답인 이유

1 내용 일치

정답 ⑤

해설 Singh 교수는 대학에서 과학을 가르친다. 그는 식당에서 모자를 벗지 않아 식당 지배인과 다툼이 일어났고 식사를 하지 않고 아내와 함께 바로 식당을 떠났기 때문에 ①, ②, ③, ④는 글의 내용과 일치하지 않는다. ⓬에서 인도 출신임을 알 수 있으므로 ⑤가 글의 내용과 일치한다.

2 주제 추론

정답 ⑤

해설 모자를 벗어야 하는 문화와 벗지 않는 문화의 차이에서 생겨난 일이므로 ⑤ '나라 간의 문화적 차이'가 주제로 가장 적절하다.

해석 이 글의 주제로 가장 적절한 것은?

① 미국의 식사 예절 ② 인도에서 모자의 인기
③ 지배인의 오해 ④ 미국에 있는 다양한 종류의 식당들
⑤ 나라 간의 문화적 차이

3 서술형

정답 (1) The (restaurant) manager (2) Professor Singh

해설

(1) 식당에서 모자를 벗지 않는 것을 무례하게 여기는 것은 식당 매니저이다.

(2) 모자를 벗는 것이 본인에게 큰 부끄러움이라고 여기는 것은 Singh 교수이다.

해석

(1) "식당에서 모자를 쓰고 있는 것은 다른 손님들을 불편하게 할 수 있다."

(2) "모자를 벗는 것은 나에게 큰 부끄러움이다."

제대로 독해법

어휘 Level Up

1 ⓔ 2 ⓓ 3 ⓞ 4 ⓑ 5 ⓖ 6 ⓝ 7 ⓐ 8 ⓚ 9 ⓕ 10 ⓘ 11 ⓛ 12 ⓙ 13 ⓒ 14 ⓗ 15 ⓜ

내신 Level Up

정답 take off

해설 remove와 take off는 '(옷·모자 등을) 벗다'를 의미한다.

구문 Level Up

정답 1. have 2. take

해설

1, 2. 제안을 나타내는 동사 suggested 다음의 that절에서 should가 생략되어 있으므로 각각 동사원형 have, take가 와야 한다.

▸ pp.86~87

시험 전 금기 사항

지문 분석

❶ Superstitions can reduce anxiety in a number of situations. ❷ Some people believe [that if a certain action is performed, some tragedy will occur]. ❸ ⓐ Since Korean students are very concerned about test results, there are some superstitions for tests. ❹ For example, Korean students do not eat seaweed soup before the test. ❺ ⓑ Seaweed is slippery, so they think [their test scores might slide down]. ❻ Also, they don't cut their nails or get their hair cut before their test either. ❼ ⓒ Strong nails and hair tell how healthy you are. ❽ ⓓ They believe [the knowledge will go out of their brains as their hair or nails get cut from their bodies]. ❾ Although they know [the superstitions don't have any direct effect], they continue to follow them. ❿ ⓔ The reason is [that it helps them focus on their tests with a more positive mind].

a number of: 많은(= many)
that if a certain ~: 명사절(believe의 목적어)
is performed: 조건절에서는 현재시제로 미래를 나타냄
Since: 접 ~ 때문에(이유)
are very concerned about: be concerned about: ~에 대해 걱정하다
there are some superstitions: there are + 복수명사: ~들이 있다
For example: 예를 들어
seaweed soup: 미역국
their test: (think의 목적어절을 이끄는 접속사 that 생략)
Also: 부 또한
cut: 동사 1
get: 동사 2
Strong nails and hair: 주어 / tell: 동사 / how healthy you are: 간접의문문(의문사 + 주어 + 동사)
the knowledge: (believe의 목적어절을 이끄는 접속사 that 생략)
go out of: ~에서 없어지다
as: 접 ~듯이, 처럼
Although: 접 ~이지만(양보)
the superstitions: (know의 목적어절을 이끄는 접속사 that 생략)
follow: = following / them: = the superstitions
that it helps ~: 명사절(보어)
helps them focus: help + 목적어 + (to) 동사원형: (목적어)가 …하는 것을 돕다

지문 해석

❶ 미신은 많은 상황에서 불안감을 줄일 수 있다. ❷ 어떤 사람들은 만약 어떤 특정한 행동이 행해지면, 어떤 비극이 발생할 것이라고 믿는다. ❸ 한국 학생들은 시험 결과에 대해 매우 걱정하기 때문에, 시험에 대한 몇 가지 미신들이 있다. ❹ 예를 들어, 한국 학생들은 시험 전에 미역국을 먹지 않는다. ❺ 미역이 미끄러워서 그들은 시험 성적이 미끄러져 떨어질 것이라고 생각한다. ❻ 또한 그들은 시험 전에 손톱을 깎거나, 머리를 자르지도 않는다. ❼ (튼튼한 손톱과 모발은 당신이 얼마나 건강한지 알려준다.) ❽ 그들은 머리카락이나 손톱이 신체에서 잘려나가듯이 지식이 그들의 머리에서 없어질 것이라고 믿는다. ❾ 그들은 미신이 직접적인 영향을 주지 않는다는 것을 알지만 그들은 계속해서 그것들을 따른다. ❿ 그 이유는 그것이 그들로 하여금 더 긍정적인 마음을 가지고 시험에 집중하도록 돕기 때문이다.

정답인 이유

1 무관한 문장

정답 ③

해설 이 글은 한국 학생들의 시험에 관련된 미신에 관한 내용이다. ⓒ '튼튼한 손톱과 모발은 당신이 얼마나 건강한지 알려준다.'는 글 전체 내용과 관계가 없다.

2 요약문 완성

정답 ④

해설 한국 학생들은 시험 결과에 관련된 미신들 때문에 시험 전에 하지 않는 행동들이 있다는 내용의 글이다.

해석 이 글의 내용에 따라 빈칸 (A), (B)에 들어갈 말로 가장 적절한 것은?

한국 학생들은 미신 때문에 시험 전에 어떤 행동들을 하지 않는다.

① 조사 - 미신 ② 행동 - 지식 ③ 조사 - 비극
④ 행동 - 미신 ⑤ 수다 - 지식

3 서술형

정답

(1) 시험 전에 (성적이 미끄러져 떨어질 것이라고 생각해서) 미역국을 먹지 않는다.

(2) 시험 전에 (지식이 빠져나간다고 생각해서) 머리나 손톱, 발톱을 깎지 않는다.

해설 ❹ For example 이후부터 한국 학생들이 시험에 관해 가지고 있는 미신의 예를 소개하고 있다.

제대로 독해법

어휘 Level Up

1 ⓗ 2 ⓞ 3 ⓙ 4 ⓛ 5 ⓡ 6 ⓢ 7 ⓚ 8 ⓘ 9 ⓑ
10 ⓒ 11 ⓕ 12 ⓖ 13 ⓜ 14 ⓟ 15 ⓠ 16 ⓝ 17 ⓓ 18 ⓐ
19 ⓔ

내신 Level Up

정답 (1) down (2) slippery (3) test

해설 한국 학생들은 미끄러운 미역 때문에 그들의 성적이 떨어질 것이라고 생각해 시험 전에 미역국을 먹지 않는다고 하였다.

구문 Level Up

정답 continues to read

해설 continue는 동명사(reading)와 to부정사(to read)를 둘 다 목적어로 쓸 수 있다.

▸ pp.88~89

슬픈 음악은 심리 치료사

지문 분석

(suggests의 목적어절을 이끄는 접속사 that 생략)

❶ New research suggests [listening to sad music can help overcome the sadness of an ended relationship]. (listening to sad music: 동명사(주어); overcome = to overcome) ❷ This is against our common sense [that cheerful music is the best when (we are) feeling the blues]. (This: 앞 문장 전체를 의미; that ~: common sense를 설명해 주는 동격절(접속사 that); when: 접 ~할 때(시간); the blues: 우울함) ❸ It might explain [why people began singing the blues in painful and tough times]. (why ~: 간접의문문(의문사+주어+동사)) ❹ Stephen Palmer, a researcher at the University of California, Berkeley, said, "Emotional experiences of art products are important to our happiness." ❺ When people experience serious emotional problems, they look for a way to replace their sadness. (When: 접 ~할 때(시간); look for: ~을 찾다; to replace: to부정사(a way 수식)) ❻ When people are in negative moods, they choose ㉠similar moods from sad music or dramas. (When: 접 ~할 때(시간))

❼ Even when pleasant songs are available, they want to experience the similar feeling from music. (Even when: ~할 때도[조차]; want to experience: want+to부정사(목적어)) ❽ In a similar way, sad movies and books provide comfort to them as well. (sad movies and books: 주어; provide: 동사; as well: ~도, 역시(= too))

지문 해석

❶ 새로운 연구는 슬픈 음악을 듣는 것이 끝난 관계의 슬픔을 극복하도록 도울 수 있다고 시사한다. ❷ 이것은 우울함을 느낄 때 즐거운 음악이 가장 좋다는 상식에 반대되는 것이다. ❸ 그것이 왜 사람들이 고통스럽고 힘든 시대에 블루스를 부르기 시작했는지 설명할 수 있을 것이다. ❹ 버클리에 있는 캘리포니아 대학 소속 연구원인 스티븐 파머는 "예술 작품의 감정적인 경험이 우리의 행복에 중요합니다."라고 말했다. ❺ 사람들이 심각한 감정적 문제를 겪을 때, 그들은 그들의 슬픔을 대체할 방법을 찾는다. ❻ 사람들이 부정적인 감정을 느낄 때 그들은 슬픈 음악이나 드라마에서 비슷한 감정을 선택한다. ❼ 즐거운 노래를 들을 수 있을 때조차, 그들은 음악에서 비슷한 감정을 경험하길 원한다. ❽ 비슷한 방식으로, 슬픈 영화와 책도 그들에게 위안을 제공한다.

정답인 이유

1 내용 일치

정답 ⑤

해설 ❽에서 슬픈 영화와 책도 위안을 제공한다고 했으므로 ⑤는 글의 내용과 일치하지 않는다.

2 빈칸 추론

정답 ③

해설 슬픈 음악이 아픈 마음을 달래준다는 중심 내용에 비추어 볼 때 블루스라는 장르가 시작된 시기는 ③ '고통스럽고 힘든' 시기였음을 유추할 수 있다.

해석 빈칸에 들어갈 말로 가장 적절한 것은?

① 행복하고 기쁜 ② 흥분되고 신이 난

③ 고통스럽고 힘든 ④ 지루하고 재미없는

⑤ 현대적이고 새로운

3 서술형

정답 sadness

해설 문맥상 밑줄 친 similar moods는 사람들이 느끼는 부정적인 감정(슬픈 감정)을 의미한다. 본문에서 슬픈 감정을 한 단어로 표현한 것은 sadness(슬픔)이다.

제대로 독해법

어휘 Level Up

1 ⓛ 2 ⓞ 3 ⓖ 4 ⓙ 5 ⓔ 6 ⓟ 7 ⓒ 8 ⓓ 9 ⓠ 10 ⓚ 11 ⓗ 12 ⓘ 13 ⓑ 14 ⓕ 15 ⓝ 16 ⓜ 17 ⓐ

내신 Level Up

정답 sad dramas, tearful movies

해설 글의 내용에 따르면 우울할 때는 슬픈 드라마, 눈물이 나는 영화가 도움이 된다.

해석 즐거운 노래, 슬픈 드라마, 눈물이 나는 영화, 재미있는 소설

구문 Level Up

정답 that

해설 news(추상명사)와 뒤에 나오는 that절은 동격 관계이다.

어휘 테스트

▸ p.90

A 1 shopping 2 busiest 3 university 4 serve 5 India 6 nails

B 1 ⓑ 2 ⓐ 3 ⓒ

해석 1 기념하다 2 미신 3 구할[이용할] 수 있는

ⓐ 인간의 이성이나 과학적 지식에 근거하지 않은 믿음

ⓑ 어떤 특별하거나 즐거운 일을 함으로써 어떤 사건이나 때가 중요하다는 것을 보여주다

ⓒ 사거나 이용할 수 있는

Chapter 8 Science · Technology

Day 15 Reading 01

▸ pp.94~95

캡슐 하나로 식사가 가능할까?

지문 분석

❶ A meal in a tiny pill(주어) is not(동사) realistic. ❷ However, many scientists tried to make it(try+to부정사: ~하려고 노력하다). ❸ Actually, concerns for lack of food(~에 대한 염려) during(전 ~ 동안) the Cold War always(항상(빈도부사 위치 주의! 일반동사 앞)) pushed people ㉠뭔가 말도 안 되는 것을 발명하도록. ❹ American scientists needed to make(need+to부정사(목적어)) a simple food to eat(to부정사(a simple food 수식)) in case of emergency. ❺ They(= Scientists) created(동사1) TV dinners and became(동사2) very confident to make(to부정사(~하기에/~하는 데)) "a meal pill." ❻ At that time(그 당시에), the U.S. president even(부 조차) promised [that (A)people would put those meal pills in every pocket](명사절(promised의 목적어)). ❼ The trouble, however, is [that it is just impossible](명사절(보어)). ❽ After a long period of the research, scientists announced [that pills are not enough for meals](명사절(announced의 목적어)) because(접 ~ 때문에(이유)) they do not fill and satisfy our stomach physically. ❾ Today, we may take pills for vitamins and minerals, but we don't eat them as dinner.

지문 해석

❶ 작은 알약에 든 식사는 현실적이지 않다. ❷ 그러나 많은 과학자들이 그것을 만들려고 노력했다. ❸ 사실, 냉전시대 동안 식량 부족에 대한 염려가 항상 사람들을 뭔가 말도 안 되는 것을 발명하도록 압박했다. ❹ 미국 과학자들은 비상사태에 대비해 먹을 수 있는 간단한 식량을 만들 필요가 있었다. ❺ 그들은 TV 디너를 만들었고 '식사 (대용) 알약'을 만드는 데 매우 자신감이 생겼다. ❻ 그 당시 미국 대통령조차 사람들이 이러한 식사 (대용) 알약을 모든 호주머니에 넣을 것이라고 약속했다. ❼ 그러나 문제는 이것이 그냥 불가능하다는 것이다. ❽ 오랜 기간의 연구 뒤에, 과학자들은 알약이 물리적으로 우리의 배(위장)를 채우지 못하고 만족시키지 못하기 때문에 알약은 식사로 충분하지 않다는 것을 발표했다. ❾ 오늘날, 우리는 비타민과 무기질 섭취를 위해 알약을 먹지만, 저녁 식사로 그것들을 먹지 않는다.

정답인 이유

1 밑줄 추론

정답 ⑤

해설 밑줄 친 내용 '사람들이 이러한 식사 (대용) 알약을 모든 호주머니에 넣을 것이다'는 ⑤ '식사 알약이 모든 사람들에게 보급될 것이다.'를 의미한다.

해석

① 사람들은 식사 알약 외에 어떤 음식도 먹지 않을 것이다.
② 식사 알약은 사람들의 생명을 구할 것이다.
③ 식사 알약은 훨씬 더 작아질 것이다.
④ 사람들은 싼 가격에 식사 알약을 살 것이다.
⑤ 식사 알약이 모든 사람들에게 보급될 것이다.

2 빈칸 추론

정답 ④

해설 빈칸에는 비타민과 무기질 섭취를 위해 알약을 먹지만, (알약으로) 식사는 하기 힘들다는 내용이 오는 게 적절하다. 따라서 ④ '우리는 저녁 식사로 그것들을 먹지 않는다'가 빈칸에 가장 적절하다.

해석 빈칸에 들어갈 말로 가장 적절한 것은?

① 그것들은 위험하다
② 우리는 식사 알약을 여전히 연구하고 있다
③ 그것들은 우리를 배부르게 한다
④ 우리는 저녁 식사로 그것들을 먹지 않는다
⑤ 우리는 그것들을 싼 가격에 살 수 없다

3 서술형

정답 **식사 (대용) 알약은 물리적으로 우리 배(위장)를 채우지 못하고 만족시키지 못하기 때문이다.**

해설 ❽에서 meal pills가 식사를 대체할 수 없는 이유를 설명하고 있다.

제대로 독해법

어휘 Level Up

1 ⓙ 2 ⓓ 3 ⓘ 4 ⓛ 5 ⓕ 6 ⓗ 7 ⓝ 8 ⓐ 9 ⓚ 10 ⓖ 11 ⓔ 12 ⓞ 13 ⓑ 14 ⓜ 15 ⓒ

내신 Level Up

정답 to invent something crazy

해설 -thing으로 끝나는 대명사는 형용사가 뒤에서 수식하므로 something crazy로 써야 한다.

구문 Level Up

정답 1. often wash 2. is sometimes late

해설

1. often은 '종종, 자주'라는 의미의 빈도부사로 일반동사(wash) 앞에 쓴다.
2. sometimes는 '가끔'이라는 의미의 빈도부사로 be동사(is) 뒤에 쓴다.

▸ pp.96~97

비밀 편지 쓰기

지문 분석

❶ Making ink [that can't be seen] ⓐis lots of fun. ❷ You can act as if you are a secret agent as you keep all your secret codes and messages ⓑhidden from others. ❸ You only need some household objects such as cups and bowls and a little lemon juice.

(동명사(주어) / 관계대명사절(주격) / 단수동사 / 마치 ~인 것처럼 / 접 ~하면서 / keep + 목적어 + 목적격보어(hidden) → 5형식 / ~와 같은)

❹ 1. Drop some lemon juice into the bowl and add a few ⓒdrops of water.

(명령문(동사원형으로 시작) / (a) few + 셀 수 있는 복수명사)

❺ 2. Mix the water and lemon juice with the spoon.

(mix A and B: A와 B를 섞다 / 전 ~을 가지고, ~로(수단))

❻ 3. Dip a brush in the mixture.

❼ 4. Write a message onto the white paper with the brush.

❽ 5. Wait for the juice to dry so that it becomes ⓓcompletely unseen.

(의미상 주어 / ~하도록(목적))

❾ All done. ❿ When you are ready to read your secret message or ⓔshows it to someone else, heat the paper by holding it close to a light bulb. ⓫ Then the hidden message will turn brown.

(접 ~할 때(시간) / 병렬구조 / (×) → (to) show (○) / by + -ing: ~함으로써 / 전구)

지문 해석

❶ 보이지 않는 잉크를 만드는 것은 아주 재미있다. ❷ 당신은 다른 사람들에게 비밀 암호나 메시지를 숨기면서 마치 첩보원인 것처럼 행동할 수 있다. ❸ 컵과 그릇 같은 주방용품과 약간의 레몬주스만 있으면 된다.

❹ 1. 약간의 레몬주스를 그릇에 떨어뜨리고 물을 몇 방울 넣어라.

❺ 2. 물과 레몬주스를 숟가락으로 섞어라.

❻ 3. 그 혼합액에 붓을 담궈 적셔라.

❼ 4. 그 붓으로 흰 종이 위에 메시지를 적어라.

❽ 5. 그것이 완전히 보이지 않도록 주스가 마르는 것을 기다려라.

❾ 다 끝났다. ❿ 당신이 비밀 메시지를 읽을 준비가 되거나 그것을 다른 누군가에게 보여줄 준비가 될 때 그것을 전구 가까이에 잡고서 종이를 가열해라. ⓫ 그러면 숨겨진 메시지가 갈색으로 변할 것이다.

정답인 이유

1 어법성 판단

정답 ⑤

해설 ⓔ to read와 병렬구조이므로 shows가 아니라 (to) show가 와야 한다.

ⓐ 동명사 주어(making)는 단수 취급하므로 단수동사 is가 적절하다.

ⓑ 「keep + 목적어 + 목적격보어」의 형태로 hidden은 '숨겨진'이라는 의미이다.

ⓒ a few가 항상 복수명사와 결합하는 수량형용사이므로 drops가 적절하다.

ⓓ unseen이라는 형용사를 꾸며주는 부사 completely가 적절하다.

2 목적 추론

정답 ①

해설 이 글은 보이지 않는 잉크를 소개하고 그 잉크로 메시지를 쓰고 읽는 방법을 알려주는 글이다. 따라서 ① '비밀 메시지 쪽지를 만드는 방법을 가르쳐 주려고'가 글의 목적으로 가장 적절하다.

해석 이 글의 목적으로 가장 적절한 것은?

① 비밀 메시지 쪽지를 만드는 방법을 가르쳐 주려고

② 레몬주스를 정기적으로 마시라고 권장하려고

③ 손으로 글씨를 더 잘 쓰게 하려고

④ 그림을 더 잘 그릴 수 있도록 도우려고

⑤ 종이 위에 잉크로 쓴 글씨를 지우는 방법을 설명하려고

3 서술형

정답 레몬주스, 그릇(컵), 물, 숟가락, 붓, 종이

해설 비밀 쪽지를 만드는 방법을 설명한 과정을 따라서 재료들을 찾을 수 있다.

제대로 독해법

어휘 Level Up

1 ⓛ 2 ⓘ 3 ⓙ 4 ⓒ 5 ⓐ 6 ⓔ 7 ⓓ 8 ⓕ 9 ⓗ
10 ⓞ 11 ⓚ 12 ⓜ 13 ⓝ 14 ⓖ 15 ⓑ

내신 Level Up

정답 ①, ⑤

해설 마지막 두 문장의 내용으로 보아 열을 가하면 레몬주스로 쓴 부분이 갈색으로 변한다는 것을 알 수 있다. 따라서 종이를 다림질하거나 전구 가까이에 대어 종이에 열을 가한 범균과 영준이가 메시지를 볼 수 있다.

구문 Level Up

정답 1. a few 2. few

해설

1. things가 복수명사이므로 a few가 알맞다.
2. friends가 복수명사이므로 few가 알맞다.

▸ pp.98~99

왜 여름엔 덥고, 겨울엔 추울까?

지문 분석

❶ In summer, we wear shorts because of the heat. (because of: ~ 때문에 / because of + 명사(구)) ❷ But in winter, we wear a coat because of the cold. ❸ Why is it hot in summer and cold in winter? (it: 비인칭 주어(날씨)) ❹ Many people think [that it is hot because the Earth is closer to the Sun in summer and it is cold because the Earth is farther from the Sun in winter]. (because: 접 ~ 때문에(이유) / because + 절; that절: 명사절(think의 목적어); closer: close의 비교급; because: 접 ~ 때문에(이유); farther: far의 비교급(far-farther-farthest)) ❺ However, the answer lies in the angle of the sunray. (However: 그러나) ❻ In summer, the sunrays hit the Earth at a ㉠sharp angle. (at a sharp angle: 가파른 각도로) ❼ This is because the Earth's axis is tilted. (This is because: 이것은 ~ 때문이다; is tilted: 수동태(be동사 + p.p.)) ❽ ⓐ The light does not spread out very much. (spread out: 퍼지다) ❾ ⓑ So, the Sun shines more strongly on certain places. (more strongly: strongly의 비교급) ❿ ⓒ But in winter, the Sun shines on the Earth at a gentle angle. (at a gentle angle: 완만한 각도로) ⓫ ⓓ The sunray to the Earth gets weaker if the Sun goes farther from it. (gets weaker: get + 비교급: 점점 더 ~해지다; it = the Earth) ⓬ ⓔ The light spreads out more and it reduces the amount of energy [that hits on certain places]. (it = the light; energy: 선행사; that절: 관계대명사절(주격))

지문 해석

❶ 여름에 우리는 더위 때문에 반바지를 입는다. ❷ 그러나 겨울에는 추위 때문에 외투를 입는다. ❸ 왜 여름에는 덥고 겨울에는 추운 걸까? ❹ 많은 사람들이 여름에는 지구가 태양에 더 가까이 있어서 덥고 겨울에는 지구가 태양으로부터 더 멀리 있기 때문에 춥다고 생각한다. ❺ 그러나 정답은 태양 광선의 각도에 있다. ❻ 여름에는 태양 광선이 지구에 가파른 각도로 내리쬔다. ❼ 이것은 지축이 기울어져 있기 때문이다. ❽ 빛이 많이 퍼지지 않는 것이다. ❾ 그래서 태양이 특정 지역에 더 강하게 비친다. ❿ 그러나 겨울에는 태양이 지구를 완만한 각도로 비춘다. ⓫ (태양이 지구에서 멀어지면 지구로 오는 태양 광선은 더 약해진다.) ⓬ 빛이 더 넓게 퍼지고 그것이 특정 지역에 내리쬐는 에너지의 양을 줄인다.

정답인 이유

1 무관한 문장

정답 ④

해설 글의 앞부분에 겨울에 지구가 태양으로부터 멀리 있기 때문에 추운 것이 아니라 태양 광선의 각도 때문이라고 했으므로 ⓓ '태양이 지구에서 멀어지면 지구로 오는 태양 광선은 더 약해진다.'는 글의 전체 흐름과 관련이 없다.

2 빈칸 추론

정답 ⑤

해설 빈칸 뒤에 '태양 광선이 들어오는 각도에 따라 지구의 온도가 달라진다.'는 설명이 오므로 빈칸에는 ⑤ '태양 광선의 각도'가 가장 적절하다.

해석 빈칸에 들어갈 말로 가장 적절한 것은?

① 지구와 태양의 거리
② 태양에서 나오는 빛의 종류
③ 하늘 위 대기의 양
④ 태양의 온도
⑤ 태양 광선의 각도

3 서술형

정답 지구의 지축이 기울어져 있기 때문에

해설 ❼에서 태양 광선이 여름과 겨울에 지구에 다른 각도로 들어오는 이유를 알 수 있다.

제대로 독해법

어휘 Level Up

1 ⓘ 2 ⓖ 3 ⓕ 4 ⓚ 5 ⓙ 6 ⓑ 7 ⓒ 8 ⓐ 9 ⓔ 10 ⓓ 11 ⓜ 12 ⓗ 13 ⓛ

내신 Level Up

정답 gentle

해설 sharp는 '가파른', gentle은 '완만한'의 뜻으로 서로 반대되는 의미를 가진다.

구문 Level Up

정답 1. because 2. because of

해설

1. 뒤에 절(it got cold)이 오므로 because가 알맞다.
2. 뒤에 구(my English test)가 오므로 because of가 알맞다.

▸ pp.100~101

고양이 발을 감지해 드립니다

지문 분석

❶ Have you ever had issues with your cat walking on your computer keyboard and deleting data when you are sending emails? ❷ Well in Tucson, Arizona, there is a man [(A) that / who / which can help you out with this]. ❸ He is the inventor of "PawSense." ❹ It is a software program especially (B) designed / designing to detect when your cats are running across your computer keyboard. ❺ Also, it can help train your cat to stay off the computer keyboard. ❻ If a cat gets on the keyboard, PawSense detects the cat typing. ❼ Then it will disable any inputs from the keyboard. ❽ At the same time it makes a sound [that annoys cats]. ❾ This teaches your cat [that getting on the keyboard is bad even if humans aren't watching].

(have issues with: ~와 문제가 있다 / 현재완료(경험) 의문문: ~해본 적 있니? / 병렬구조(현재분사) / 접 ~할 때(시간) / 관계대명사절(주격) / to부정사(~하도록) / 접 ~할 때(시간) / help + (to) 동사원형: ~하는 것을 돕다 / to부정사(~하도록) / 접 ~라면(조건) / detect + 목적어 + 현재분사(목적격보어): ~가 …하는 것을 감지하다 / 동시에 / 관계대명사절(주격) / teach + 목적어 + that절: (목적어)가 ~라는 것을 깨닫게 하다 / 명사절(보어) / 동명사(주어) / 단수동사 / 접 ~하더라도)

지문 해석

❶ 당신이 이메일을 보내고 있을 때 고양이가 컴퓨터 키보드 위를 걸어 다니고 자료를 삭제하는 문제를 겪은 적이 있는가? ❷ 자, 애리조나 주의 투손에 이러한 문제를 겪고 있는 당신을 도와줄 수 있는 한 남자가 있다. ❸ 그는 'PawSense'의 발명가이다. ❹ 그것은 당신의 고양이가 컴퓨터 키보드를 가로질러 뛰어갈 때를 감지하도록 특별하게 고안된 소프트웨어 프로그램이다. ❺ 또한, 그것은 당신의 고양이가 컴퓨터 키보드에서 멀리 있도록 훈련시키는 것도 도와줄 수 있다. ❻ 고양이가 키보드 위에 올라가면 PawSense는 그 고양이가 키보드를 치는 것을 감지한다. ❼ 그런 다음 그것은 키보드로부터의 어떠한 입력도 못하게 할 것이다. ❽ 동시에 그것은 고양이를 짜증나게 하는 소리를 낸다. ❾ 이것은 당신의 고양이가 인간이 보고 있지 않더라도 키보드 위에 있는 것은 나쁜 일이라는 것을 깨닫게 한다.

정답인 이유

1 어법성 판단

정답 ③

해설 (A) 선행사가 사람(a man)이고 관계대명사절 속에서 주어 역할을 해야 하므로 주격 관계대명사 who 또는 that이 적절하다. (B) a software program을 수식하며 프로그램은 능동적으로 만드는 것이 아니라 사람에 의해 수동적으로 만들어지므로 designed가 적절하다.

2 빈칸 추론

정답 ③

해설 빈칸에는 고양이가 키보드를 건드리지 못하도록 하는 장치의 역할이 드러나야 하므로 ③ '고양이를 짜증나게 하는'이 내용상 가장 적절하다.

해석 빈칸에 들어갈 말로 가장 적절한 것은?

① 고양이를 유혹하는 ② 도움을 요청하는
③ 고양이를 짜증나게 하는 ④ 고양이의 소리와 비슷한
⑤ 오류를 막는

3 서술형

정답

(1) 고양이가 컴퓨터 키보드 위를 뛰어가는 것을 감지한다.
(2) 고양이가 컴퓨터 키보드에서 떨어져 있도록 훈련시킨다.

해설 PawSense는 고양이가 컴퓨터 키보드 위로 올라오는 것을 감지하고, 고양이를 성가시게 하는 소리를 내서 키보드 위로 올라오지 않도록 훈련시키는 소프트웨어이다.

제대로 독해법

어휘 Level Up

1ⓓ 2ⓖ 3ⓙ 4ⓕ 5ⓔ 6ⓗ 7ⓜ 8ⓐ 9ⓚ 10ⓑ 11ⓛ 12ⓒ 13ⓘ

내신 Level Up

정답 (1) disable (2) train (3) stay off

해설 'PawSense'는 고양이가 타이핑하는 것이 입력되지 못하게 하는 데 사용될 수 있고 고양이가 컴퓨터 키보드에서 떨어져 있도록 훈련시키는 소프트웨어 프로그램이다.

구문 Level Up

정답 Have, eaten

해설 '~해본 적이 있니?'라는 의미의 현재완료(경험) 의문문(Have / Has + 주어 + p.p. ~?)으로 나타낼 수 있다.

어휘 테스트

▸ p.102

A 1 pill 2 confident 3 hidden 4 brush 5 detects 6 train

B 1ⓒ 2ⓐ 3ⓑ

해석 1 염려 2 발표하다 3 문제, 주제

ⓐ 공식적으로 어떤 것에 대해 사람들에게 말하거나 알리다
ⓑ 사람들이 생각하거나 이야기하는 주제나 문제
ⓒ 무언가에 대해 걱정하거나 불안해하는 감정

Jobs · People

Reading 01

▸ pp.106~107

인터넷 콘텐츠 크리에이터는 괜찮은 직업일까?

지문 분석

항상 대문자로 시작
❶ Once you connect to the Internet, you will find lots
접 ~하자마자(시간) 시간 부사절에서 현재시제가 미래를 나타냄
of new videos. ❷ These videos are generally fun and
interesting and usually ⓐexclude advertisements.
(×) → include (○)
❸ A number of people make a huge income from
많은(= many)
㉠them, so people think [creating these videos for a living
(think의 목적어절을 이끄는 접속사 that 생략)
is a successful job]. ❹ However, it doesn't seem to be
~해 보이다
ⓑpositive for two reasons. ❺ First of all, the field is very
먼저
ⓒcompetitive. ❻ Anyone can do this job with simple
누구나
skills. ❼ Even if you had a big talent for this and became
동사 1 동사 2
ⓓsuccessful, there would be new challengers with
전 ~을 가진
bigger passion and better ability. ❽ Second, it is not
가주어
ⓔsure [that they get paid every day]. ❾ Most of media
└ 진주어(that절) 돈을 벌다 주어
creators earn money from advertisements. ❿ But if
동사 접 ~라면(조건)
the Internet site goes broke and nobody reaches your
아무도 ~않다 (단수 취급) 단수동사
contents, you will get nothing.

지문 해석

❶ 인터넷에 접속하자마자, 당신은 많은 새로운 영상을 발견할 것이다. ❷ 이러한 영상들은 일반적으로 재밌고 흥미롭고 보통 광고를 제외한다(→ 포함한다). ❸ 많은 사람들이 그것(광고)으로부터 큰 소득을 만들어서, 사람들은 생계 수단으로 이러한 영상을 만드는 것을 성공적인 직업으로 여긴다. ❹ 하지만, 그것은 두 가지 이유로 긍정적으로 보이지 않는다. ❺ 먼저, 그 분야는 매우 경쟁이 심하다. ❻ 누구나 간단한 기술들을 가지고 이 일을 할 수 있다. ❼ 당신이 이것에 엄청난 재능을 가지고 있고 성공하더라도, 더 큰 열정과 더 나은 능력을 가진 새로운 도전자들이 있을 것이다. ❽ 두 번째로, 돈을 매일 벌 수 있을지 확실하지 않다. ❾ 대부분의 미디어 창작자들은 광고로 돈을 번다. ❿ 그러나 인터넷 사이트가 파산하고 아무도 당신의 콘텐츠에 도달하지 못하면, 당신은 아무것도 얻을 수 없을 것이다.

정답인 이유

1 주제 추론

정답 ①

해설 이 글은 인터넷 콘텐츠 크리에이터의 직업 전망이 어두운 이유를 서술한 글이다. 따라서 ① '직업으로서 인터넷 콘텐츠 크리에이터가 되는 것의 부정적인 면'이 주제로 적절하다.

해석

① 직업으로서 인터넷 콘텐츠 크리에이터가 되는 것의 부정적인 면
② 콘텐츠 제작 시장에 참여하는 방법
③ 광고에 사용되는 돈의 양
④ 인터넷 콘텐츠의 최신 유행
⑤ 인터넷 콘텐츠의 부작용

2 어휘 파악

정답 ①

해설 마지막 부분에서 콘텐츠 제작자들이 광고를 통해 돈을 번다고 했으므로 ⓐ는 '광고를 포함한다'는 의미가 되어야 한다. 그러므로 exclude(제외하다)가 아니라 include(포함하다)가 오는 것이 적절하다.

해석 ⓐ~ⓔ 중에서 낱말의 쓰임이 적절하지 않은 것은?

3 서술형

정답 **부정적이다.**
(1) 매우 경쟁이 심하다.
(2) 매일 돈을 벌 수 있을지 확실하지 않다.

해설 ❹ 이하에서 인터넷 콘텐츠 크리에이터의 직업 전망을 부정적으로 보는 이유를 설명하고 있다.

제대로 독해법

어휘 Level Up

1 ⓛ 2 ⓚ 3 ⓜ 4 ⓒ 5 ⓗ 6 ⓐ 7 ⓓ 8 ⓙ 9 ⓖ 10 ⓑ 11 ⓕ 12 ⓘ 13 ⓔ 14 ⓝ 15 ⓞ

내신 Level Up

정답 advertisements

해설 '많은 사람들이 광고로부터 큰 소득을 만든다.'는 내용이다.

구문 Level Up

정답 1. were 2. do

해설

1. 「half of + 복수명사(the houses)」는 복수 취급하므로 were가 알맞다.
2. 「most of + 복수명사(the students)」는 복수 취급하므로 do가 알맞다.

▸ pp.108~109

특이한 직업들

지문 분석

❶ There are various, unique jobs as well as commonly heard of jobs such as teachers, doctors, and police officers. ❷ Here are two examples. ❸ (ⓐ) You might have heard of a sommelier, someone [who is in charge of wines at a restaurant]. ❹ (ⓑ) In the past few years, however, some restaurants have been employing experts to taste various mineral waters. ❺ (ⓒ) A "water sommelier" recommends [which type of mineral water tastes best with a particular food].

❻ (ⓓ Another unique job is a location manager.)

❼ A location manager is someone [who works for movie companies]. ❽ It is his job [to find the best sites for filming scenes outside the studio]. ❾ Once he has found the appropriate places, he has to make a schedule. ❿ (ⓔ) Though the efforts of location managers are often unknown, depending on the type of the movie, it can be a really interesting job.

(as well as: A as well as B: B뿐만 아니라 A도 / such as: ~와 같은(= like) / Here are + 복수명사 ~: 여기에 ~들이 있다 / might have p.p.: ~했을지도 모른다(추측) / 동격 / 선행사 / 관계대명사절(주격) / be in charge of: ~을 담당하다 / 형 지난 / however: 그러나 / to부정사(experts 수식) / 간접의문문(의문사 + 주어 + 동사) / 선행사 / 관계대명사절(주격) / 가주어 / 진주어(to부정사구) / 전치사 + 동명사 / 접 일단 ~하면(조건) / = must / 스케줄을 짜다 / 접 ~이지만(양보) / 수동태(be동사 + p.p.) / ~에 따라서)

지문 해석

❶ 교사, 의사, 경찰과 같이 흔히 들어본 직업들뿐만 아니라 다양하고 독특한 직업들이 있다. ❷ 여기 두 가지 예가 있다. ❸ 여러분은 아마 소믈리에, 즉 레스토랑에서 와인을 담당하는 사람을 들어봤을지도 모른다. ❹ 그러나 지난 몇 년 동안, 몇몇 레스토랑이 다양한 생수를 맛보는 전문가들을 고용하고 있다. ❺ '워터 소믈리에'는 어떤 종류의 생수가 특정한 요리에 가장 맛있는지를 추천한다. ❻ 또 다른 독특한 직업은 로케이션 매니저이다. ❼ 로케이션 매니저는 영화 회사를 위해 일하는 사람이다. ❽ 스튜디오 밖에서 촬영하기에 가장 좋은 장소를 찾는 것이 그의 일이다. ❾ 일단 그가 적합한 장소를 찾으면, 그는 스케줄을 짜야 한다. ❿ 로케이션 매니저들의 수고는 종종 알려지지 않지만 영화의 종류에 따라 아주 흥미로운 직업이 될 수도 있다.

정답인 이유

1 목적 추론

정답 ①

해설 이 글은 잘 알려진 직업뿐만 아니라 독특한 직업이 있다는 것을 강조하고 워터 소믈리에와 로케이션 매니저라는 두 가지 독특한 직업을 소개하고 있다. 따라서 ① '독특한 직업을 소개하려고'가 글의 목적으로 적절하다.

2 문장 삽입

정답 ④

해설 글의 흐름상 '워터 소믈리에'에 대한 내용이 끝나고 '로케이션 매니저'에 대한 구체적인 내용이 시작되기 전인 ⓓ에 들어가는 것이 가장 적절하다.

해석 주어진 문장이 들어가기에 가장 적절한 곳은?
또 다른 독특한 직업은 로케이션 매니저이다.

3 서술형

정답

(1) 어떤 생수와 음식이 잘 어울리는지 추천한다.

(2) 영화를 찍을 최고의 장소를 찾아 스케줄을 짠다.

해설

(1) ❺에 워터 소믈리에가 하는 일이 잘 나타나 있다.

(2) ❽, ❾에 로케이션 매니저가 하는 일이 잘 나타나 있다.

제대로 독해법

어휘 Level Up

1ⓒ 2ⓓ 3ⓐ 4ⓖ 5ⓑ 6ⓘ 7ⓕ 8ⓛ 9ⓙ 10ⓜ 11ⓔ 12ⓝ 13ⓚ 14ⓗ

내신 Level Up

정답 ①

해설 '워터 소믈리에'와 '로케이션 매니저'를 예로 들어 독특한 직업을 소개하고 있다.

구문 Level Up

정답 cannot

해설 「should have p.p.」는 '~했어야 했는데 (하지 않았다)'의 의미이고, 「cannot have p.p.」는 '~했을 리가 없다'라는 의미이므로 문맥상 cannot이 알맞다.

▸ pp.110~111

일하는 백만장자

지문 분석

❶ Most people want to earn much money, so they work hard. (much+셀 수 없는 명사) ❷ If you became a millionaire, or if you had very rich parents, would you want to keep working hard? (병렬구조 / keep+-ing: 계속 ~하다) ❸ Maybe not. ❹ Here is a story about a Chinese millionaire. (Here is+단수명사: 여기에 ~이 있다) ❺ This 53-year-old Chinese millionaire, Yu Youzhen, works very hard. ❻ She has worked hard for about 40 years as a farmer, cook, driver, and street cleaner. (현재완료(계속) / 전 ~동안 / 전 ~로서) ❼ Being a diligent woman, she finally became very rich. (분사구문(= Because she was a diligent woman)) ❽ However, she keeps working. (그러나) ❾ These days, she works as a street cleaner six days a week. (요즘에 / 전 ~로서 / 일주일에 6일) ❿ A reporter asked her [why she keeps working so hard]. (간접의문문(의문사+주어+동사)) ⓫ She said [that this is because of her son]. (명사절(said의 목적어) / because of+명사(구): ~ 때문에) ⓬ She didn't want her son to be lazy because of her wealth, so she wanted to be her son's role model. (want+목적어+to부정사: (목적어)가 ~하기를 원하다 / want+to부정사(목적어)) ⓭ It reminds us of the saying, 'Examples are better than precepts.' (remind A of B: A에게 B가 생각나게 하다) ⓮ She is not only a great worker, but also a wise mother. (not only A but also B: A뿐만 아니라 B도)

지문 해석

❶ 대다수의 사람들은 돈을 많이 벌기를 원해서 일을 열심히 한다. ❷ 만약 당신이 백만장자가 된다면, 혹은 만약 당신에게 매우 부유한 부모가 있다면 당신은 계속 열심히 일하고 싶을까? ❸ 아마 아닐 것이다. ❹ 여기 한 중국 백만장자의 이야기가 있다. ❺ 이 53세의 중국인 백만장자 유 유진(Yu Youzhen)은 매우 열심히 일한다. ❻ 그녀는 약 40년간 농부, 요리사, 운전사 그리고 거리 청소부로서 열심히 일해 왔다. ❼ 근면한 여성이었기 때문에, 그녀는 마침내 매우 부유해졌다. ❽ 그러나, 그녀는 계속 일하고 있다. ❾ 요즘에 그녀는 거리 청소부로서 일주일에 6일을 일한다. ❿ 한 리포터가 그녀에게 왜 그렇게 계속 열심히 일하는지 물었다. ⓫ 그녀는 이것이 그녀의 아들 때문이라고 말했다. ⓬ 그녀는 아들이 그녀의 재산 때문에 게을러지는 것을 원하지 않아서, 그녀가 아들의 역할 모델이 되길 원했다. ⓭ 그것은 우리에게 '교훈보다 본보기가 더 낫다.'는 속담을 생각나게 한다. ⓮ 그녀는 훌륭한 노동자일 뿐만 아니라 지혜로운 어머니이다.

정답인 이유

1 목적 추론

정답 ③

해설 이 글은 성실하게 일해서 백만장자가 되고 난 후에도 거리 청소부로 일하는 한 여성의 이야기를 통해 일하는 것에 관한 교훈을 주는 내용이므로 ③ '열심히 일하는 것에 관한 교훈을 주려고'가 글의 목적으로 적절하다.

해석
① 중국의 다양한 직업들을 소개하려고
② 부자가 되는 것에 관한 조언을 하려고
③ 열심히 일하는 것에 관한 교훈을 주려고
④ 노동자들에게 돈 버는 방법을 가르쳐 주려고
⑤ 사람들에게 위험한 직업에 대해 경고하려고

2 빈칸 추론

정답 ②

해설 돈이 많아도 계속 일을 함으로써 아들에게 근면함을 몸소 가르치고 있는 어머니를 나타내는 것으로 빈칸에는 ② '교훈보다 본보기가 더 낫다.'가 가장 적절하다.

해석 빈칸에 들어갈 말로 가장 적절한 것은?
① 백지장도 맞들면 낫다.
② 교훈보다 본보기가 더 낫다.
③ 서툰 일꾼이 연장 탓한다.
④ 손 안에 든 새 한마리가 숲에 있는 두 마리보다 낫다.
⑤ 일만하고 놀지 않으면 바보가 된다.

3 서술형

정답 diligent

해설 유 유진은 그녀의 아들이 본인처럼 부지런해지기를 원하므로 빈칸에는 '부지런한'이라는 뜻의 'diligent'가 가장 적절하다.

해석 유 유진은 그녀의 아들이 부지런해지기를 원했다.

제대로 독해법

어휘 Level Up

1 ⓐ 2 ⓕ 3 ⓚ 4 ⓒ 5 ⓔ 6 ⓓ 7 ⓑ 8 ⓙ 9 ⓘ 10 ⓖ 11 ⓗ 12 ⓜ 13 ⓛ

내신 Level Up

정답 (1) Yu (2) 53 (3) 40 (4) cook

해설 유 유진은 53세의 중국인 백만장자이다. 그녀는 농부, 요리사, 운전사, 그리고 거리 청소부로서 40년간 열심히 일해 왔다.

구문 Level Up

정답 Having spare time

해설 분사구문을 만들 때 ① 부사절의 접속사를 삭제하고, ② 부사절의 주어와 주절의 주어가 같으면 부사절의 주어를 삭제하고, ③ 부사절과 주절의 동사의 시제가 일치할 경우, 부사절의 동사를 현재분사(동사원형+-ing)로 바꾼다.

▸ pp.112~113

괴짜 왕 루이 14세

지문 분석

❶ Louis XIV built a huge palace at Versailles. ❷ The gardens of the palace had 1,400 fountains. ❸ (ⓐ) The fountains used water, but Louis himself ㉠did not! ❹ (ⓑ) He hated to wash. ❺ He washed only one part of his body — the tip of his nose. ❻ Louis had other unusual habits. ❼ He liked being watched by many people when he got dressed. ❽ (ⓒ) Also, only the king and queen were allowed to sit on chairs with arms. ❾ Louis had problems sleeping. ❿ (ⓓ He had 413 beds.) ⓫ He went from one bed to another until he fell asleep. ⓬ But he had a good appetite. ⓭ (ⓔ) His cook served him plenty of food. ⓮ A normal dinner was four bowls of soup, two whole chickens, ham, lamb, a salad, cakes, fruit, and hardboiled eggs. ⓯ According to records, his stomach was two times the size of a normal stomach.

built: build-built-built
himself: 재귀대명사(강조 용법)
did not (use water)
to wash: = washing
the tip of his nose: 코끝
when: 접 ~할 때(시간)
got dressed: get dressed: 옷을 입다
were allowed to: be allowed to부정사: ~을 허락받다
chairs with arms: 팔걸이 의자
had problems sleeping: have a problem -ing: ~하는 데 어려움을 겪다
until: 접 ~ (때)까지(시간)
fell asleep: fall asleep: 잠들다
But: 하지만
served him plenty of food: 4형식: 수여동사(served) + 간접목적어(사람) + 직접목적어(사물)
whole chickens: 통닭
According to: ~에 따르면
two times the size of a: 배수사 + the size of ~: ~의 …배

지문 해석

❶ 루이 14세는 베르사유에 커다란 궁전을 지었다. ❷ 그 궁전의 정원에는 1,400개의 분수가 있었다. ❸ 그 분수들은 물을 사용했지만 루이 자신은 그렇지 않았다(물을 쓰지 않았다)! ❹ 그는 씻는 것을 싫어했다. ❺ 그는 오직 몸의 한 부분 — 그의 코끝만 씻었다. ❻ 루이는 다른 특이한 버릇들도 있었다. ❼ 그는 그가 옷을 입을 때 많은 사람들에게 보여지는 것을 좋아했다. ❽ 또한 오직 왕과 왕비만이 팔걸이가 있는 의자에 앉을 수 있도록 했다. ❾ 루이는 잠자는 데 어려움을 겪었다. ❿ 그에게는 413개의 침대가 있었다. ⓫ 그는 잠이 들 때까지 한 침대에서 또 다른 침대로 옮겨 다녔다. ⓬ 하지만 식욕은 좋았다. ⓭ 그의 요리사는 그에게 많은 음식을 제공했다. ⓮ 보통 저녁 식사는 수프 네 그릇, 통닭 두 마리, 햄, 양고기, 샐러드, 케이크, 과일, 그리고 삶은 달걀들이었다. ⓯ 기록에 따르면, 그의 위는 크기가 보통 위의 두 배였다고 한다.

정답인 이유

1 내용 일치

정답 ③

해설 ❽의 왕과 왕비만 팔걸이가 있는 의자에 앉도록 했다는 내용으로 미루어 볼 때 루이 14세가 팔걸이가 있는 의자를 선호했음을 알 수 있으므로 ③은 내용과 일치하지 않는다.

2 문장 삽입

정답 ④

해설 글의 흐름상 잠자는 것에 문제가 있었다는 내용과 잠들 때까지 침대를 옮겨 다녔다는 내용 사이에 주어진 문장이 오는 것이 자연스러우므로 ⓓ에 들어가는 것이 적절하다.

해석 주어진 문장이 들어가기에 가장 적절한 곳은?
그에게는 413개의 침대가 있었다.

3 서술형

정답 **정원에 1,400개의 분수가 있다, 팔걸이가 없는 의자가 많다, 많은 침대가 있다, 요리사가 많은 음식을 준비한다.**

해설 베르사유 궁전 정원에는 1,400개의 분수가 있고, 왕과 왕비만 팔걸이가 있는 의자에 앉을 수 있게 했으므로 팔걸이가 없는 의자가 많았을 것을 유추할 수 있다. 또한 413개의 침대가 있고, 요리사가 많은 음식을 준비했다는 내용을 알 수 있다.

제대로 독해법

어휘 Level Up

1ⓐ 2ⓗ 3ⓚ 4ⓑ 5ⓕ 6ⓔ 7ⓜ 8ⓓ 9ⓙ 10ⓝ 11ⓒ 12ⓖ 13ⓛ 14ⓘ 15ⓞ

내신 Level Up

정답 use water

해설 '그 분수들은 물을 사용했지만 루이 자신은 물을 쓰지 않았다.'는 내용이다.

구문 Level Up

정답 1. herself 2. itself

해설

1. 주어 She가 3인칭 단수, 여성이므로 재귀대명사 herself를 써야 한다.
2. 목적어 the report를 강조하므로 itself를 써야 한다.

어휘 테스트

▸ p.114

Ⓐ 1 filming 2 palace 3 fountains 4 fell asleep 5 cook 6 reporter

Ⓑ 1ⓐ 2ⓒ 3ⓑ

해석 1 소득, 수입 2 식욕 3 생각나게 하다
ⓐ 일을 해서 벌거나 투자를 해서 받은 돈
ⓑ 잊었거나 잊었을지도 모를 것을 생각나게 하다
ⓒ 음식을 먹고 싶어 하는 감정

Stories · Origins

▸ pp.118~119

생일 때 촛불을 끄는 이유

지문 분석

❶ Once a year, you celebrate the day [when you were born]. ❷ It's your birthday. ❸ Everybody sings the Happy Birthday song with candles burning. ❹ When the song finishes, it's time ⓐfor you to make a wish and blow out the candles. ❺ By the way, have you ever ⓑwonder [why you blow out the candles on your birthday]? ❻ (A) A long time ago, people believed [that their wishes could reach God better with smoke]. ❼ (B) The greater the amount of smoke was, ⓒthe better it was. ❽ (C Therefore, blowing out all the candles at once was the best way to make a wish.) ❾ To make a wish come true, people started to blow candles all at the same time on birthdays. ❿ (D) Now, when you blow your candles on your birthday this year, take a deep breath and ⓓblow out all the candles at once to make the biggest smoke ever. ⓫ (E) Tell God your wish and make it ⓔspecial among all the other wishes [you've made so far].

관계부사절(시간) / 주어(단수 취급) / 단수 동사 / with+명사+분사: (명사)가 ~한 채로[하면서] / to부정사구(time 수식) / 의미상 주어 / 간접의문문(의문사+주어+동사) / 그런데 / (×) → wondered (○) / 명사절(believed의 목적어) / The 비교급 ~, the 비교급 …: ~하면 할수록 더 …하다 / to부정사(~하기 위해서) / = blowing / 동시에 / 접 ~할 때(시간) / 명령문 / 한 번에 / to부정사(~하기 위해서) / 4형식(동사+간접목적어+직접목적어) / 5형식(동사+목적어+목적격보어) / 지금껏 / 관계대명사절(목적격 관계대명사 that 생략)

지문 해석

❶ 일 년에 한 번, 당신은 당신이 태어난 날을 기념한다. ❷ 그날은 당신의 생일이다. ❸ 초가 타고 있는 가운데 모두가 생일 축하 노래를 부른다. ❹ 노래가 끝나면, 당신이 소원을 빌고 초를 끌 차례다. ❺ 그런데, 당신은 생일에 왜 초를 끄는지 궁금해 해본 적이 있는가? ❻ 오래전에, 사람들은 그들의 소원이 연기와 함께 신에게 더 잘 닿을 수 있다고 믿었다. ❼ 연기의 양이 많을수록, 더 좋았다. ❽ 따라서, 한 번에 초를 불어 끄는 것이 소원을 비는 가장 좋은 방법이었다. ❾ 소원이 이뤄지게 하기 위해, 사람들은 생일에 초를 모두 동시에 불기 시작했다. ❿ 이제, 올해 당신의 생일에 초를 불 때, 심호흡을 하고 가장 큰 연기를 만들기 위해 한 번에 모든 초를 꺼라. ⓫ 신에게 당신의 소원을 말하고 그것을 지금껏 빌었던 모든 다른 소원들 중에서 특별하게 만들어보라.

정답인 이유

1 어법성 판단

정답 ②

해설

ⓑ 문장의 시제가 현재완료이므로 wonder가 아니라 과거분사형(p.p.)인 wondered가 와야 한다.

ⓐ to부정사의 의미상 주어(for+목적격)이므로 for가 적절하다.

ⓒ 「the 비교급 (+주어+동사), the 비교급 (+주어+동사)」: ~할수록 더 …하다

ⓓ 앞에 나온 take a deep breath와 병렬구조이므로 동사원형(명령문)이 오는 것이 적절하다.

ⓔ make의 목적어 it을 수식하는 목적격보어로 형용사 special은 적절하다.

2 문장 삽입

정답 ③

해설 글의 흐름상 연기가 많을수록 더 좋은 것이라는 내용과 사람들이 초를 모두 동시에 불어서 끄기 시작했다는 내용 사이에 오는 것이 자연스러우므로 (C)가 적절하다.

해석 주어진 문장이 들어가기에 가장 적절한 곳은?

따라서, 한 번에 초를 불어 끄는 것이 소원을 비는 가장 좋은 방법이었다.

3 서술형

정답 birthday

해설 빈칸 앞 문장 ❶에서 빈칸에 들어갈 단어의 정의를 알 수 있다. 일 년에 한 번 당신이 태어난 날을 축하하는 것은 생일(birthday)이다.

제대로 독해법

어휘 Level Up

1 ⓖ 2 ⓚ 3 ⓑ 4 ⓘ 5 ⓐ 6 ⓕ 7 ⓔ 8 ⓗ 9 ⓓ 10 ⓛ 11 ⓜ 12 ⓙ 13 ⓟ 14 ⓞ 15 ⓒ 16 ⓝ

내신 Level Up

정답 (1) T (2) T (3) F

해석

(1) 과거에 사람들은 연기가 그들의 소원을 신에게 전달되게 도와준다고 생각했다.

(2) 초의 연기의 양이 많을 때 더 좋은 것으로 여겨졌다.

(3) 한 번에 초를 불어 끄는 것은 불운으로 여겨졌다.(→ 불운이 아니라 소원을 비는 가장 좋은 방법이라고 말하고 있다.)

구문 Level Up

정답 more

해설 「The 비교급(+주어+동사), the 비교급(+주어+동사)」 형태로 비교급 more가 알맞다.

▸ pp.120~121

애물단지 '흰 코끼리'

지문 분석

❶ "Every time you go to a garage sale, you come home with another white elephant!" ❷ This is [what my mom yelled at my father yesterday]. ❸ You might see people selling "white elephants" at a flea market or school fair.

(Every time: ~할 때마다 / garage sale: 차고 세일 / another: 또 다른 하나의(+단수명사) / what: 선행사를 포함하는 관계대명사 what / see people selling: 지각동사+목적어+현재분사(목적격보어))

❹ ㉠Don't look for any white-colored animals. ❺ "White elephants" are just some junk [that people don't want anymore and would like to sell to you]. ❻ A long time ago in Thailand, a white elephant was a holy animal.

(Don't look for ~: 부정명령문(Don't+동사원형 ~.) / junk: 선행사 / that people don't want anymore: 관계대명사절(목적격) / want: 동사1 / would like to sell: 동사2 / ~하고 싶어 하다)

❼ When the king of Thailand was angry at someone, he gave that person a white elephant as a "present." ❽ The white elephant could never be made to work. ❾ It would live only in comfortable and luxurious condition, so its new owner would run out of money caring for it. ❿ This is why we call useless stuff a "white elephant."

(When: 접 ~할 때(시간) / be angry at: ~에게 화나다 / gave that person a white elephant: 4형식 → gave a white elephant to that person (3형식) / as: 전 ~로서 / be made to work: 사역동사(make)의 수동태(be동사+p.p.+to부정사) / its = the white elephant's / would: ~하곤 했다 / run out of: ~을 다 써버리다 / This is why: 이것이 ~하는 이유이다)

지문 해석

❶ "차고 세일을 갈 때마다, 당신은 또 다른 흰 코끼리를 가지고 오네요!" ❷ 이 말은 어제 엄마가 아빠에게 외친 말이다. ❸ 당신은 사람들이 벼룩시장이나 학교 장터에서 '흰 코끼리'를 파는 것을 볼 수 있을 것이다. ❹ 흰색의 동물을 찾지 마라. ❺ '흰 코끼리'는 사람들이 더 이상 원하지 않아 당신에게 팔고 싶어 하는 고물일 뿐이다. ❻ 오래전에 태국에서, 흰 코끼리는 성스러운 동물이었다. ❼ 태국의 왕이 누군가에게 화가 났을 때, 그는 그 사람에게 흰 코끼리를 '선물'로 주었다. ❽ 흰 코끼리는 일하도록 시킬 수가 없었다. ❾ 그것은 오직 편안하고 호화로운 상태에서 살아서 그것(흰 코끼리)의 새 주인은 그것(흰 코끼리)을 돌보느라 돈을 다 써버리곤 했다. ❿ 이것이 우리가 쓸모없는 것을 '흰 코끼리'라고 부르는 이유이다.

정답인 이유

1 밑줄 추론

정답 ④

해설 ❺에서 'white elephants'라는 표현이 '불필요한 물건'을 의미한다고 했으므로 밑줄 친 ㉠ '흰색의 동물을 찾지 마라'고 한 이유는 ④ '실제 흰 코끼리를 의미하는 게 아니므로'가 적절하다.

2 빈칸 추론

정답 ②

해설 돌보느라 돈만 들고 일을 시킬 수 없다는 내용을 통해 흰 코끼리가 '쓸모없는' 물건을 빗대어 말하는 표현이라는 것을 알 수 있으므로 ②가 적절하다.

해석 빈칸에 들어갈 말로 가장 적절한 것은?

① 가벼운 ② 쓸모없는 ③ 귀중한 ④ 호화로운 ⑤ 중요한

3 서술형

정답 (1) present (2) money (3) junk (4) sell

해석 옛날에, 태국의 왕은 누군가에게 화가 나면 그 사람에게 흰 코끼리를 선물로 주었다. 그것(흰 코끼리)은 편안하고 호화로운 상태에서만 살아서 그 새 주인은 그것(흰 코끼리)을 돌보느라 돈을 다 써버리곤 했다. 오늘날 'white elephant'라는 표현은 사람들이 필요로 하지 않고 팔아버리고 싶어 하는 고물을 나타낸다.

제대로 독해법

어휘 Level Up

1 ⓚ 2 ⓗ 3 ⓔ 4 ⓘ 5 ⓓ 6 ⓛ 7 ⓖ 8 ⓜ 9 ⓕ 10 ⓙ 11 ⓐ 12 ⓑ 13 ⓒ

내신 Level Up

정답 junk

해설 ❺에서 '흰 코끼리'는 사람들이 더 이상 원하지 않아 팔고 싶어 하는 고물(junk)이라고 했다.

구문 Level Up

정답 was made to fix

해설 사역동사 make가 쓰인 수동태 문장에서는 목적격보어로 to fix가 와야 한다.

Day 20 Reading 01

▸ pp.122~123

남자와 펭귄

지문 분석

❶ One day, a police officer was walking down the street.
(과거의) 어느 날 / walk down the street: 거리를 걷다 / 과거진행시제(was/were+-ing)

❷ As he was walking, he saw a man with a penguin following him.
접 ~할 때(시간) / 현재분사구

(C) ❸ "What are you doing with that penguin?" the police officer asked. ❹ "Well, I don't know. ❺ I saw the penguin on the street and then it started following me," the man answered.
it = the penguin / following = to follow

(A) ❻ "You should take it to the zoo," the officer said.
it = the penguin
❼ "That's a good idea," the man said, and he went off with the penguin.
he = the man / go off: 자리를 뜨다

(B) ❽ The next day, the police officer saw the man on the street again, with the penguin still behind him.
다음 날 / 전 ~와 함께
❾ "I thought [I told you to take the penguin to the zoo]," the officer said. ❿ "Oh, I did," the man replied, "and today I'm taking it to the amusement park."
(목적어절을 이끄는 접속사 that 생략) / tell+목적어+to부정사: (목적어)에게 ~하라고 말하다 / it = the penguin

지문 해석

❶ 어느 날 한 경찰관이 거리를 걷고 있었다. ❷ 그는 길을 걷다가 한 남자와 그를 따라가는 한 마리의 펭귄을 보았다. (C) ❸ "펭귄이랑 뭘 하는 겁니까?"라고 경찰관이 물었다. ❹ "음, 저도 모르겠어요. ❺ 길에서 펭귄을 봤는데 이 녀석이 저를 따라오기 시작했어요."라고 남자는 대답했다. (A) ❻ "당신은 그것을 동물원에 데려가야 합니다."라고 경찰관이 말했다. ❼ "그거 좋은 생각이군요."라고 말하고는 그는 펭귄과 함께 자리를 떴다. (B) ❽ 다음 날, 경찰관은 길에서 여전히 뒤에 펭귄을 데리고 있는 그 남자를 다시 보았다. ❾ "제가 그 펭귄을 동물원에 데려가라고 말했던 것 같은데요."라고 경찰관이 말했다. ❿ "오, 그렇게 했어요." 남자가 말했다. "그리고 오늘은 놀이공원에 데려가는 중이에요."

정답인 이유

1 순서 파악

정답 ④

해설 (C) 경찰이 길에서 남자와 펭귄을 만남 → (A) 경찰이 남자에게 펭귄을 동물원에 데려가라고 함 → (B) 다음 날 경찰은 펭귄을 놀이공원에 데려가는 남자를 다시 만남

2 내용 일치

정답 ①

해설 ❷에서 경찰관이 남자를 따라가고 있는 펭귄을 보았다는 내용이 언급되었으므로 ①이 글의 내용과 일치한다.

해석 이 글의 내용과 일치하는 것은?
① 경찰관은 한 남자를 따라가고 있는 한 펭귄을 보았다.
② 경찰관은 한 남자에게 펭귄을 데리고 놀아주라고 조언했다.
③ 한 남자가 펭귄을 거리에서 보고 따라가기 시작했다.
④ 한 남자는 펭귄을 동물원에 돌려보냈다.
⑤ 그 펭귄은 그 남자의 애완동물이었다.

3 서술형

정답
(1) 동물원에 데려가 (동물 전문가에게) 펭귄을 맡겨야 한다.
(2) 펭귄과 함께 동물원에 가서 놀아줘야 한다.

해설 (B)에서 경찰관이 "I thought I told you to take the penguin to the zoo."라고 말한 것에서 미루어볼 때, 길을 잃어버린 펭귄이 보호받을 수 있도록 동물원에 맡겨야 한다고 의도한 반면, 남자는 경찰관의 물음에 "~ and today I'm taking it to the amusement park."라고 대답한 것으로 보아 동물원을 놀이공원(amusement park)처럼 펭귄과 놀아주는 장소로 생각한 것임을 알 수 있다.

제대로 독해법

어휘 Level Up

1 ⓛ 2 ⓒ 3 ⓑ 4 ⓐ 5 ⓝ 6 ⓙ 7 ⓖ 8 ⓗ 9 ⓔ 10 ⓜ 11 ⓘ 12 ⓕ 13 ⓓ 14 ⓚ 15 ⓕ

내신 Level Up

정답 ①

해설 경찰이 동물 보호를 위해 펭귄을 동물원에 데리고 가라고 했는데 남자가 말귀를 못 알아듣고 펭귄을 데리고 놀러가라는 뜻으로 오해한 상황이므로 ① '소귀에 경 읽기'가 글의 내용과 가장 잘 어울린다.

해석
① 소귀에 경 읽기 ② 나쁜 소식은 빨리 퍼진다.
③ 쥐구멍에도 볕들 날이 있다. ④ 정직이 최선의 방책이다.
⑤ 젊음은 두 번 다시 오지 않는다.

구문 Level Up

정답 were eating

해설 과거진행시제는 「was/were+-ing」의 형태로 쓴다. 주어가 Tony and Tom 복수명사이므로 복수동사 were가 알맞다.

▸ pp.124~125

가짜 깃발, 진짜 깃발!

지문 분석

❶ Have you ever heard the old expression, "㉠to sail under false colors?" (현재완료(경험) 의문문(Have/Has+주어+p.p. ~?)) ❷ Linguists say [that it was born more than two hundred and fifty years ago]. (명사절(say의 목적어), ~보다 더) ❸ At that time, (그 당시에) pirates sailed the seas, attacking trade ships. (분사구문(= and they attacked)) ❹ ⓐThey flew the flag of a friendly country, (A) [sail / to sail / **sailing**] toward other ships. (fly-flew-flown, = and they sailed) ❺ ⓑThey sailed under the false flag until ⓒthey were close enough to attack the ships. (접 ~(때)까지, 형용사+enough to부정사: ~할 수 있을 만큼 충분히 …한) ❻ When the time came, the pirates pulled down the false flag, showing ⓓtheir true flag. (접 ~할 때(시간), 분사구문(= and they showed)) ❼ As you can imagine, there was a skull and cross bones in their true flag. (접 ~대로, a skull과 cross bones가 and로 나눠져 있을 때는 a skull에 맞춰 단수동사 was를 씀.) ❽ Today, the expression is applied to a person, not a ship. (수동태(be동사+p.p.)) ❾ Such people pretend to be nice with their true colors (B) [hiding / **hidden**]. (pretend+to부정사: ~인 척하다, with+명사+분사: ~가 …한 채로[하면서]) ❿ ⓔThey may try to get something from you. (try+to부정사: ~하려고 애쓰다) ⓫ If you are careful, however, you will soon see their true colors. (조건의 부사절에서는 현재시제로 미래를 나타냄)

지문 해석

❶ 'to sail under false colors'라는 오래된 표현을 들어본 적이 있는가? ❷ 언어학자들은 그것이 250년 보다 더 이전에 생겼다고 말한다. ❸ 그 당시에 해적들은 바다를 항해하면서 무역선들을 공격했다. ❹ 그들은 우호적인 국가의 국기를 달고 다른 배들을 향해 항해를 했다. ❺ 그들은 그 배들을 공격할 수 있을 만큼 충분히 가까워질 때까지 가짜 깃발을 달고 항해를 했다. ❻ 때가 되면 해적들은 가짜 깃발을 내리고 그들의 진짜 깃발을 드러냈다. ❼ 당신이 상상한 대로, 그들의 진짜 깃발에는 해골과 엇갈린 뼈가 있었다. ❽ 오늘날 그 표현은 배가 아니라 사람에게 적용된다. ❾ 그런 사람들은 자신의 본색을 감춘 채 좋은 (사람인) 척한다. ❿ 그들은 당신으로부터 무엇인가를 얻고자 애쓸지도 모른다. ⓫ 하지만 주의한다면 당신은 곧 그들의 본색을 알아볼 것이다.

정답인 이유

1 밑줄 추론

정답 ④

해설 글의 마지막 부분(❽~⓫)의 내용을 통해 오늘날 이 표현이 자신의 본색을 감추고 접근하는 사람을 나타낼 때 쓰이는 것임을 알 수 있으므로 ④가 가장 적절하다.

2 어법성 판단

정답 ⑤

해설

(A) and they sailed toward other ships를 분사구문으로 고친 것이므로 sailing이 적절하다.

(B) 「with+명사+분사」는 '~가 …한 채로[하면서]'의 의미로 명사와 분사의 관계가 능동이면 현재분사, 수동이면 과거분사를 쓴다. 여기서 '그들의 본색이 감춰지는 것'이므로 수동의 의미를 나타내는 hidden이 적절하다.

해석 (A), (B)의 각 네모 안에서 어법에 맞는 표현으로 가장 적절한 것은?

3 서술형

정답 true colors

해설 빈칸 앞의 ❾에서 그런 사람들은 자신의 본색을 감추고 있다는 것을 알 수 있다. 따라서 주의한다면 그들의 본색을 알아볼 수 있다는 내용이 이어지는 것이 자연스러우므로 '본모습, 본색'이라는 뜻의 true colors가 빈칸에 적절하다.

제대로 독해법

어휘 Level Up

1 ⓝ 2 ⓠ 3 ⓞ 4 ⓕ 5 ⓗ 6 ⓐ 7 ⓖ 8 ⓚ 9 ⓒ 10 ⓔ 11 ⓑ 12 ⓘ 13 ⓟ 14 ⓛ 15 ⓓ 16 ⓙ 17 ⓜ

내신 Level Up

정답 ⑤

해설 ⓔ는 '본색을 감추는 사람들'을 가리키고, ⓐ, ⓑ, ⓒ, ⓓ는 '해적들'을 가리킨다.

구문 Level Up

정답 breaking

해설 분사구문을 만들 때 접속사와 주어를 생략하고 동사를 「동사원형+-ing」의 형태로 쓴다.

어휘 테스트

▸ p.126

A 1 street 2 penguin 3 amusement park 4 pirates 5 sailed 6 skull

B 1 ⓑ 2 ⓐ 3 ⓒ

해석 1 숨 2 벼룩시장 3 공격하다

ⓐ 중고 물품을 싸게 파는 시장

ⓑ 폐에 들어가고 나오는 공기

ⓒ 폭력을 사용하여 다치게 하거나 이기려고 하다

READING